Workbook K

Recipe for Reading

Connie Russo and Ruth Emler

EDUCATORS PUBLISHING SERVICE
Cambridge and Toronto

Acquisitions/Development: Bonnie Lass
Cover Design: Karen Lomigora
Typesetting and Interior design: Sarah Cole
Illustrator: Ruth Linstromberg
Cover Photo: Becky Sharpe
Editor: Becky Ticotsky
Senior Editorial Manager: Sheila Neylon

ISBN 0-8388-0489-6
978-0-8388-0489-6
3 4 5 PPG 10 09

Printed in U.S.A.

Contents

Lesson 1

c /k/ cat

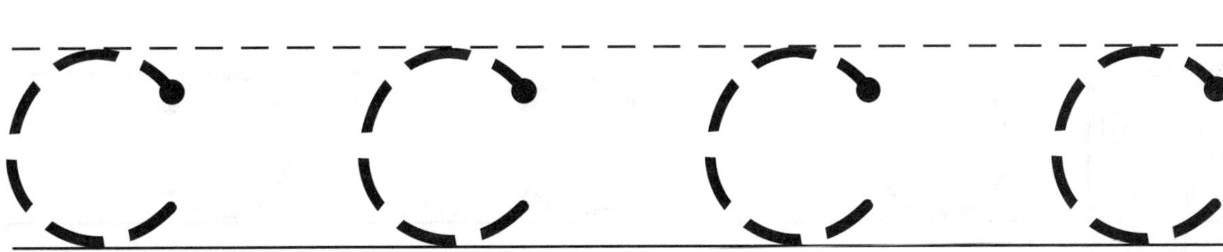

Have children trace all of the *c*'s on this page. Tell them to start at the dot and say /k/ as in *cat* as they trace each *c*.

c /k/ cat

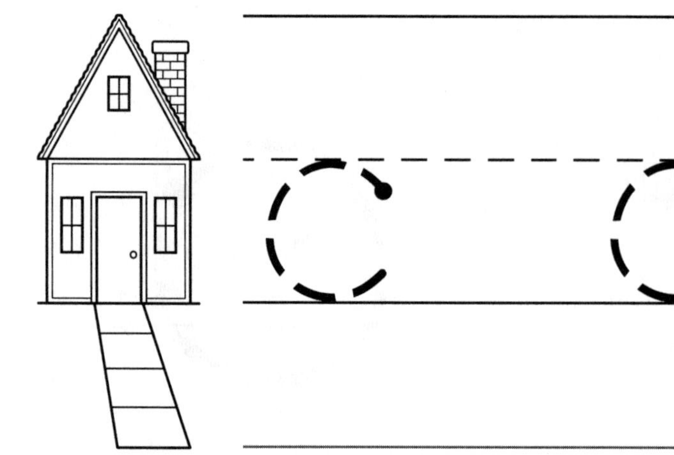

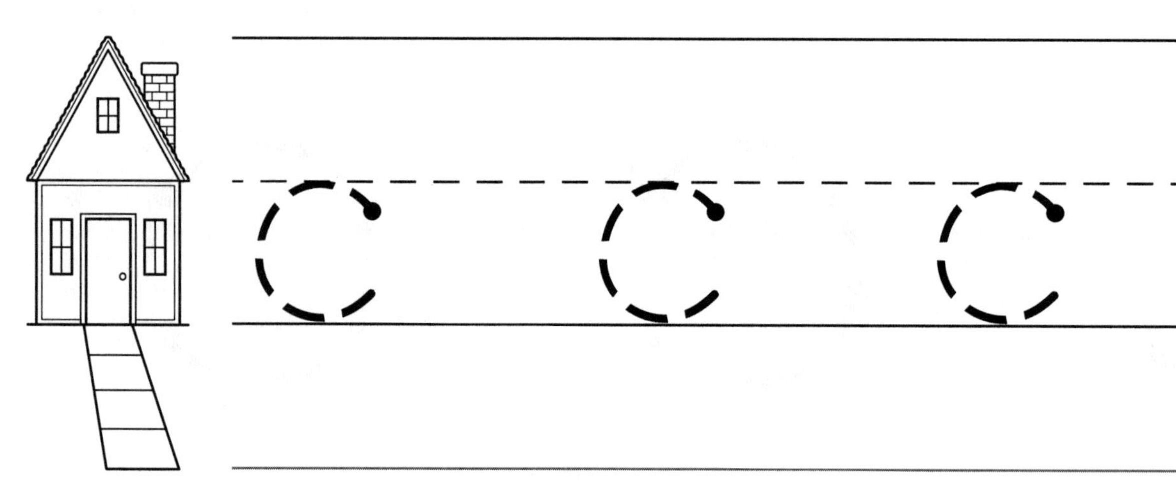

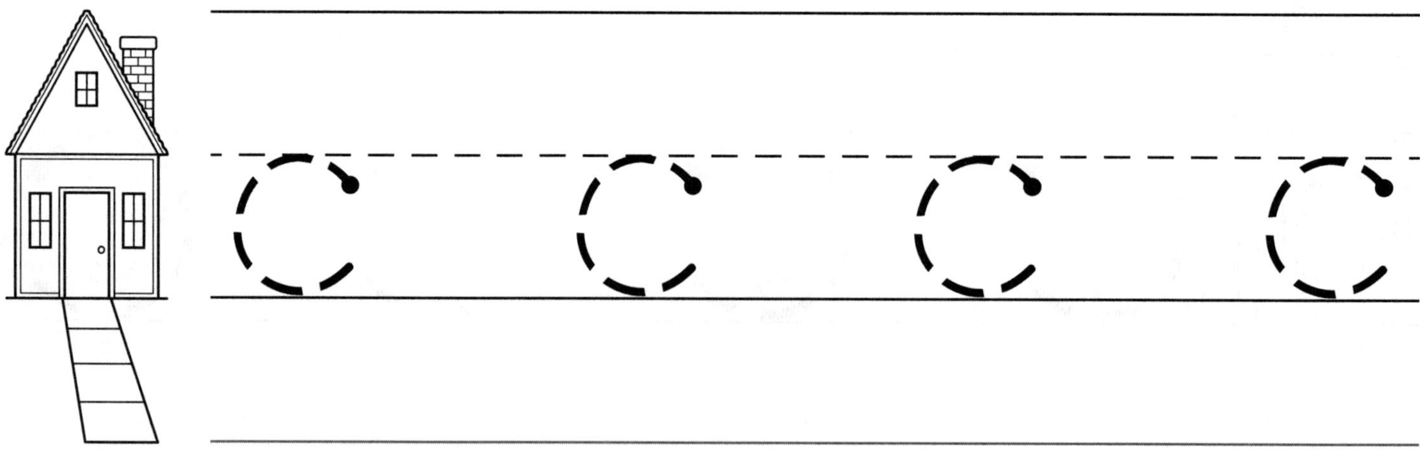

Direct children to trace the *c*'s and say /k/ as in *cat* as they trace each letter.

c /k/ cat

Identify the pictures with children. Have them circle the pictures in each row that begin with /k/ as in *cat*.

c /k/ cat 

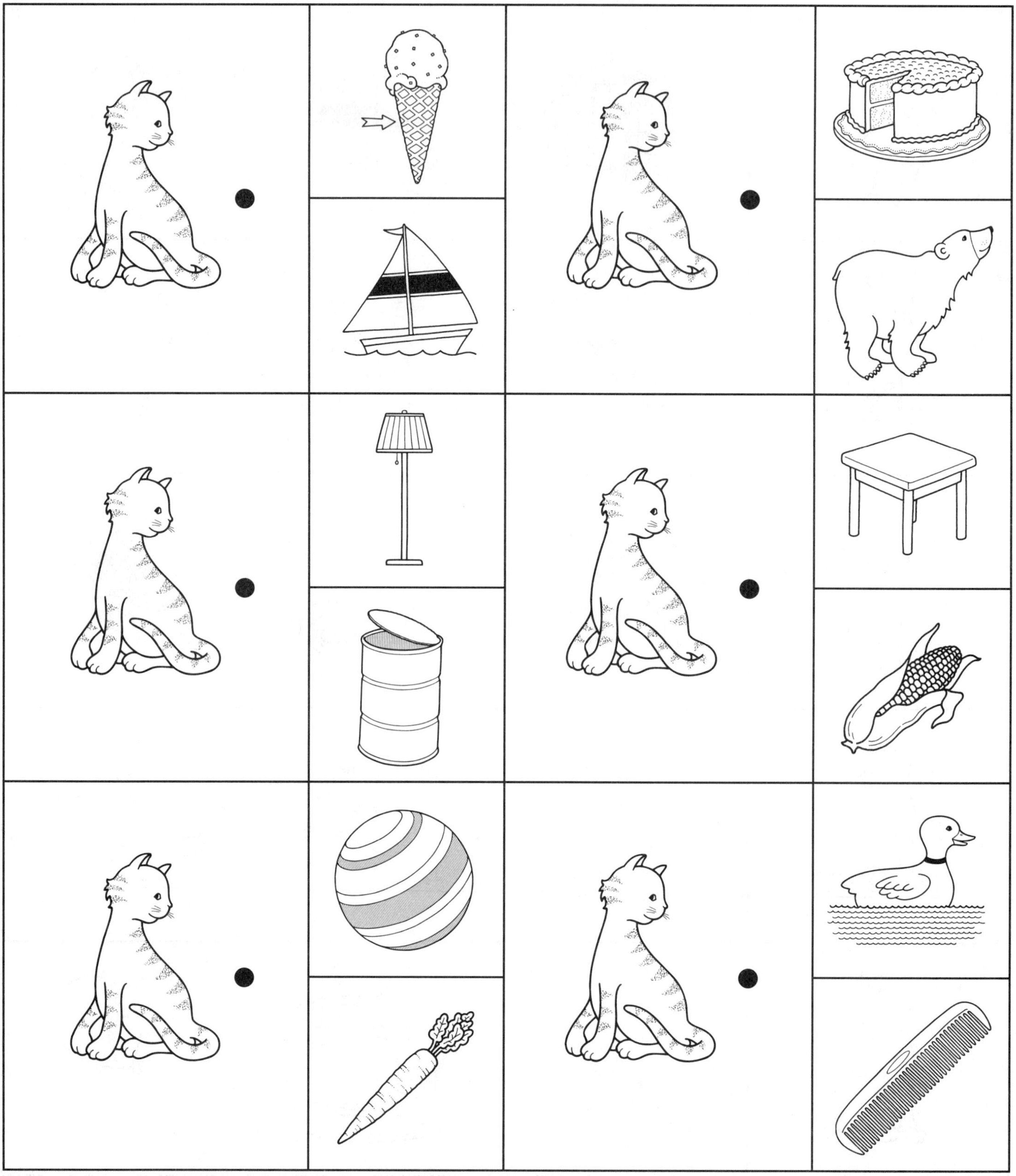

Identify the pictures with children. Tell them to start at the dot next to the cat and draw a line to the picture that begins with /k/ as in *cat*.

c /k/ cat

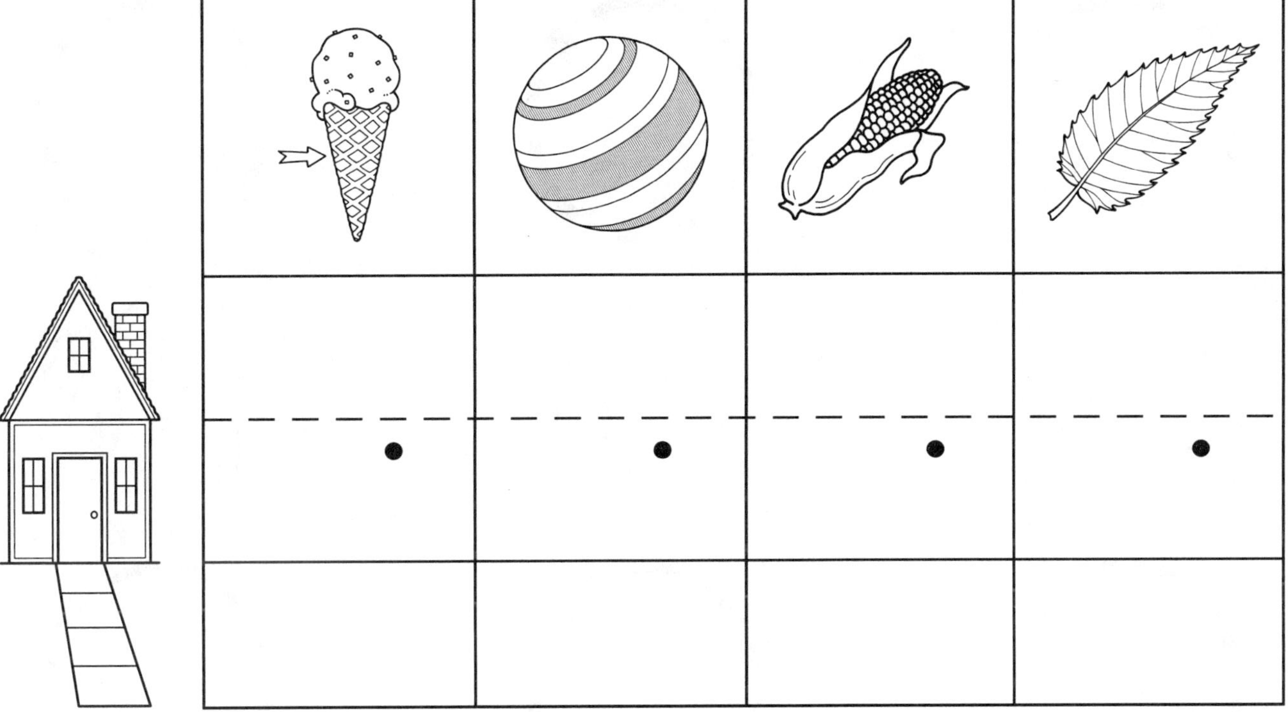

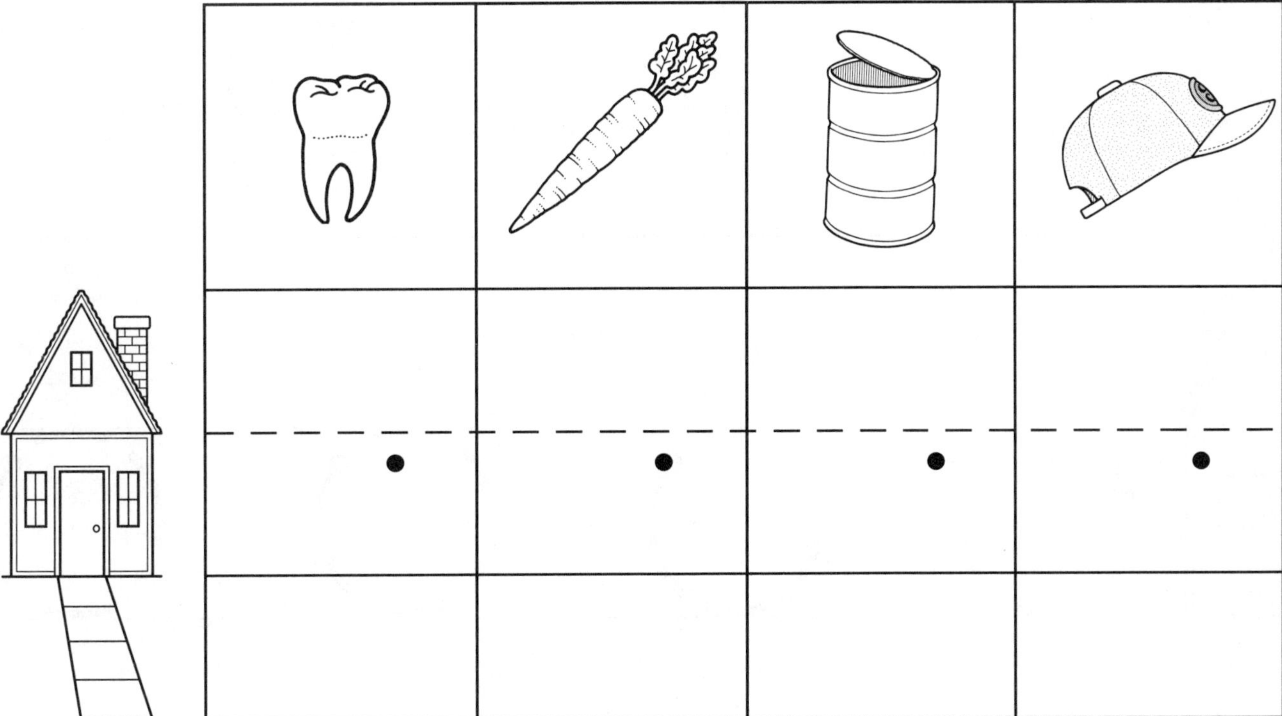

Identify the pictures with children. Direct them to circle each picture that begins with /k/ as in *cat* and print the letter *c* under it, starting at the dot.

Lesson 2

o /ŏ/ octopus

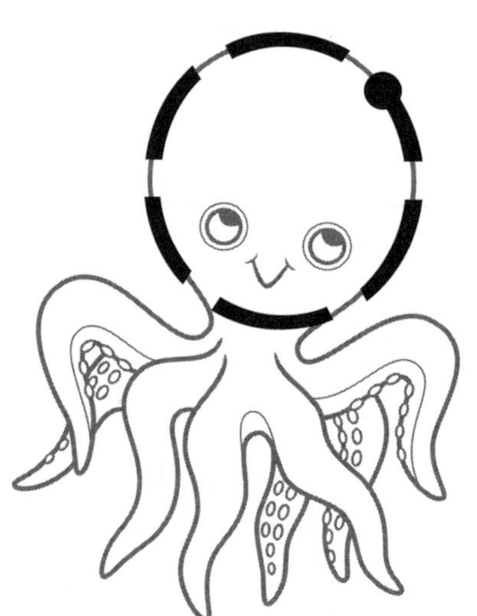

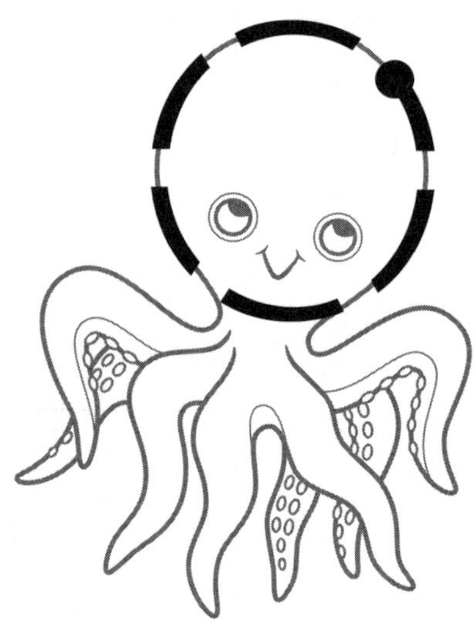

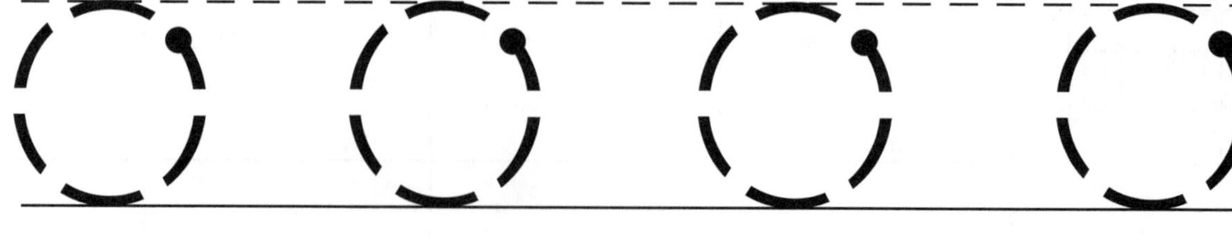

Have children trace all of the *o*'s on this page. Tell them to start at the dot and say /ŏ/ as in *octopus* as they trace each *o*.

o /ŏ/ octopus 

Direct children to trace the *o*'s and say /ŏ/ as in *octopus* as they trace each letter.

o /ŏ/ octopus 

Identify the pictures with children. Have them circle the pictures in each row that begin with /ŏ/ as in *octopus.*

o /ŏ/ octopus

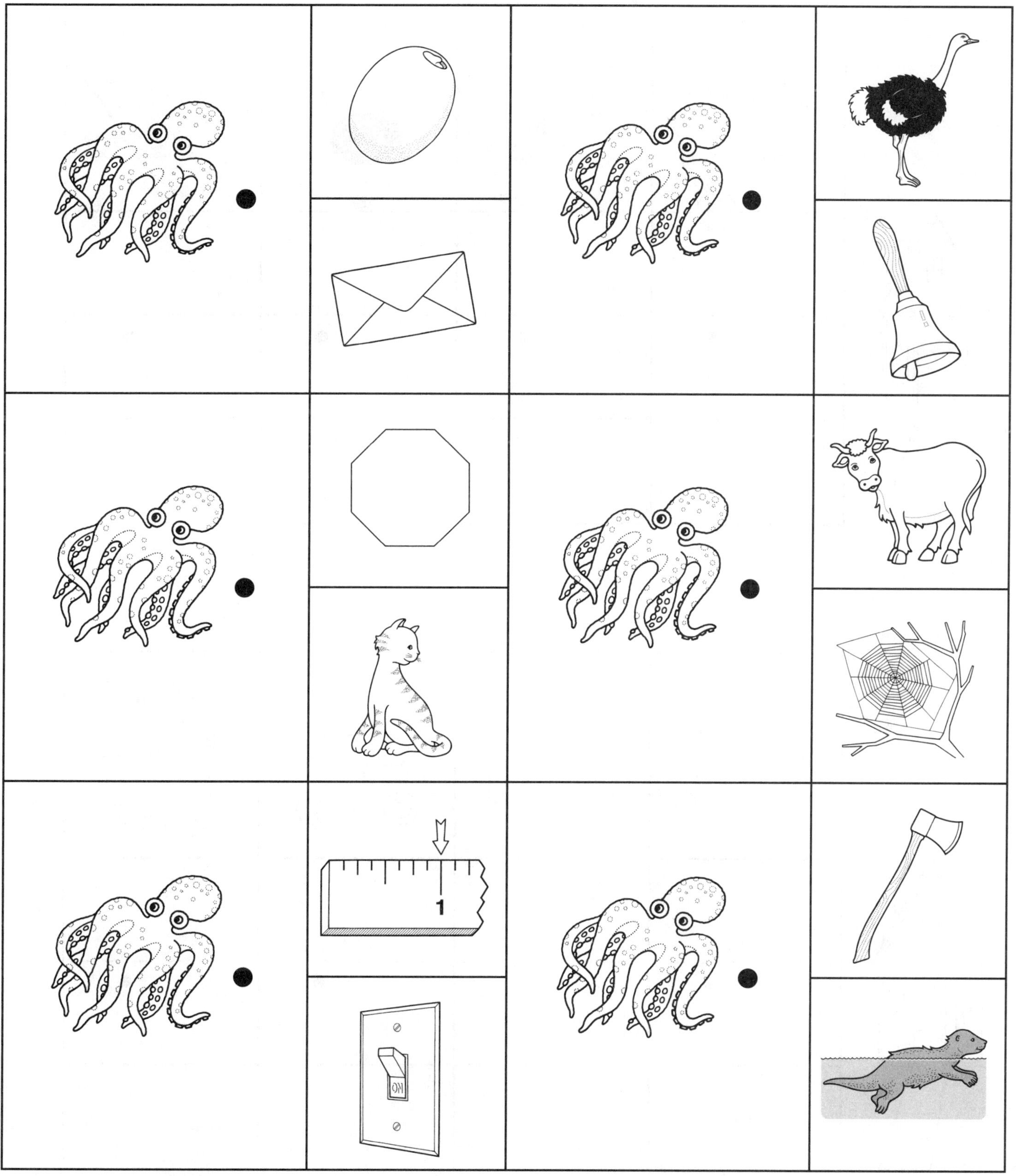

Identify the pictures with children. Tell them to start at the dot next to the octopus and draw a line to the picture that begins with /ŏ/ as in *octopus*.

o /ŏ/ octopus 

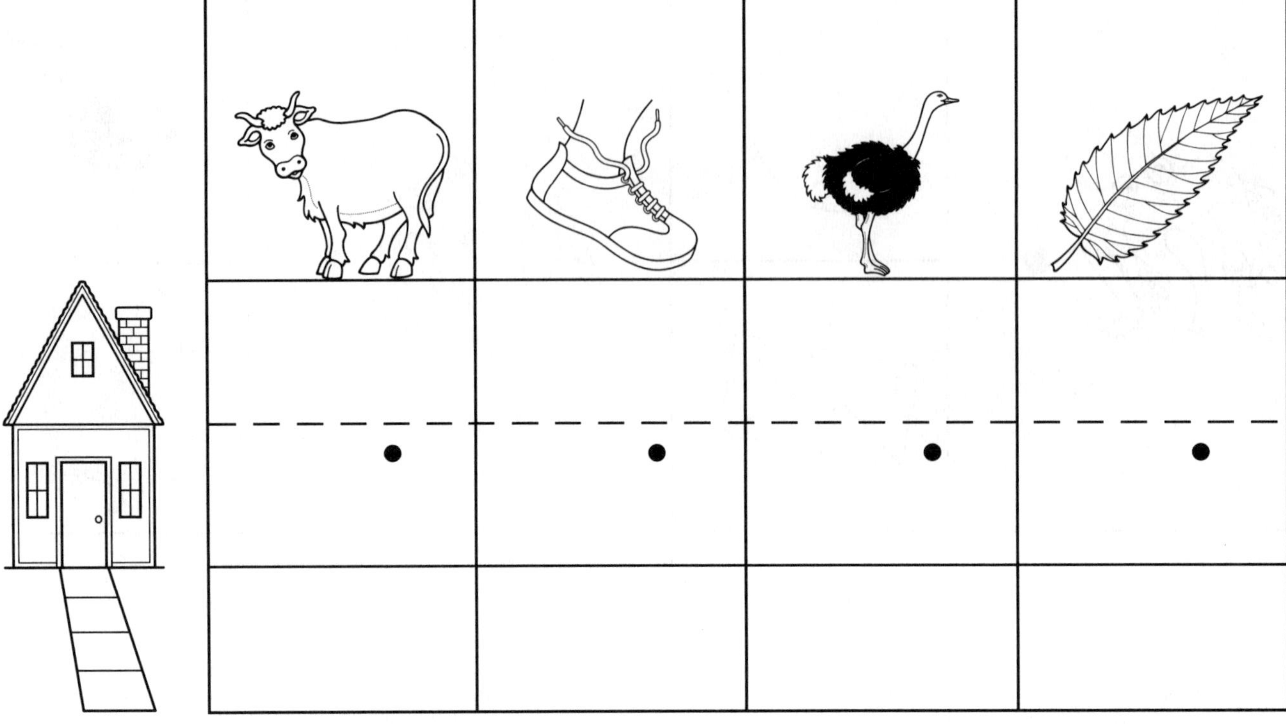

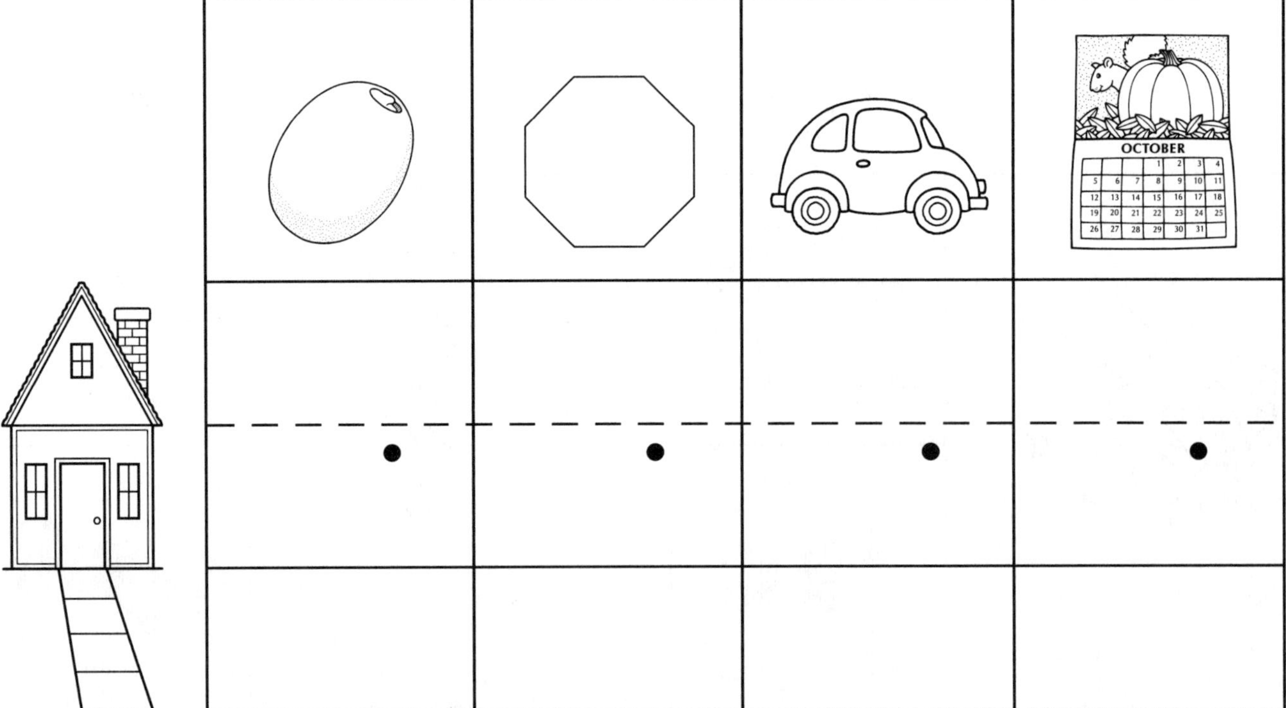

Identify the pictures with children. Direct them to circle each picture that begins with /ŏ/ as in *octopus* and print the letter *o* under it, starting at the dot.

Lesson 3

a /ă/ apple

Have children trace all of the *a*'s on this page. Tell them to start at the dot and say /ă/ as in *apple* as they trace each *a*.

a /ă/ apple

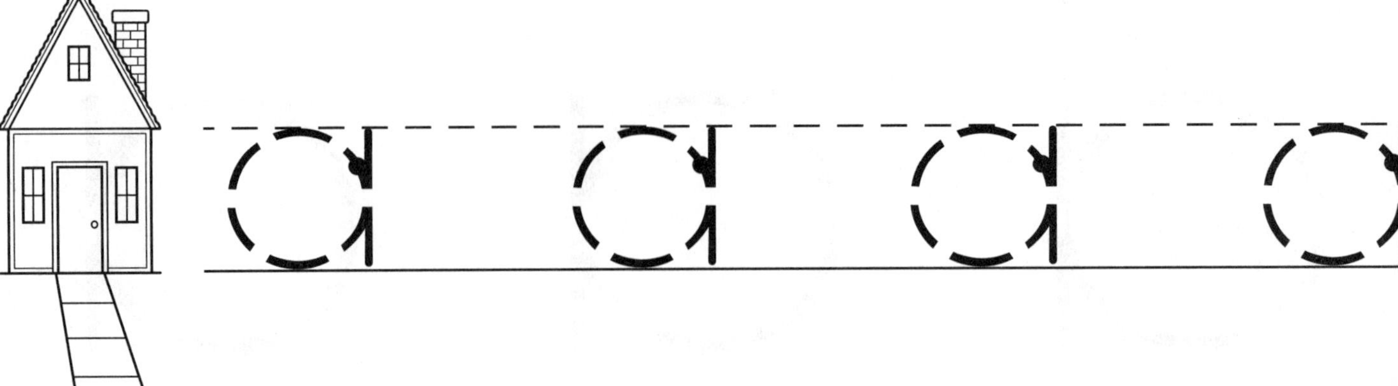

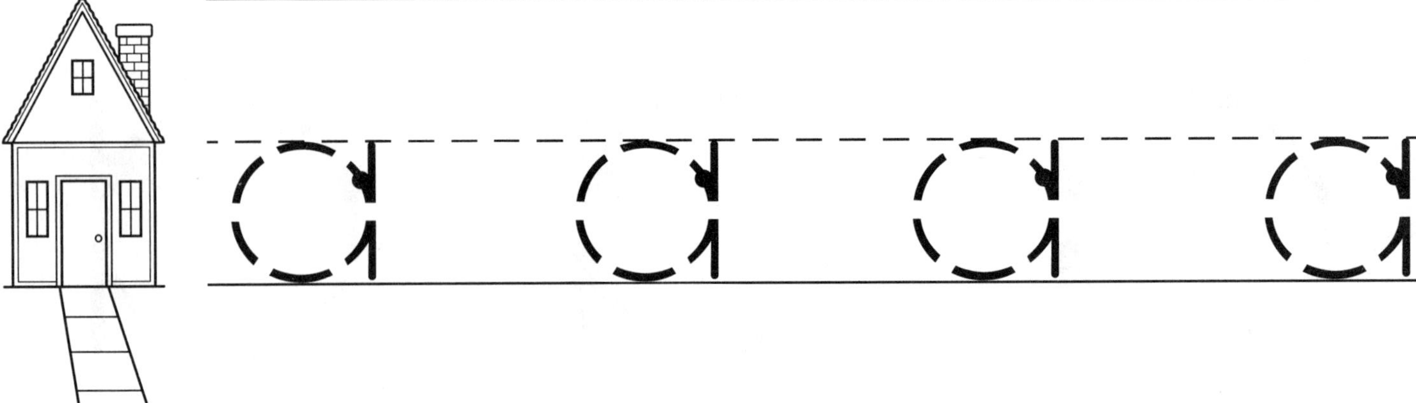

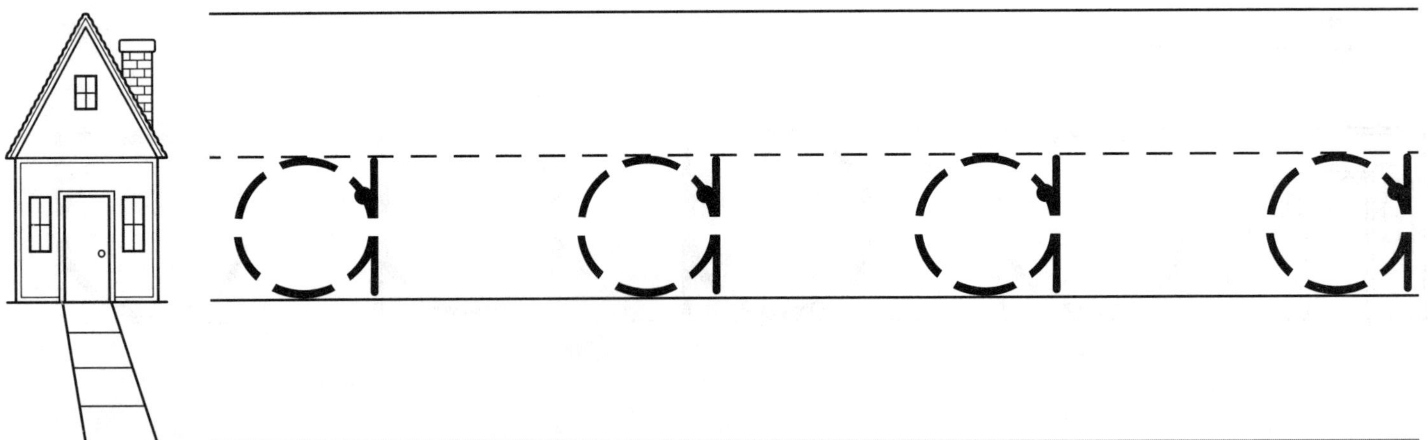

Direct children to trace the *a*'s and say /ă/ as in *apple* as they trace each letter.

a /ă/ apple

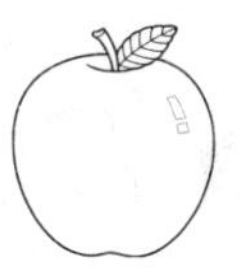

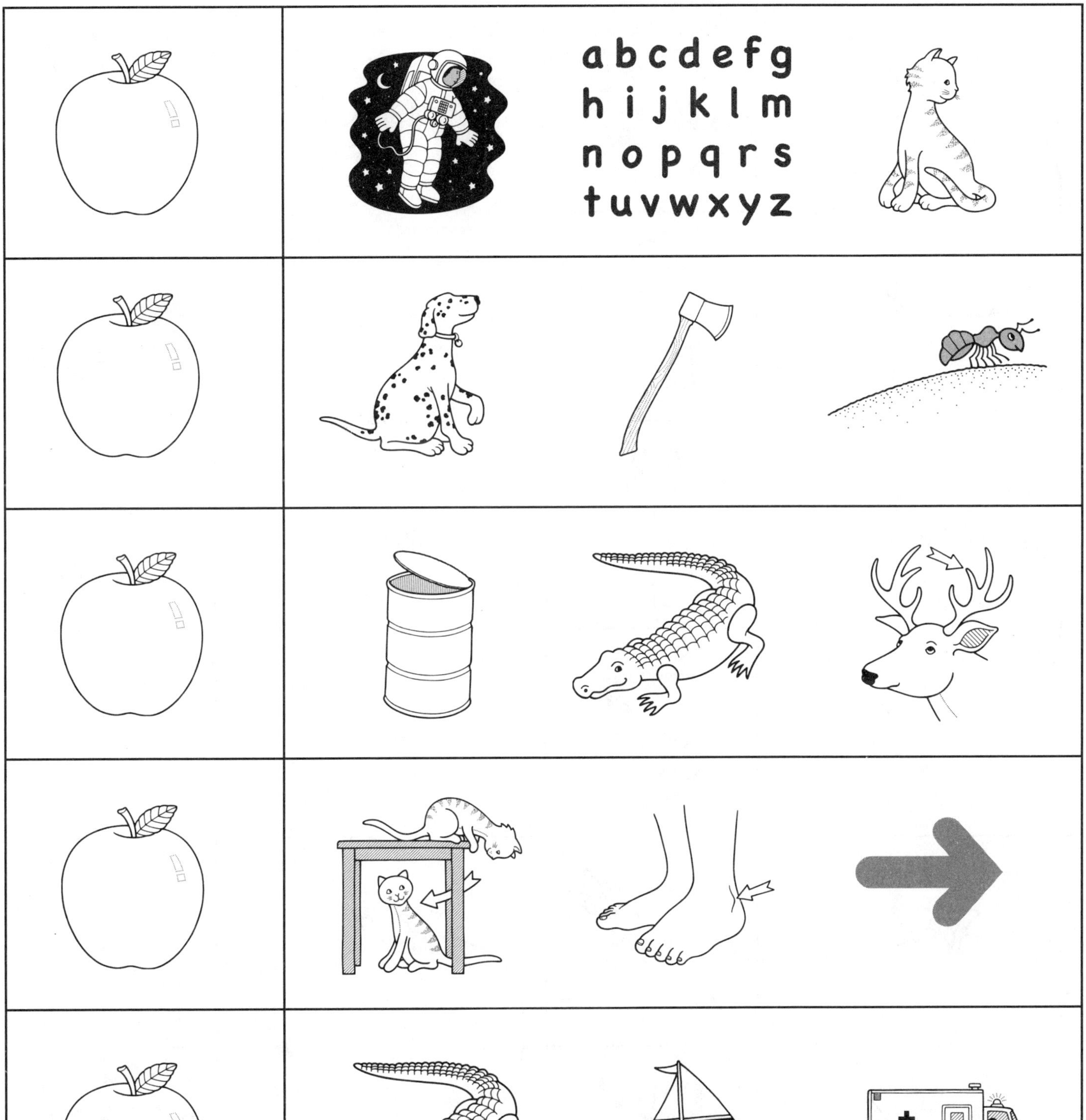
abcdefg
hijklm
nopqrs
tuvwxyz
AMBULANCE

Identify the pictures with children. Have them circle the pictures in each row that begin with /ă/ as in *apple*.

a /ă/ apple

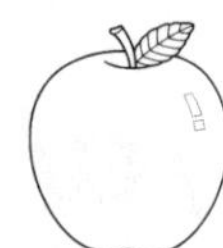

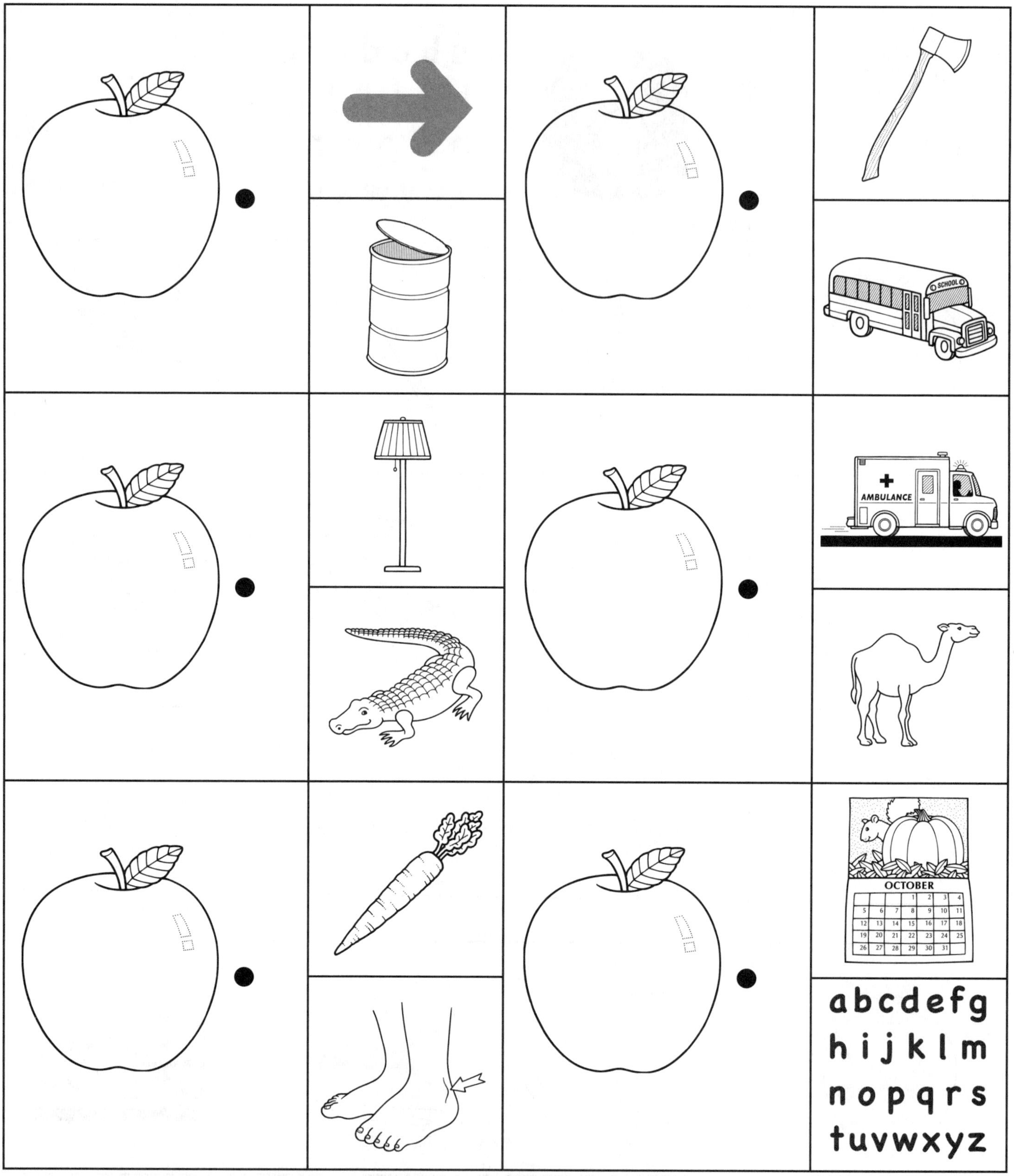
SCHOOL
AMBULANCE
OCTOBER
abcdefg
hijklm
nopqrs
tuvwxyz

Identify the pictures with children. Tell them to start at the dot next to the apple and draw a line to the picture that begins with /ă/ as in *apple*.

a /ă/ apple 

abcdefg
hijklm
nopqrs
tuvwxyz

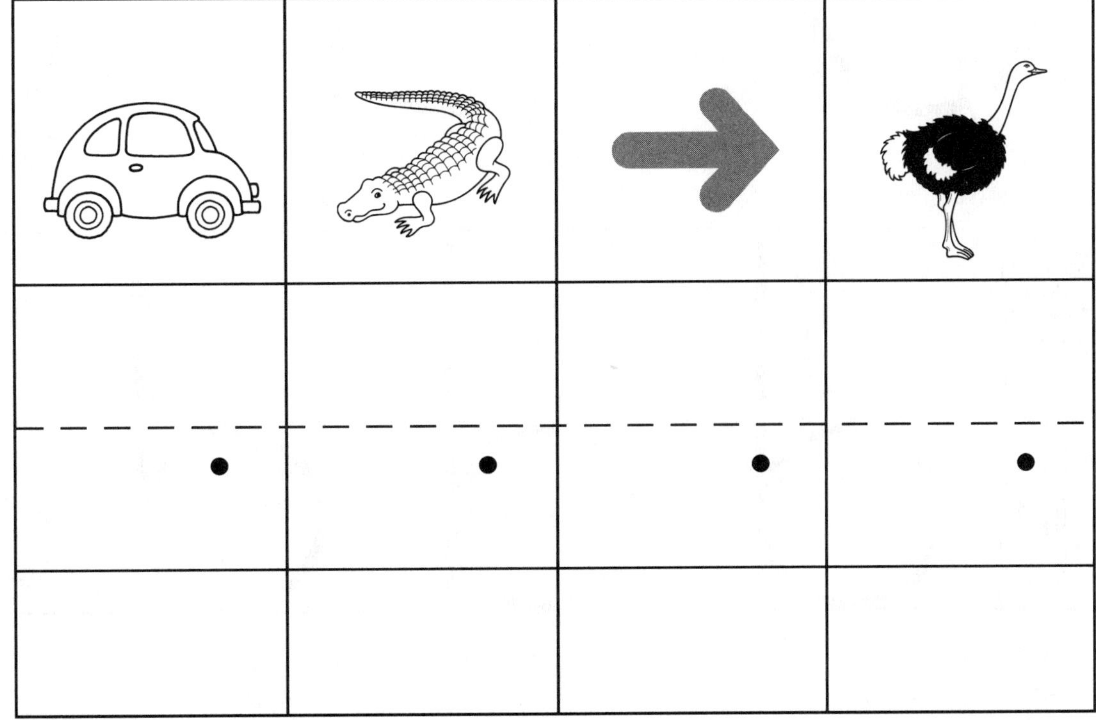

Identify the pictures with children. Direct them to circle each picture that begins with /ă/ as in *apple* and print the letter *a* under it, starting at the dot.

Lesson 4

d /d/ dog

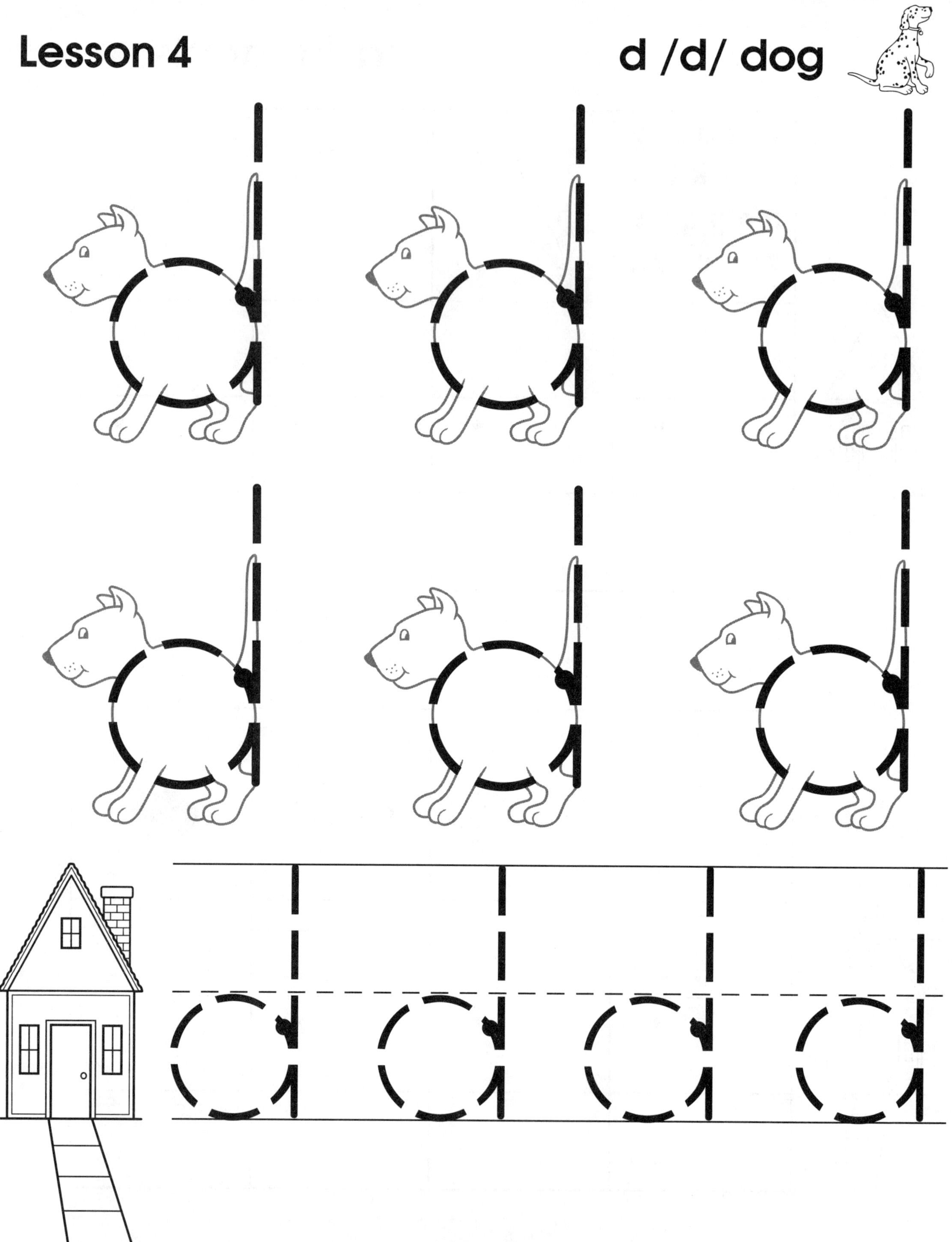

Have children trace all of the *d*'s on this page. Tell them to start at the dot and say /d/ as in *dog* as they trace each *d*.

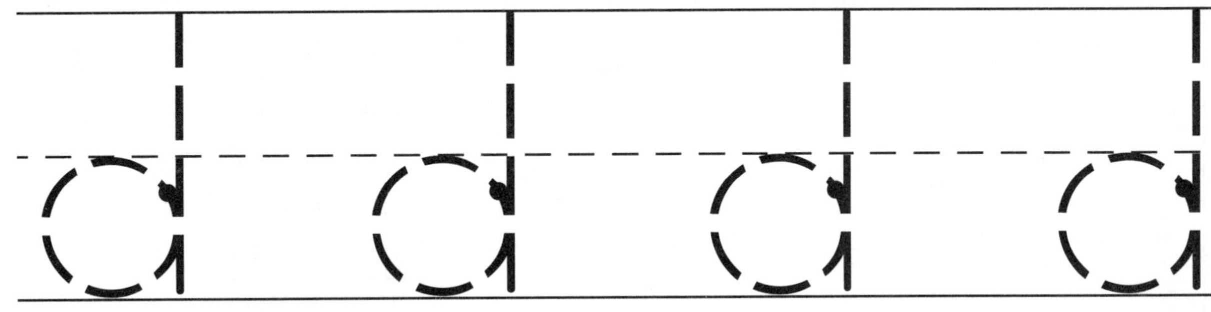

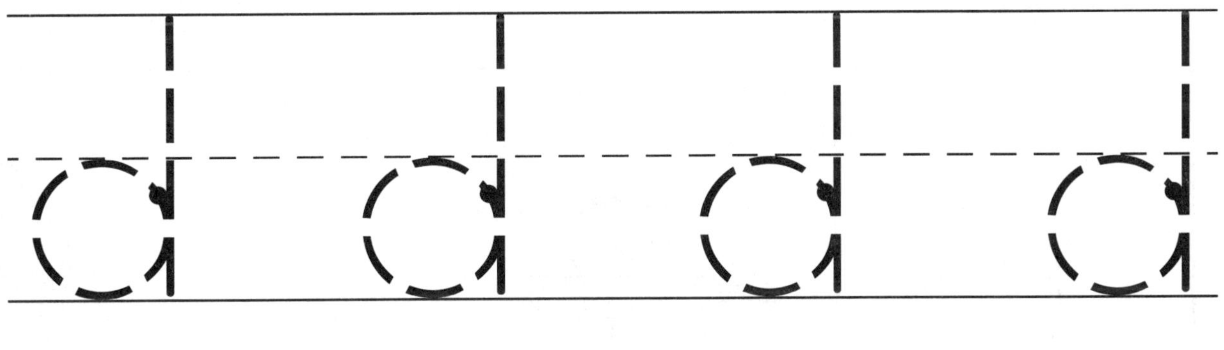

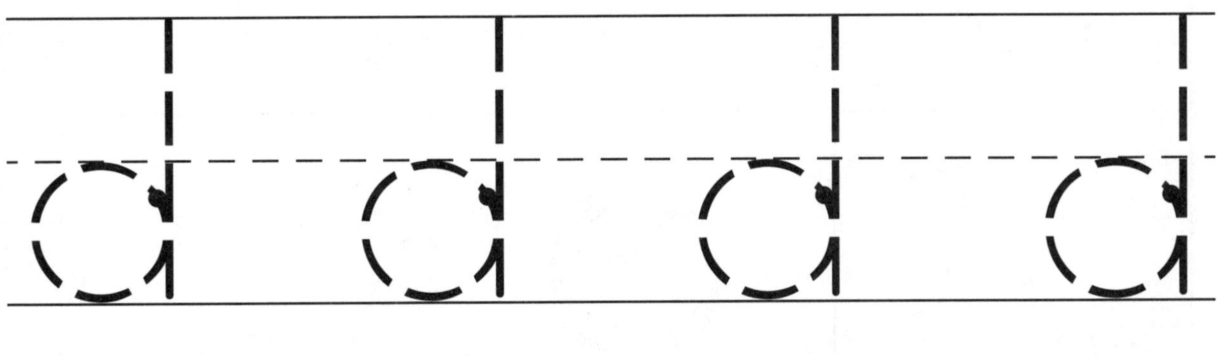

Direct children to trace the *d*'s and say /d/ as in *dog* as they trace each letter.

d /d/ dog 

Identify the pictures with children. Have them circle the pictures in each row that begin with /d/ as in *dog.*

d /d/ dog

Identify the pictures with children. Tell them to start at the dot next to the dog and draw a line to the picture that begins with /d/ as in *dog*.

d /d/ dog 

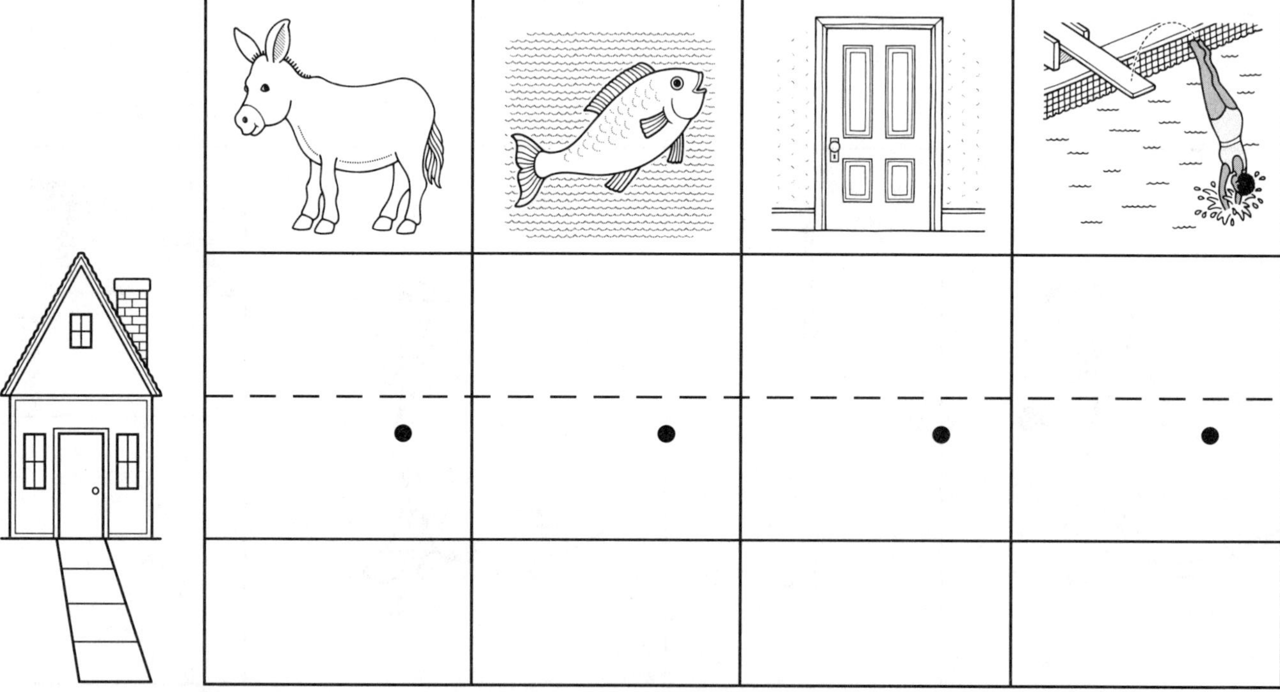

Identify the pictures with children. Direct them to circle each picture that begins with /d/ as in *dog* and print the letter *d* under it, starting at the dot.

Lesson 5

g /g/ goat

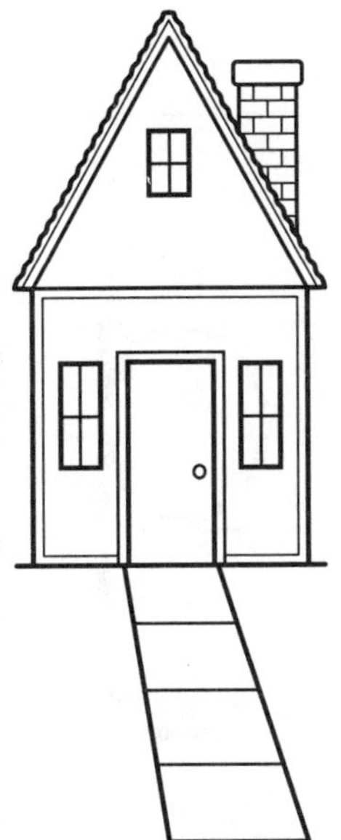

Have children trace all of the *g*'s on this page. Tell them to start at the dot and say /g/ as in *goat* as they trace each *g*.

g /g/ goat

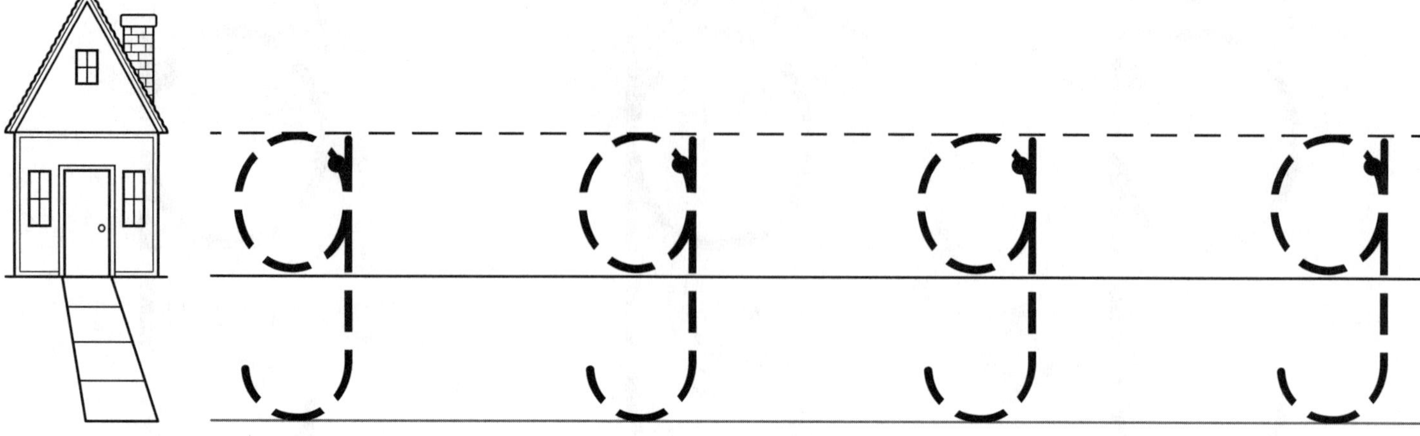

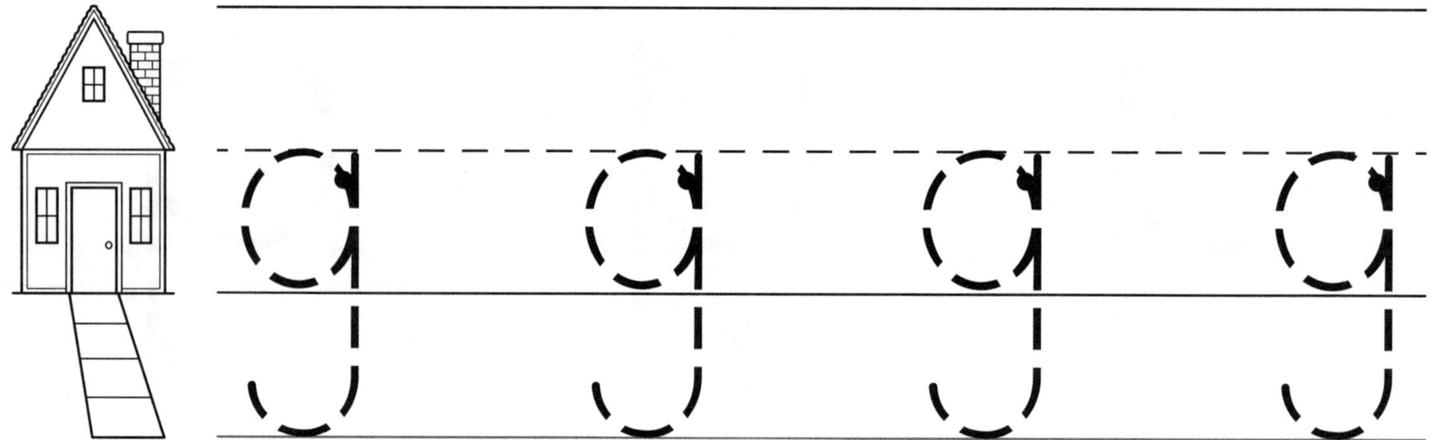

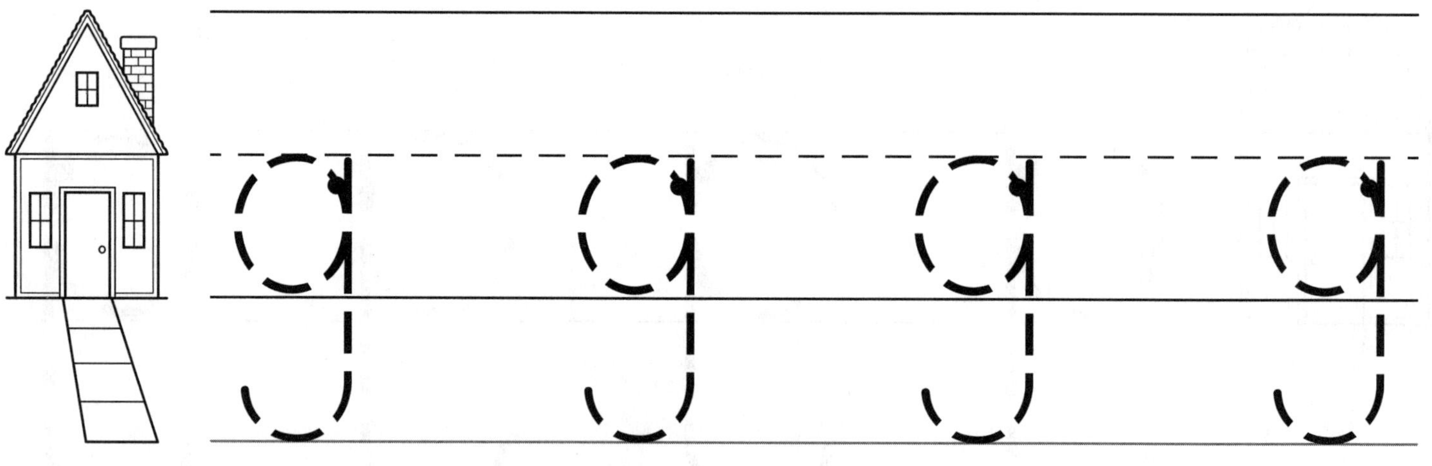

Direct children to trace the *g*'s and say /g/ as in *goat* as they trace each letter.

g /g/ goat

Identify the pictures with children. Have them circle the pictures in each row that begin with /g/ as in *goat*.

g /g/ goat 

Identify the pictures with children. Tell them to start at the dot next to the goat and draw a line to the picture that begins with /g/ as in *goat*.

g /g/ goat

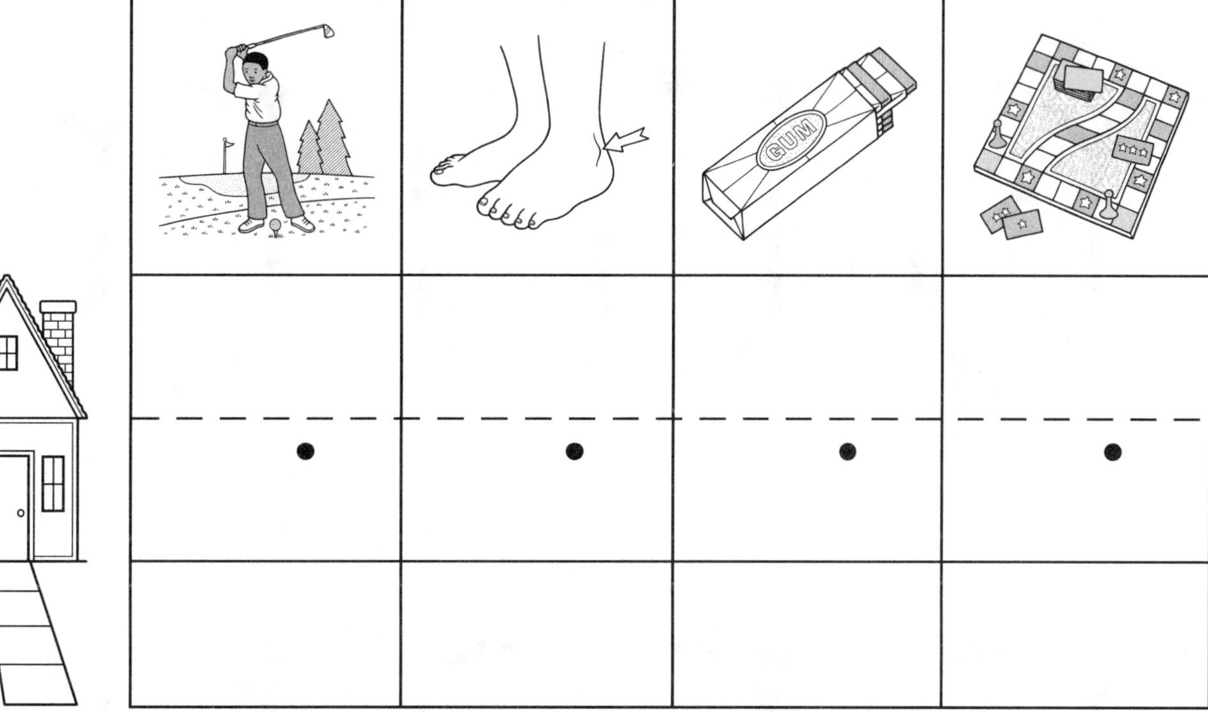

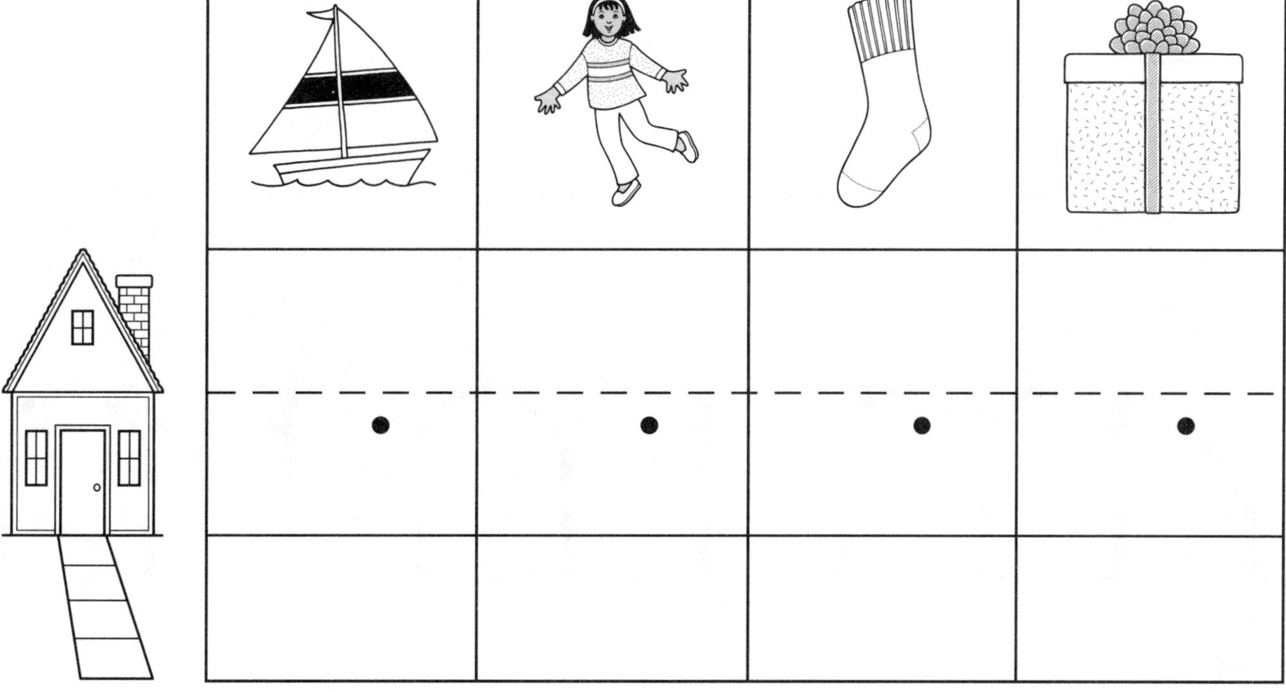

Identify the pictures with children. Direct them to circle each picture that begins with /g/ as in *goat* and print the letter *g* under it, starting at the dot.

Lesson 6

m /m/ moon 

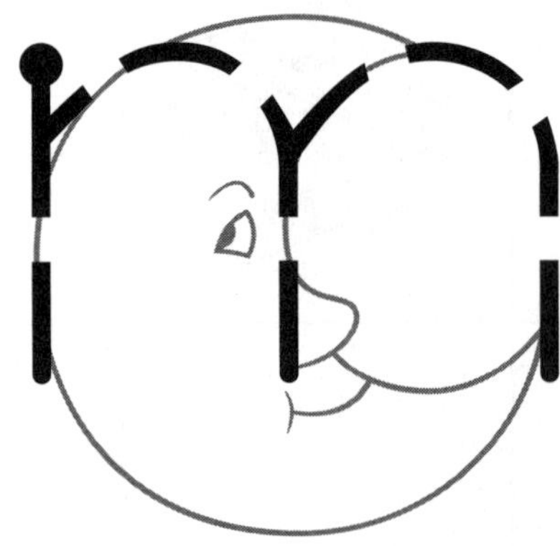

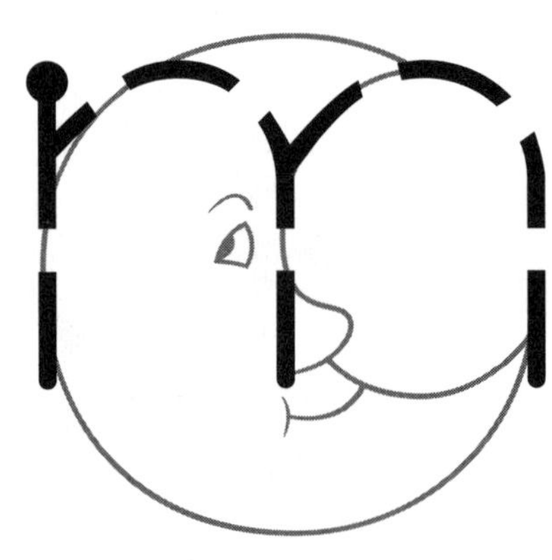
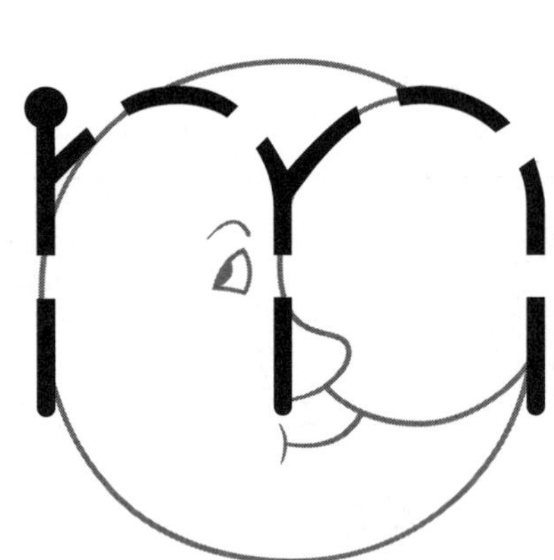
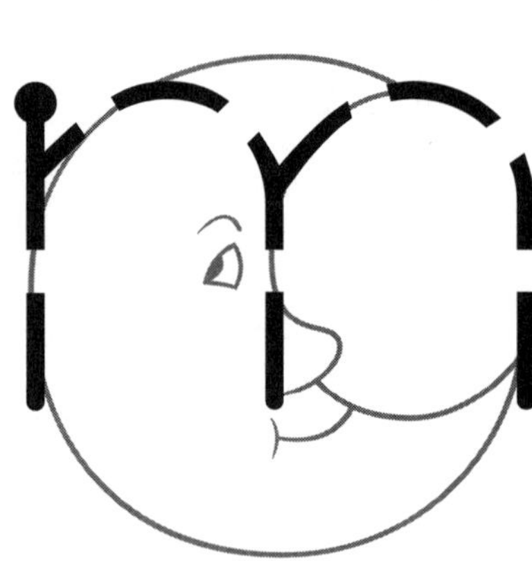

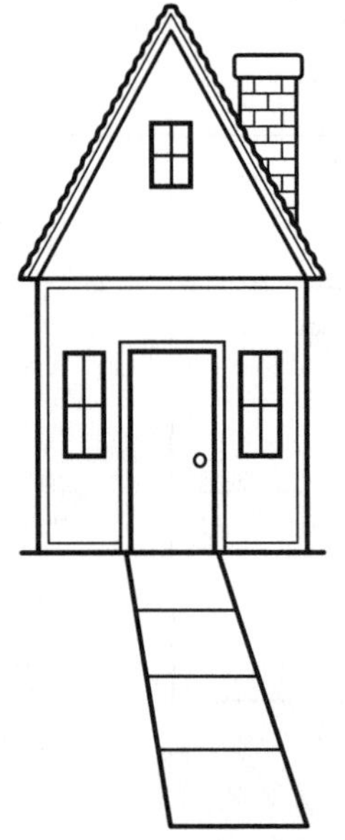
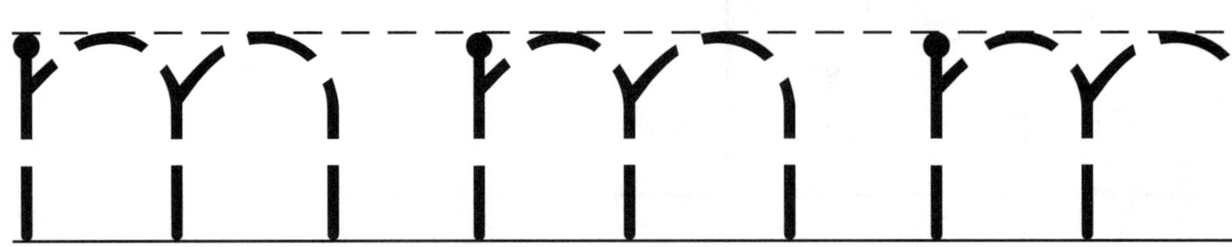

Have children trace all of the *m*'s on this page. Tell them to start at the dot and say /m/ as in *moon* as they trace each *m*.

m /m/ moon

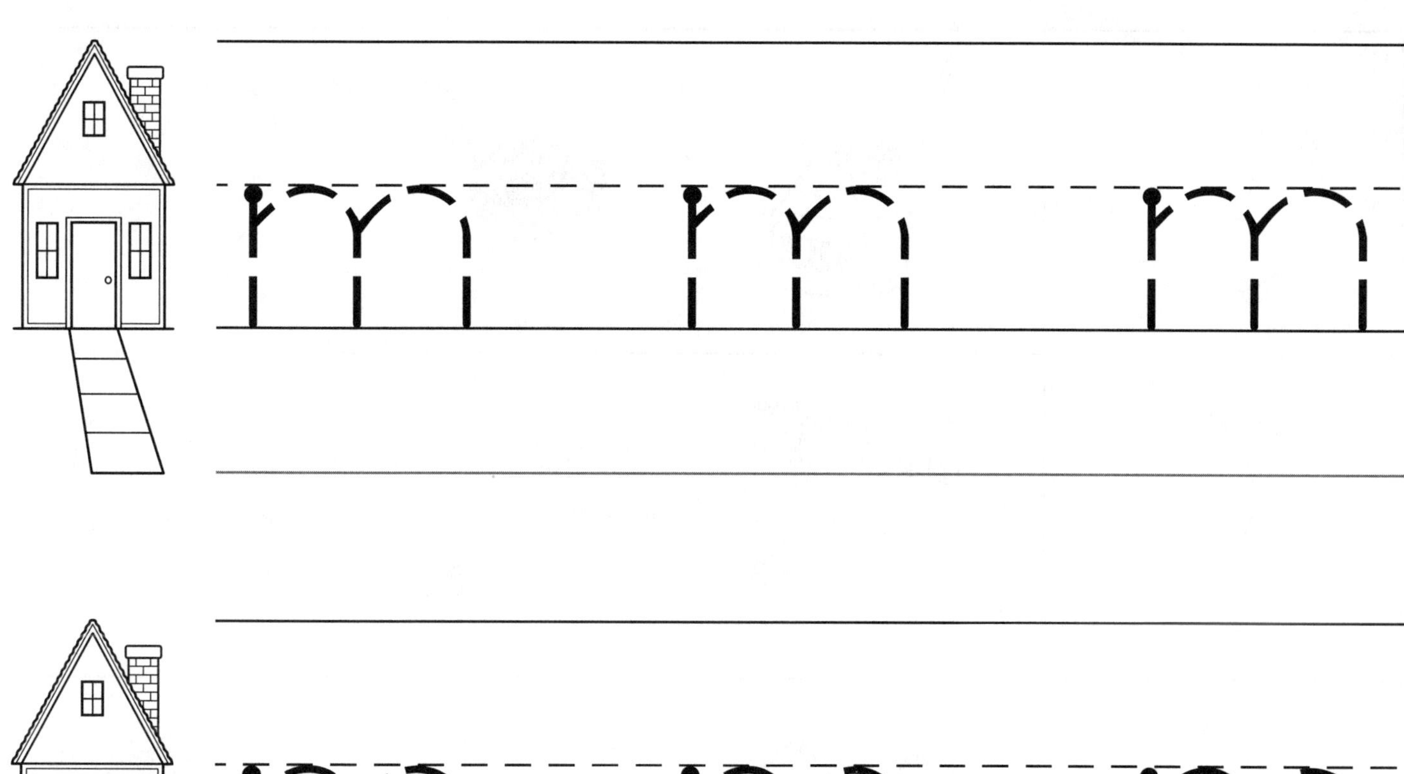

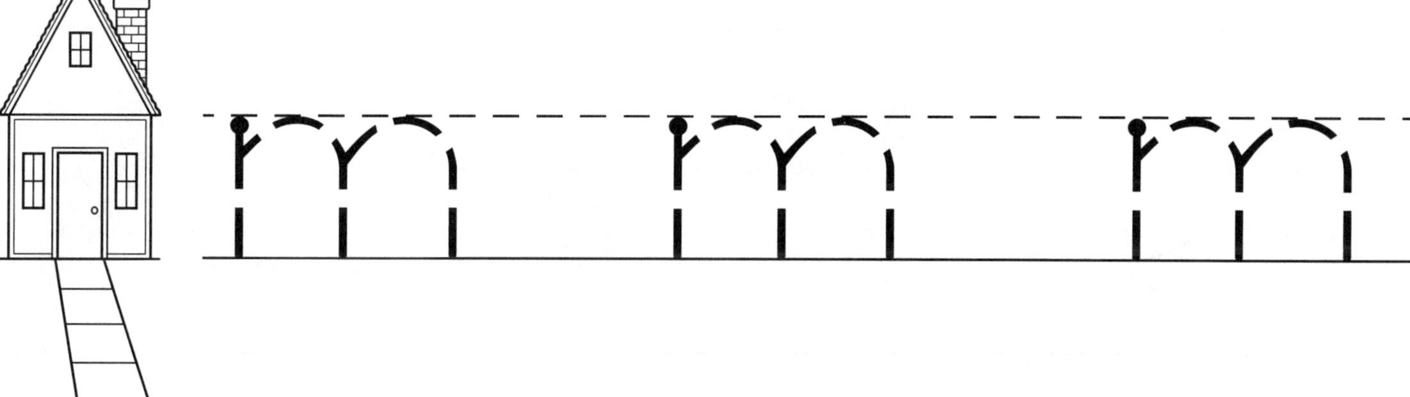

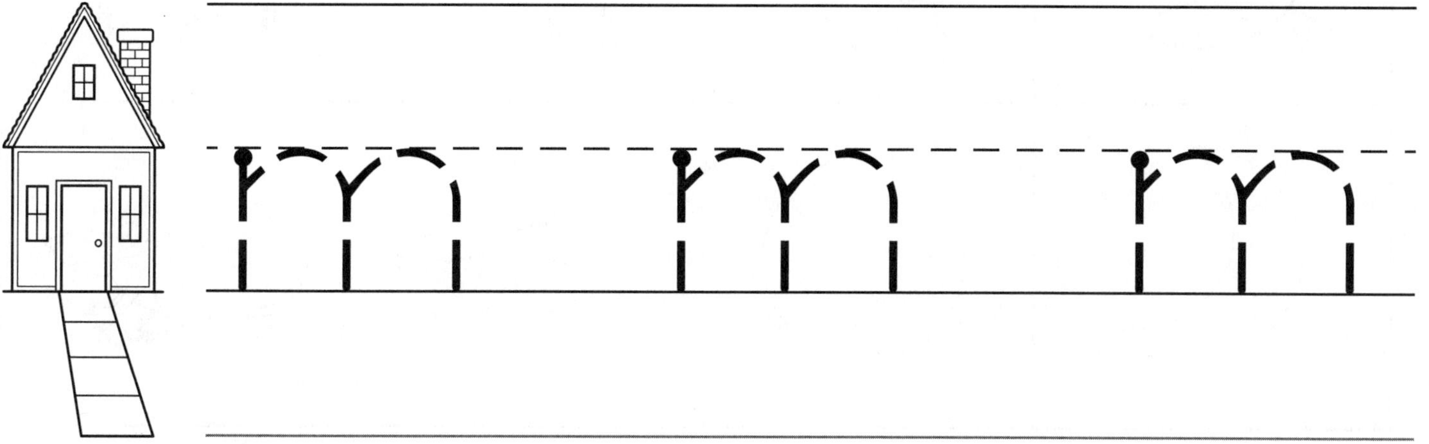

Direct children to trace the *m*'s and say /m/ as in *moon* as they trace each letter.

m /m/ moon

Identify the pictures with children. Have them circle the pictures in each row that begin with /m/ as in *moon*.

m /m/ moon 

Identify the pictures with children. Tell them to start at the dot next to the moon and draw a line to the picture that begins with /m/ as in *moon* .

m /m/ moon

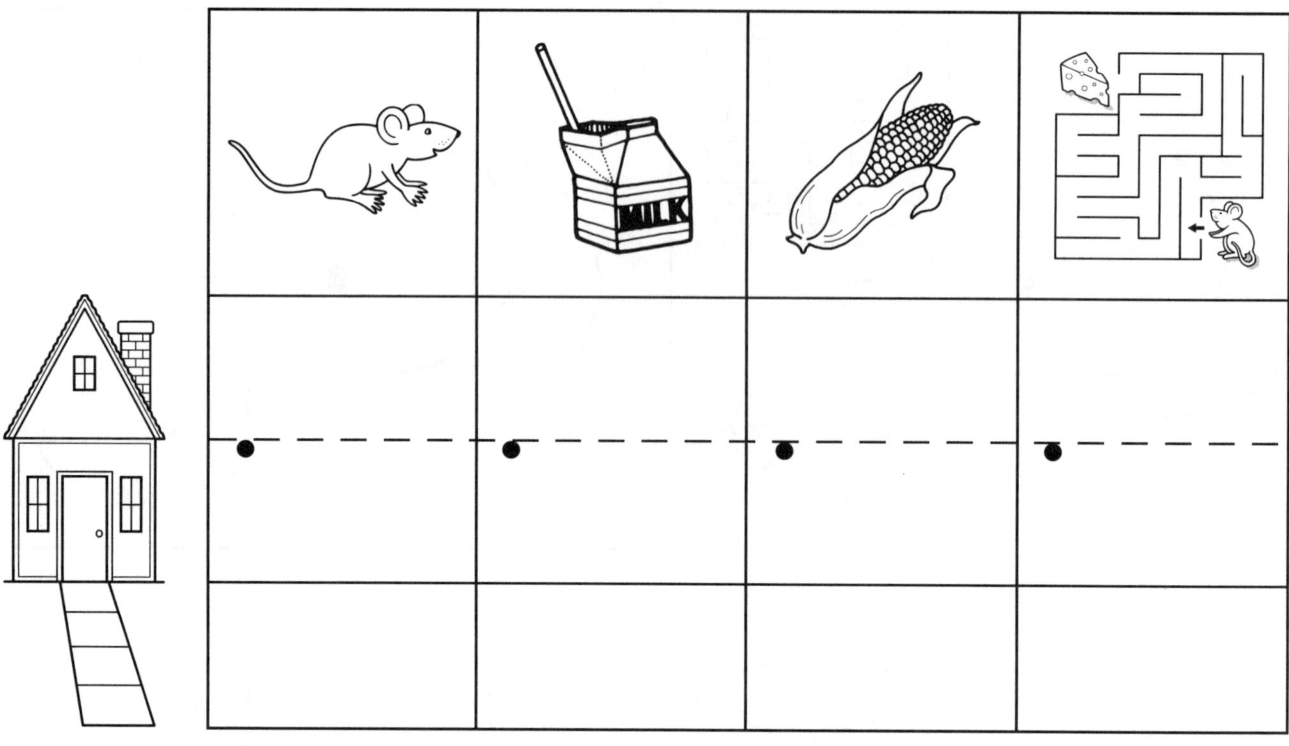

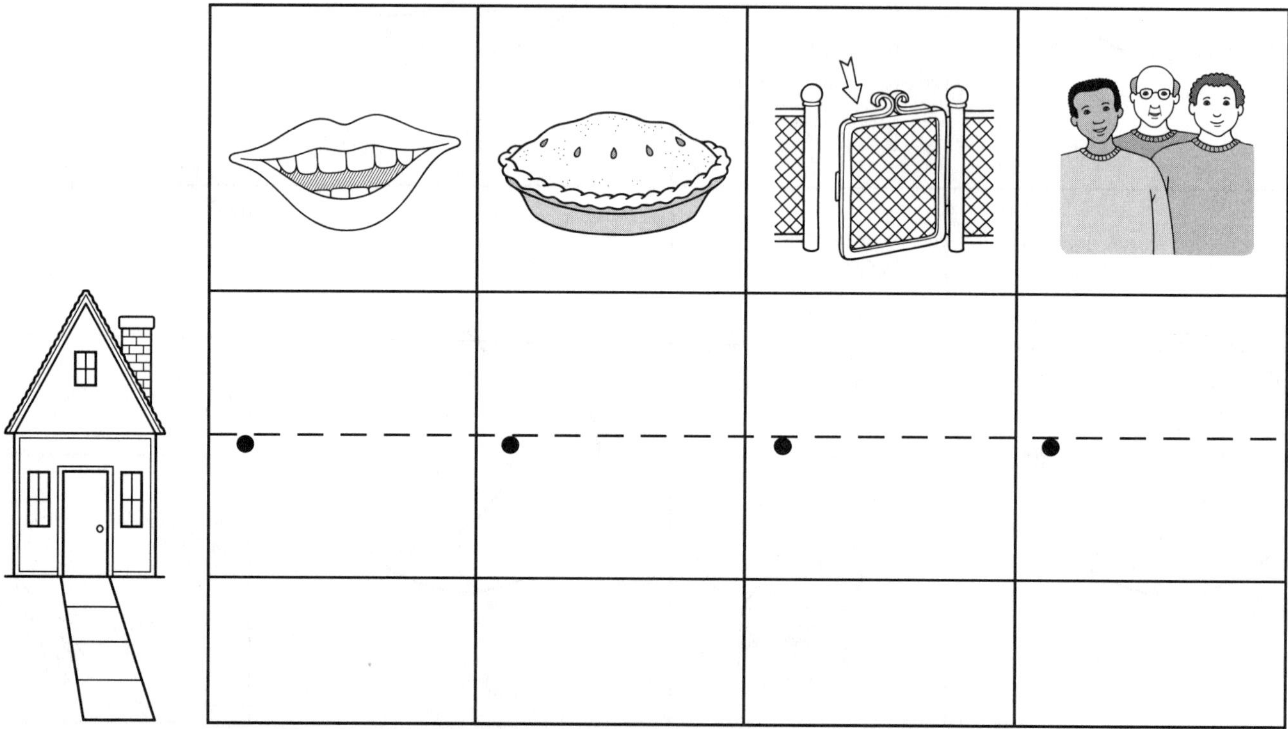

Identify the pictures with children. Direct them to circle each picture that begins with /m/ as in *moon* and print the letter *m* under it, starting at the dot.

Lesson 7

l /l/ log

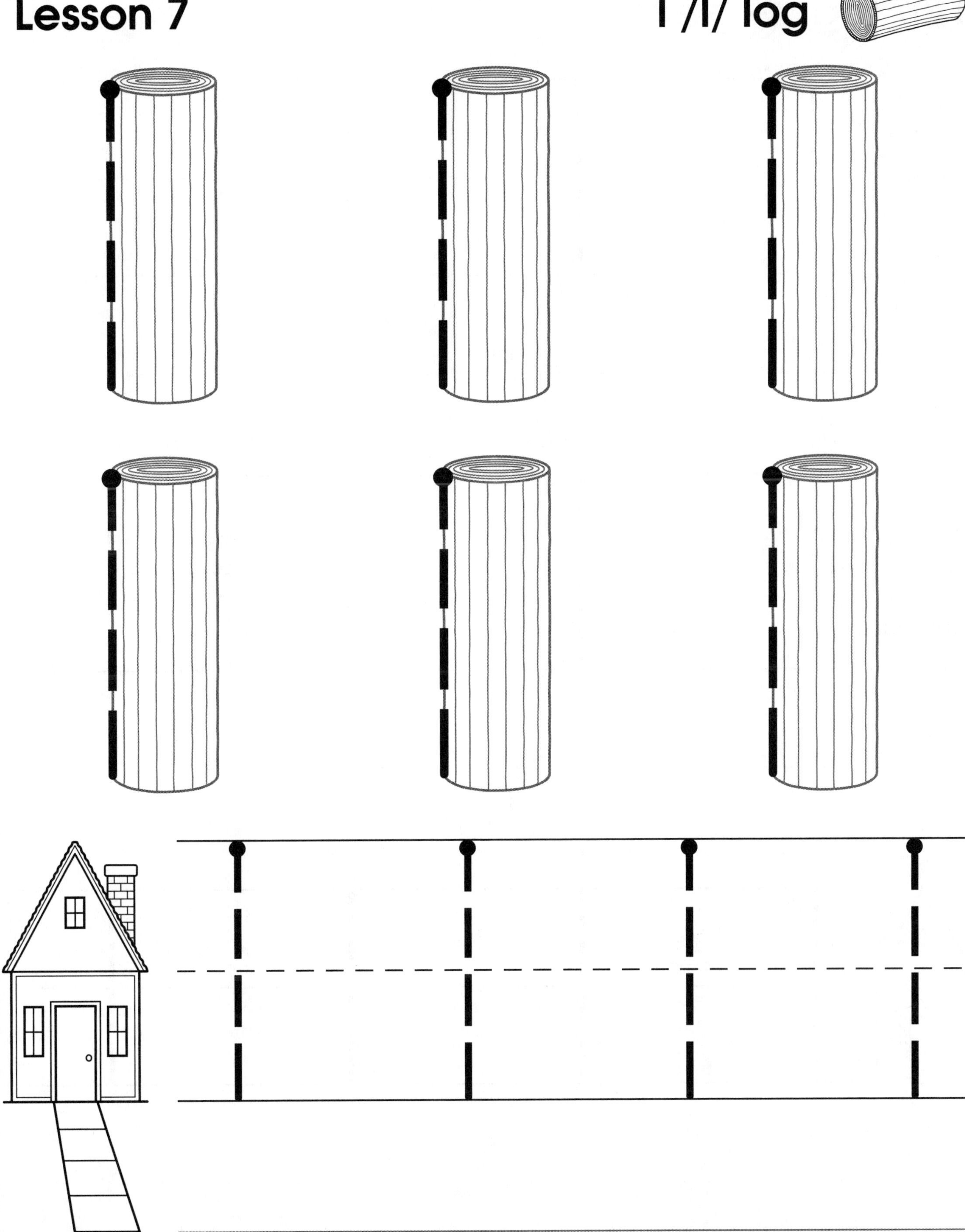

Have children trace all of the *l*'s on this page. Tell them to start at the dot and say /l/ as in *log* as they trace each *l*.

l /l/ log

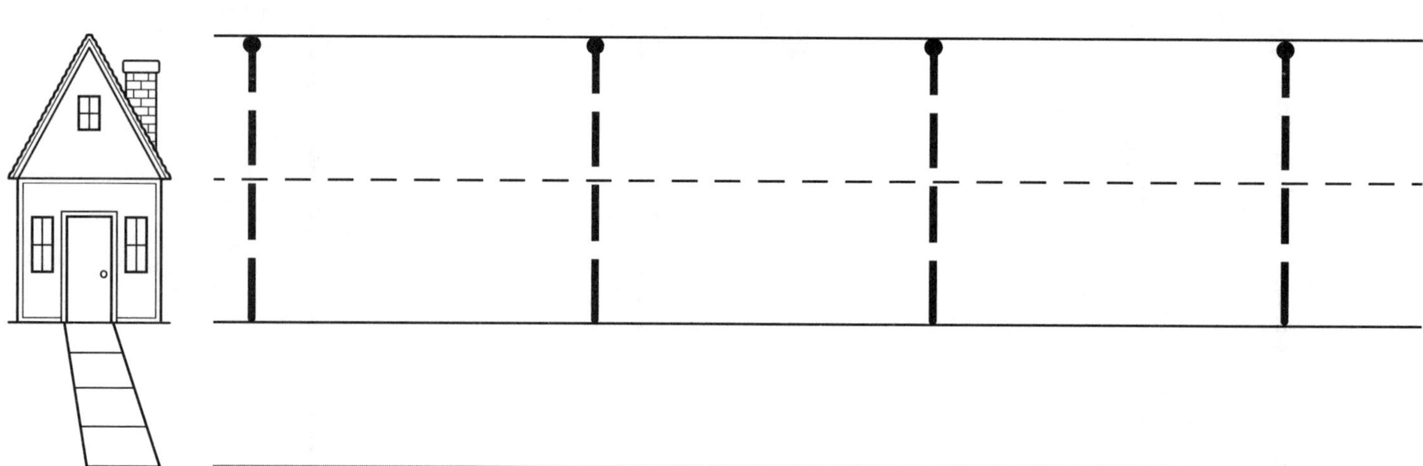

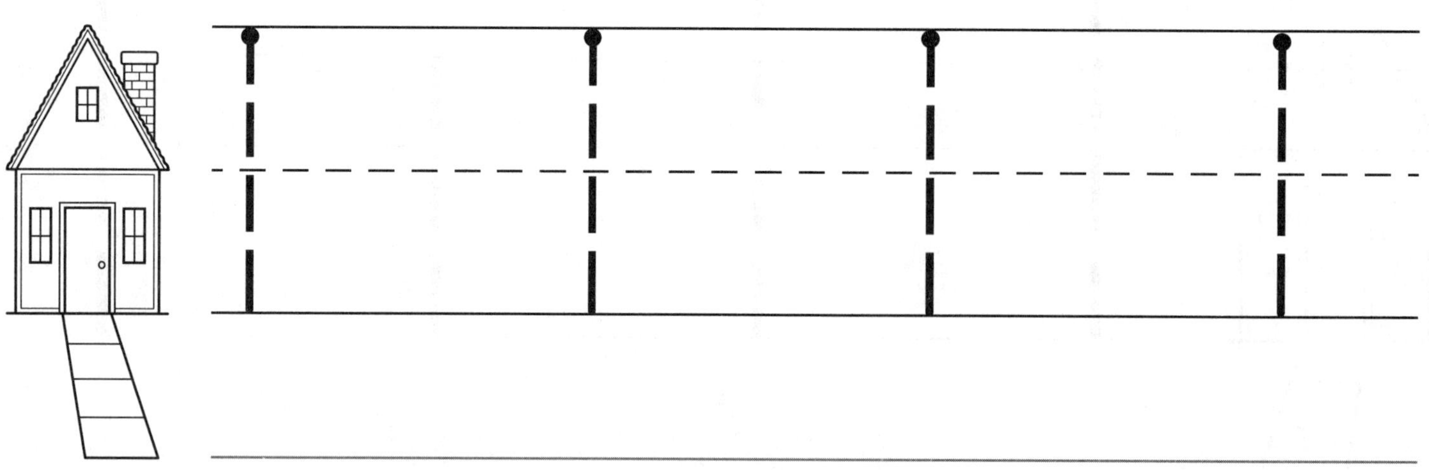

Direct children to trace the *l*'s and say /l/ as in *log* as they trace each letter.

l /l/ log 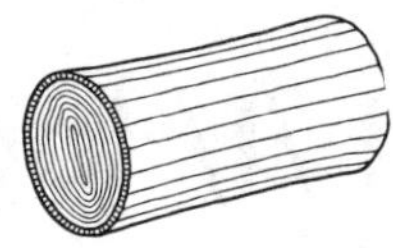

Identify the pictures with children. Have them circle the pictures in each row that begin with /l/ as in *log*.

l /l/ log

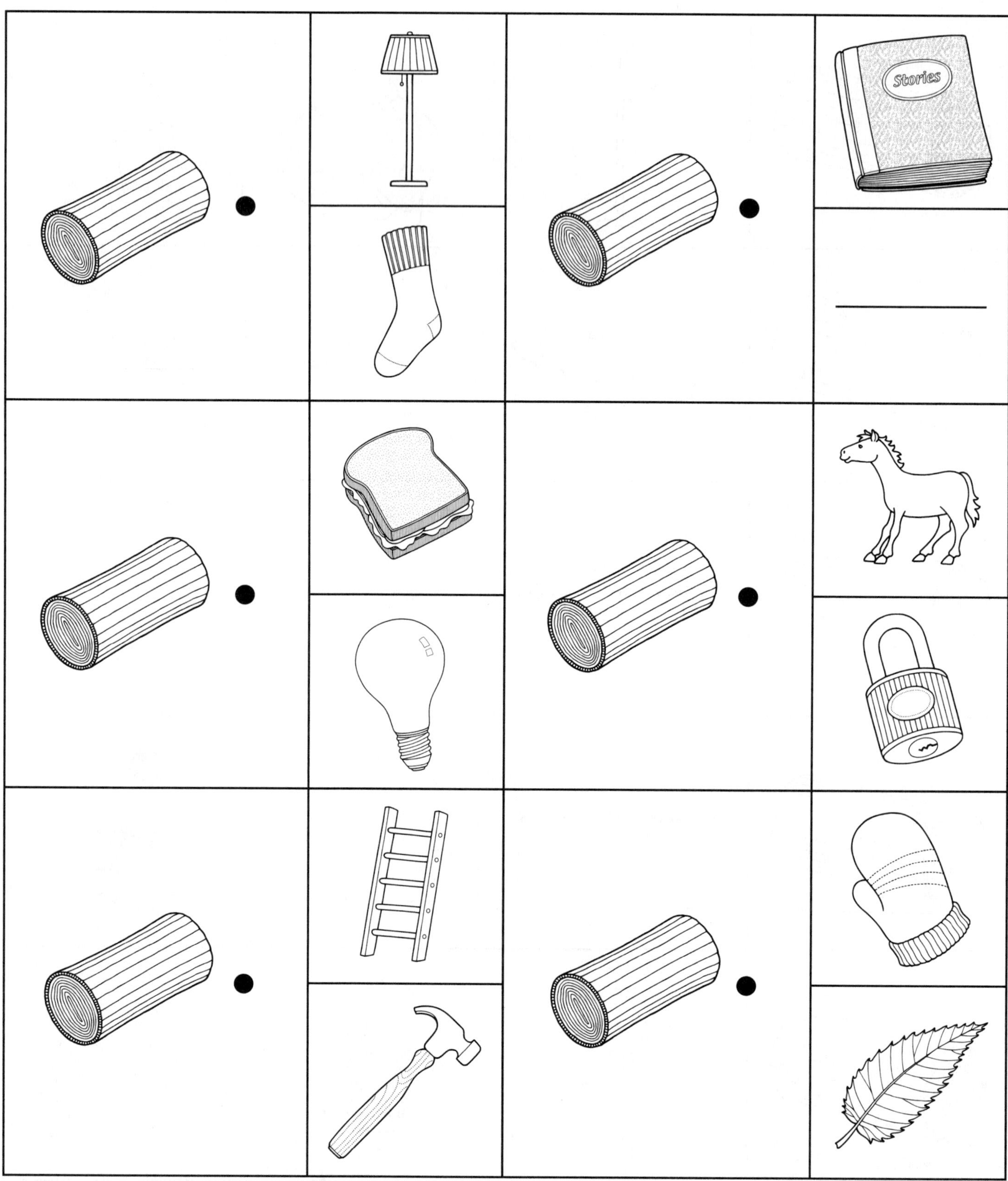

Identify the pictures with children. Tell them to start at the dot next to the log and draw a line to the picture that begins with /l/ as in *log*.

l /l/ log

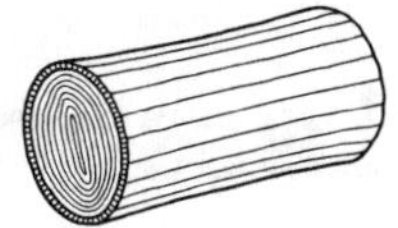

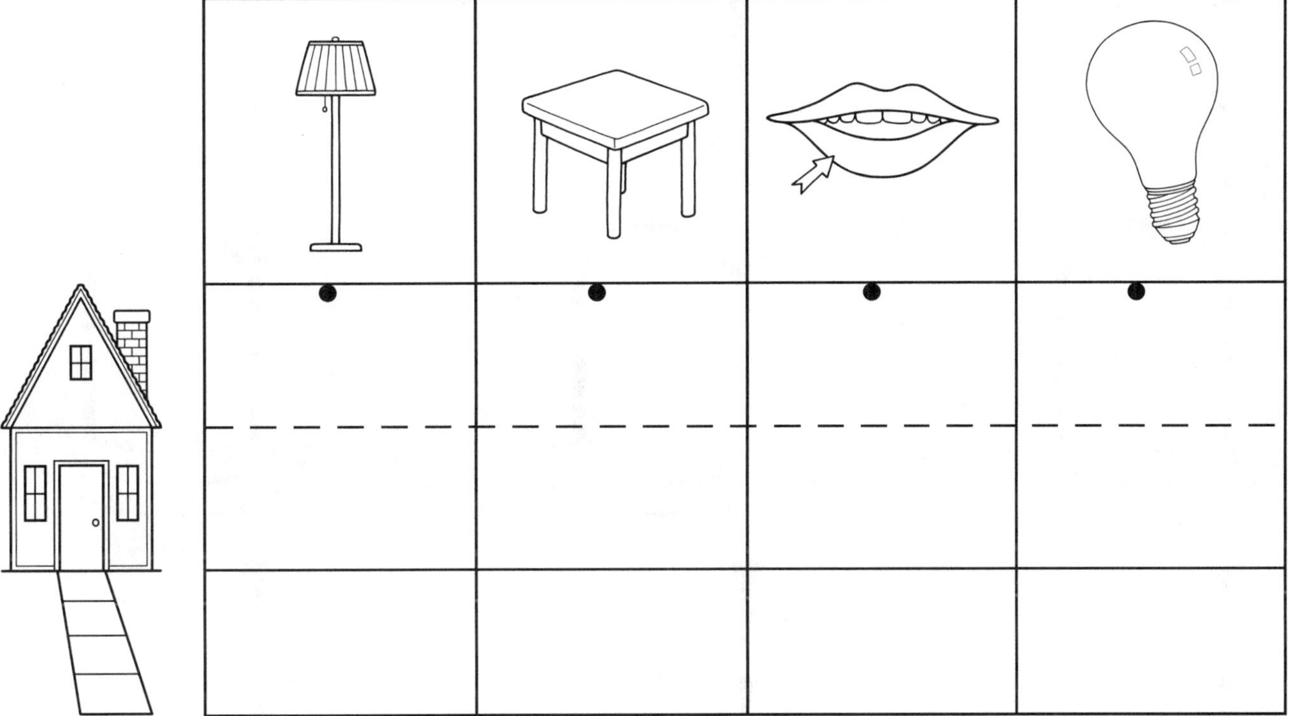

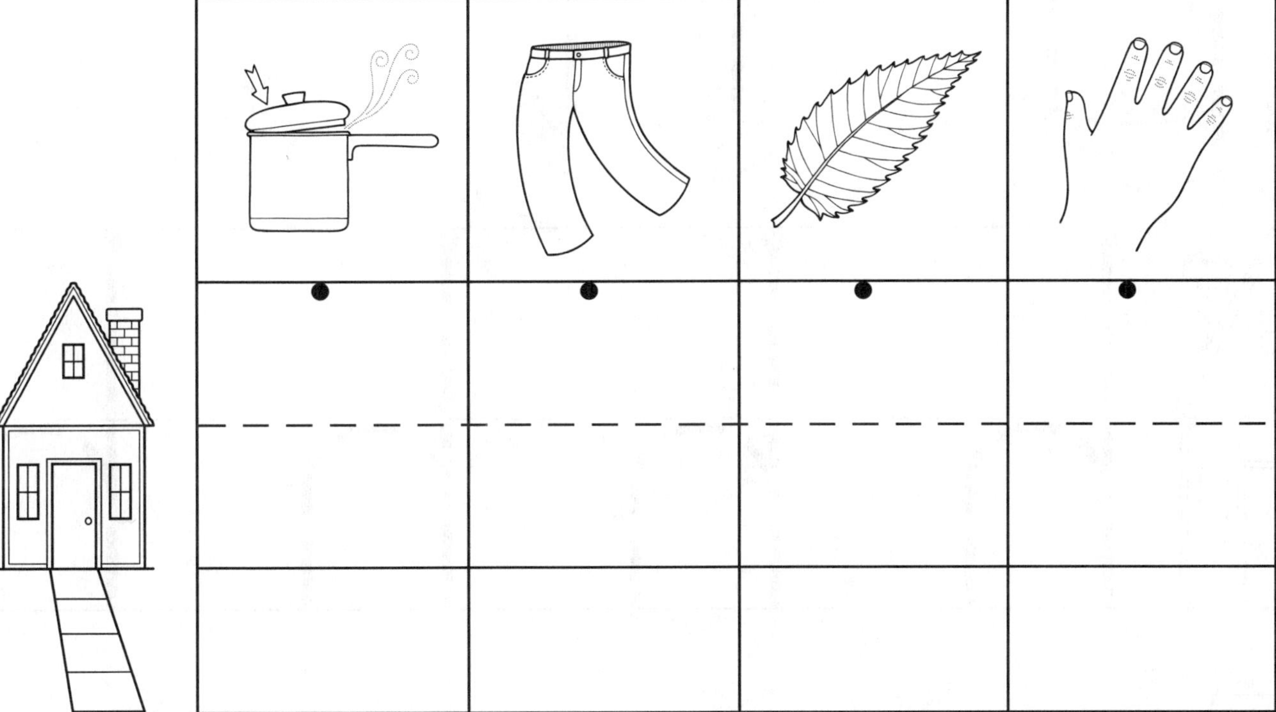

Identify the pictures with children. Direct them to circle each picture that begins with /l/ as in *log* and print the letter *l* under it, starting at the dot.

Lesson 8

h /h/ hat

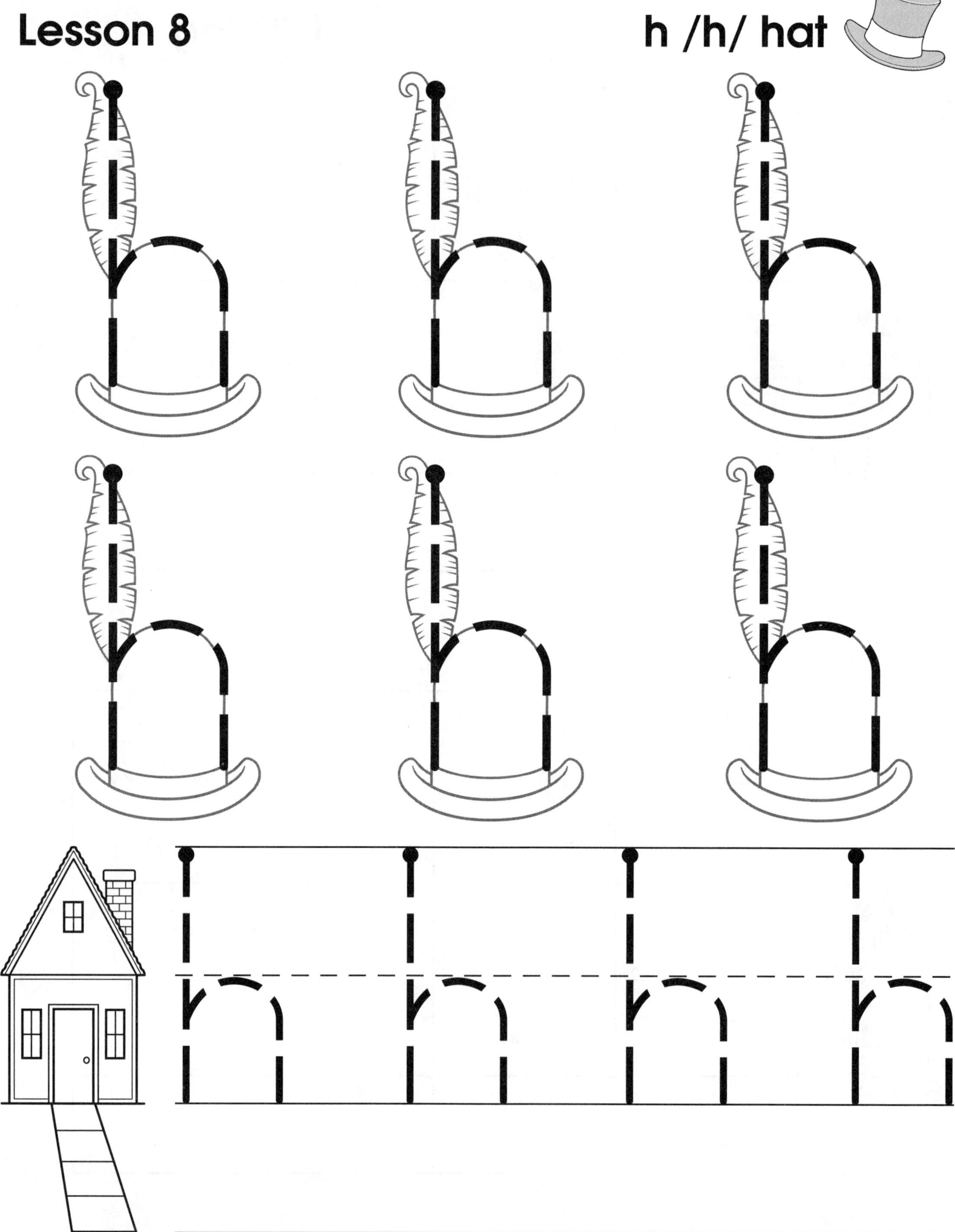

Have children trace all of the *h*'s on this page. Tell them to start at the dot and say /h/ as in *hat* as they trace each *h*.

h /h/ hat

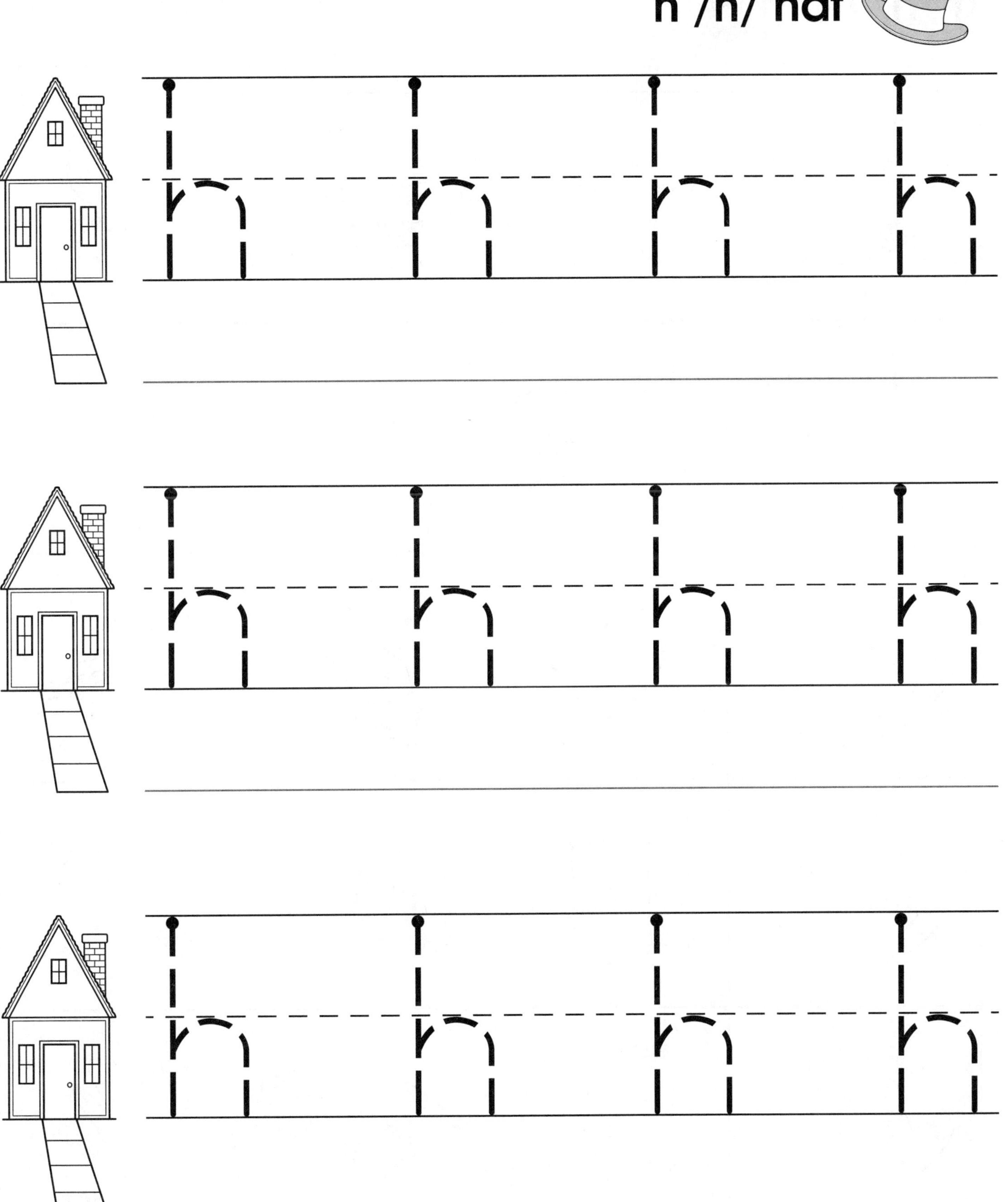

Direct children to trace the *h*'s and say /h/ as in *hat* as they trace each letter.

h /h/ hat

Identify the pictures with children. Have them circle the pictures in each row that begin with /h/ as in *hat.*

h /h/ hat

Identify the pictures with children. Tell them to start at the dot next to the hat and draw a line to the picture that begins with /h/ as in *hat*.

h /h/ hat 

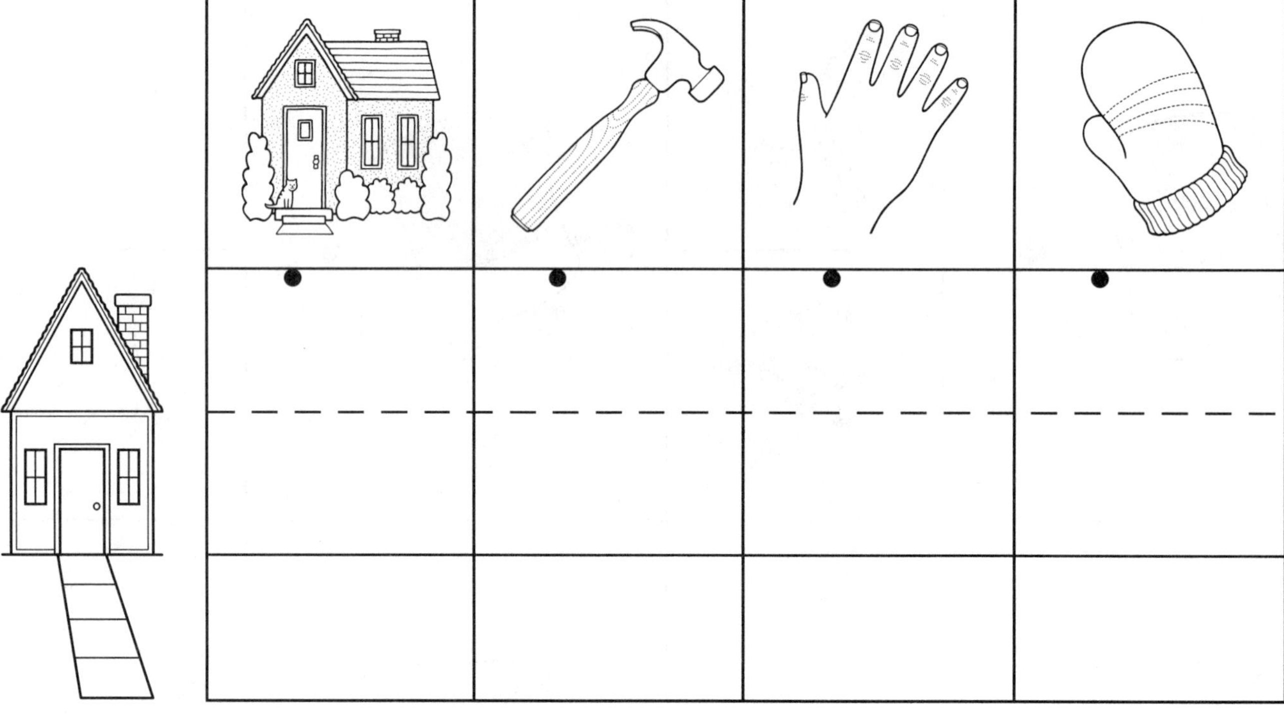

Identify the pictures with children. Direct them to circle each picture that begins with /h/ as in *hat* and print the letter *h* under it, starting at the dot.

Lesson 9

t /t/ turtle

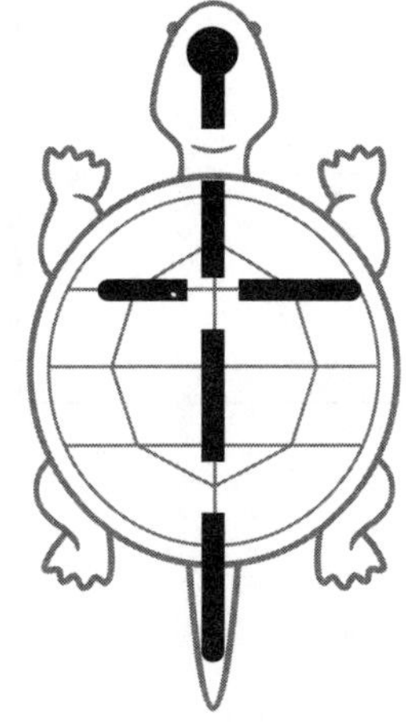
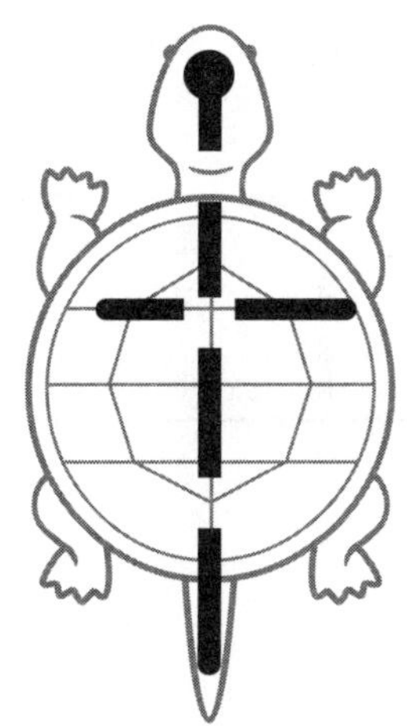

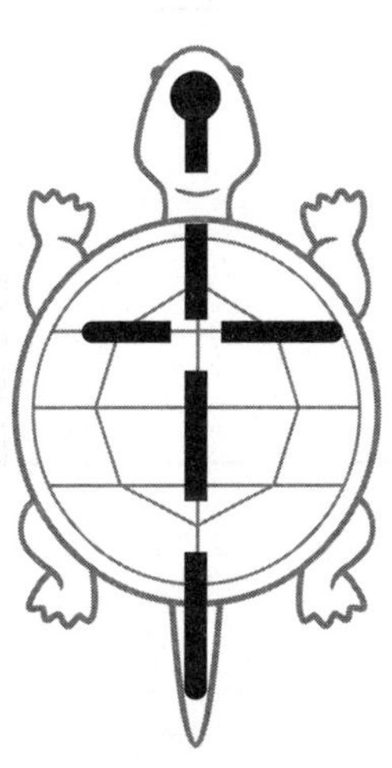

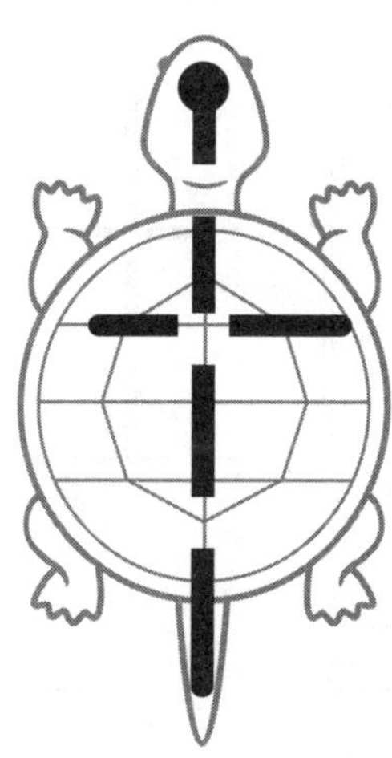

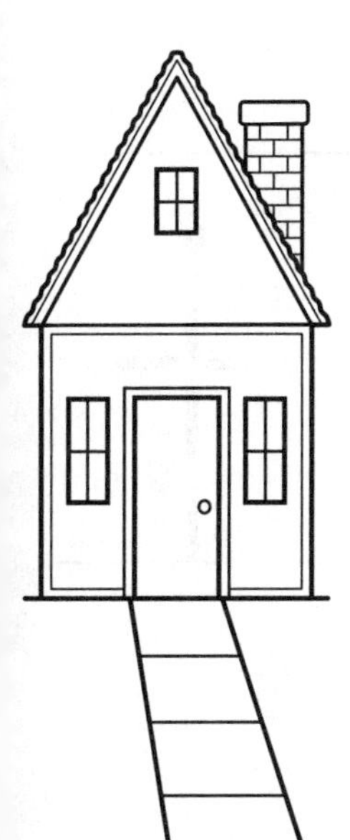
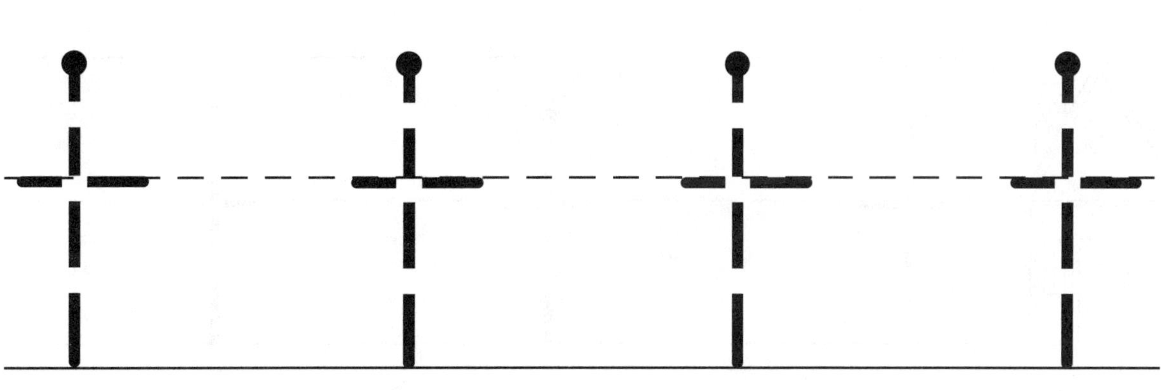

Have children trace all of the *t*'s on this page. Tell them to start at the dot and say /t/ as in *turtle* as they trace each *t*.

t /t/ turtle 

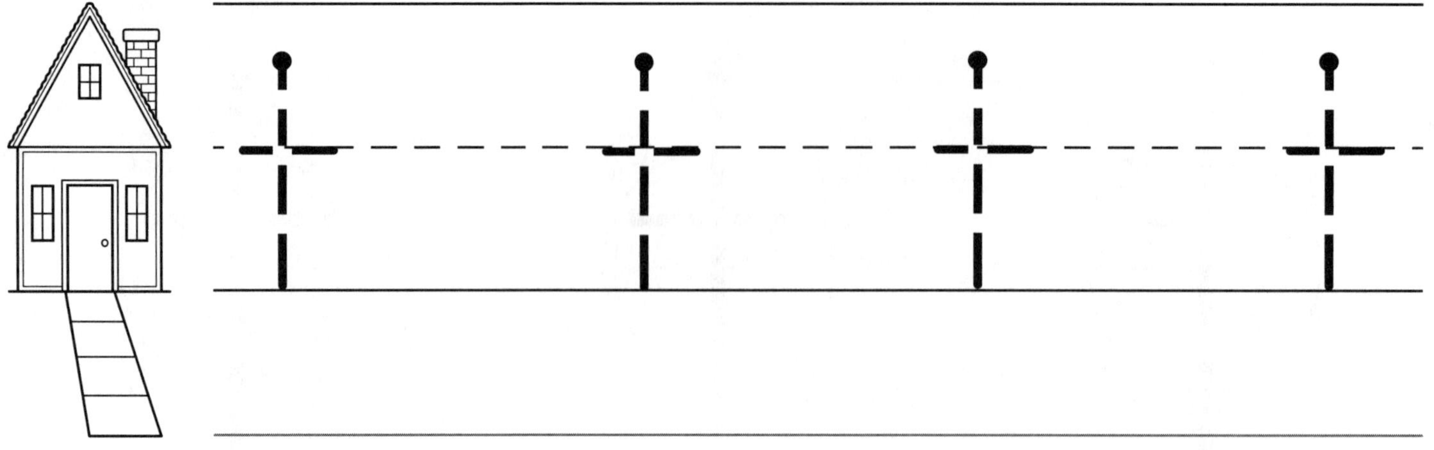

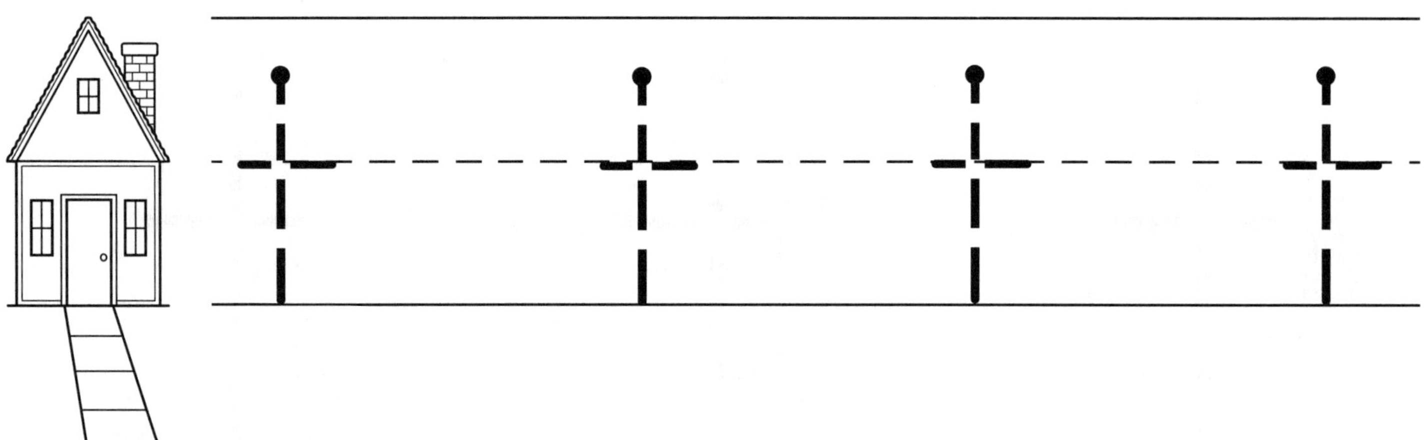

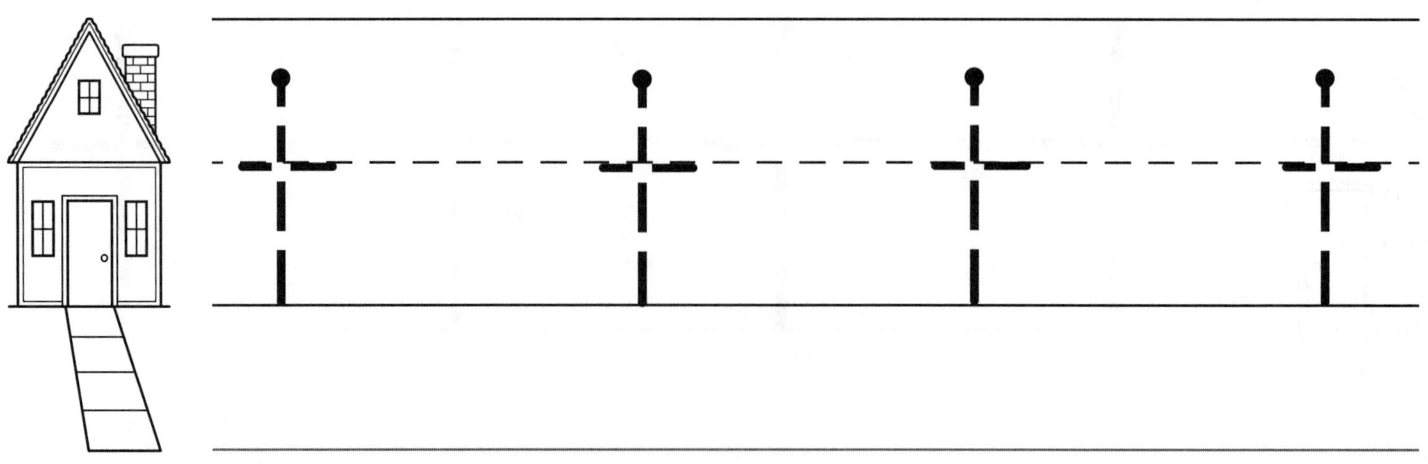

Direct children to trace the *t*'s and say /t/ as in *turtle* as they trace each letter.

t /t/ turtle

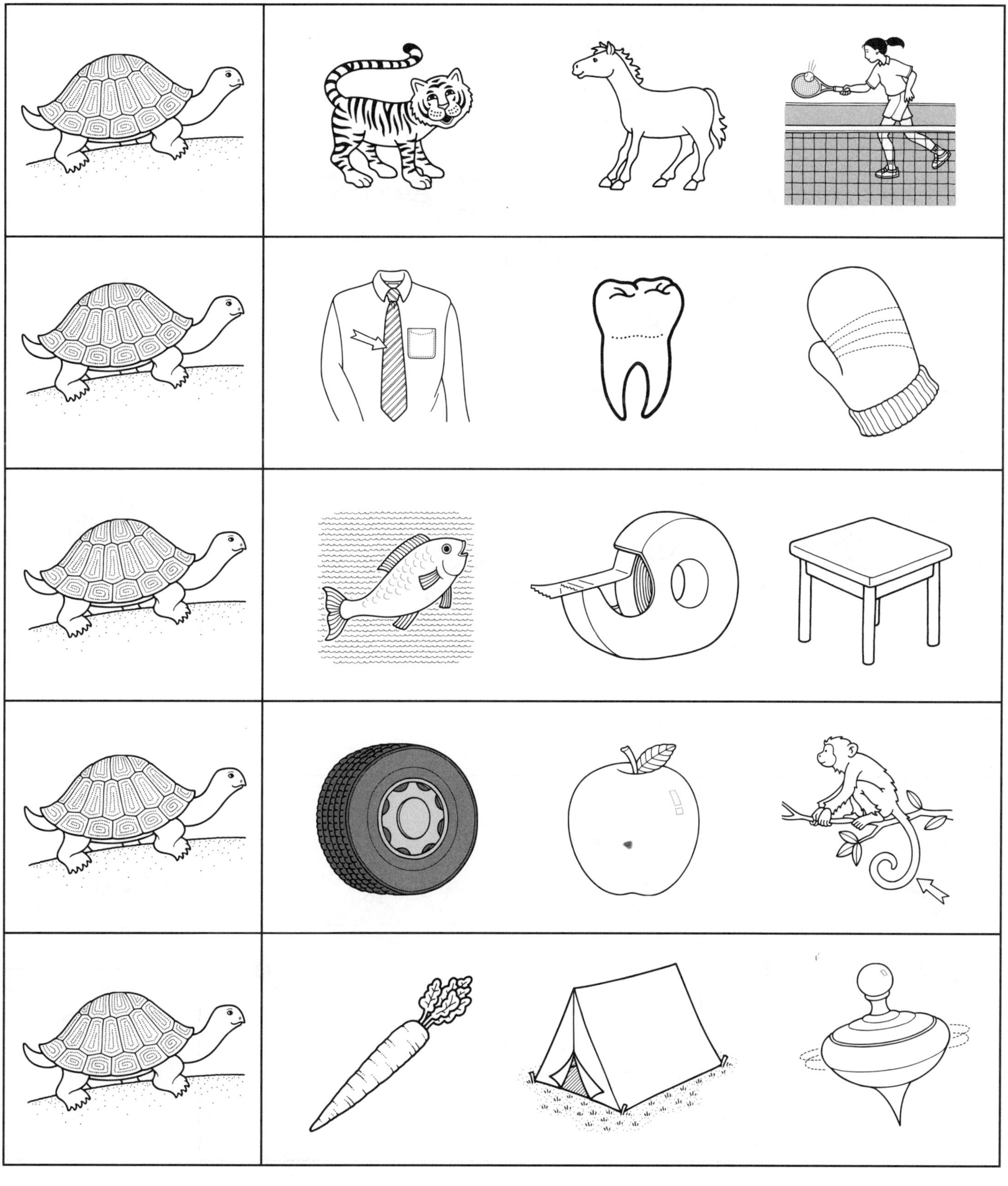

Identify the pictures with children. Have them circle the pictures in each row that begin with /t/ as in *turtle*.

t /t/ turtle 

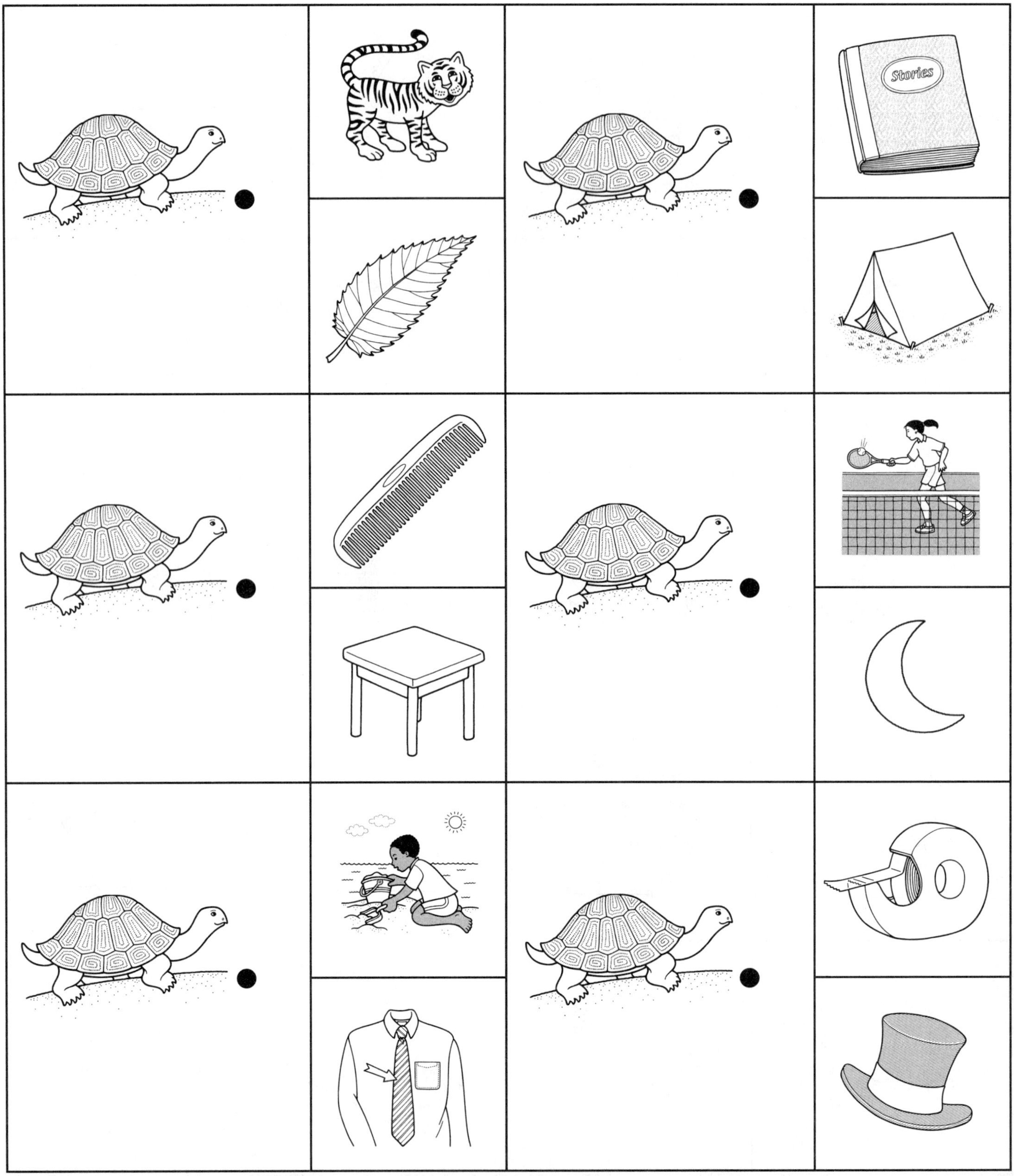

Identify the pictures with children. Tell them to start at the dot next to the turtle and draw a line to the picture that begins with /t/ as in *turtle*.

t /t/ turtle

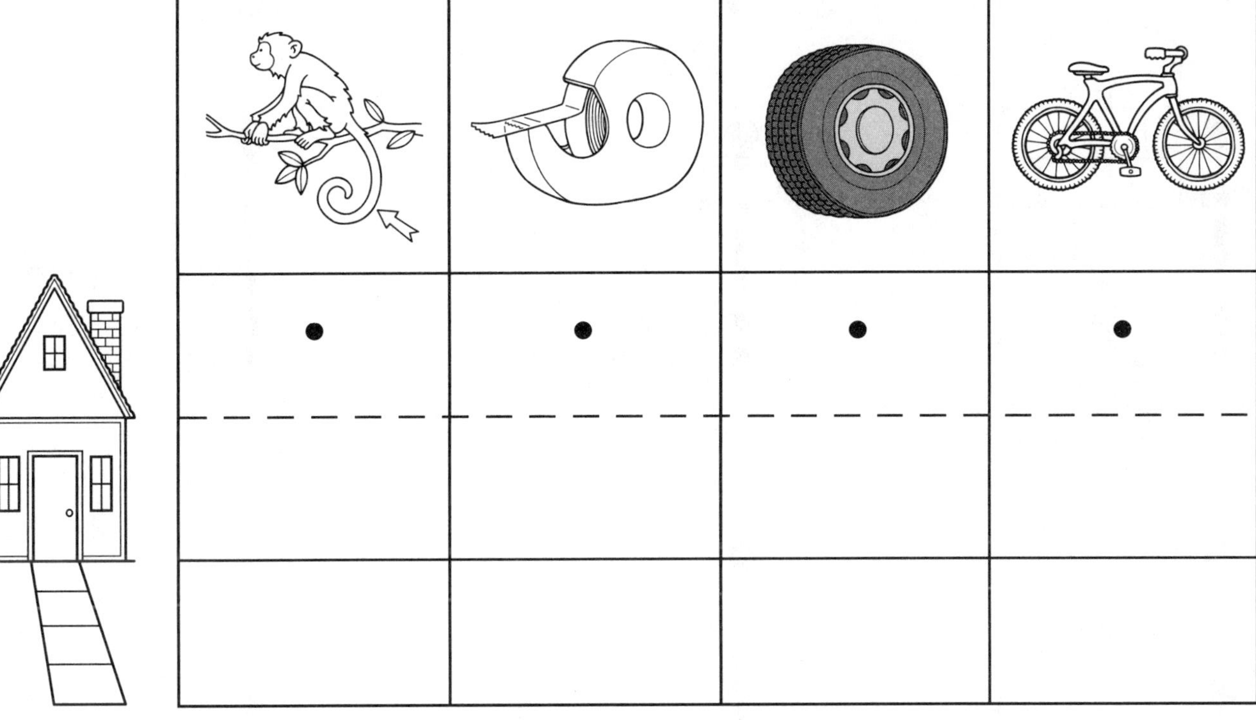

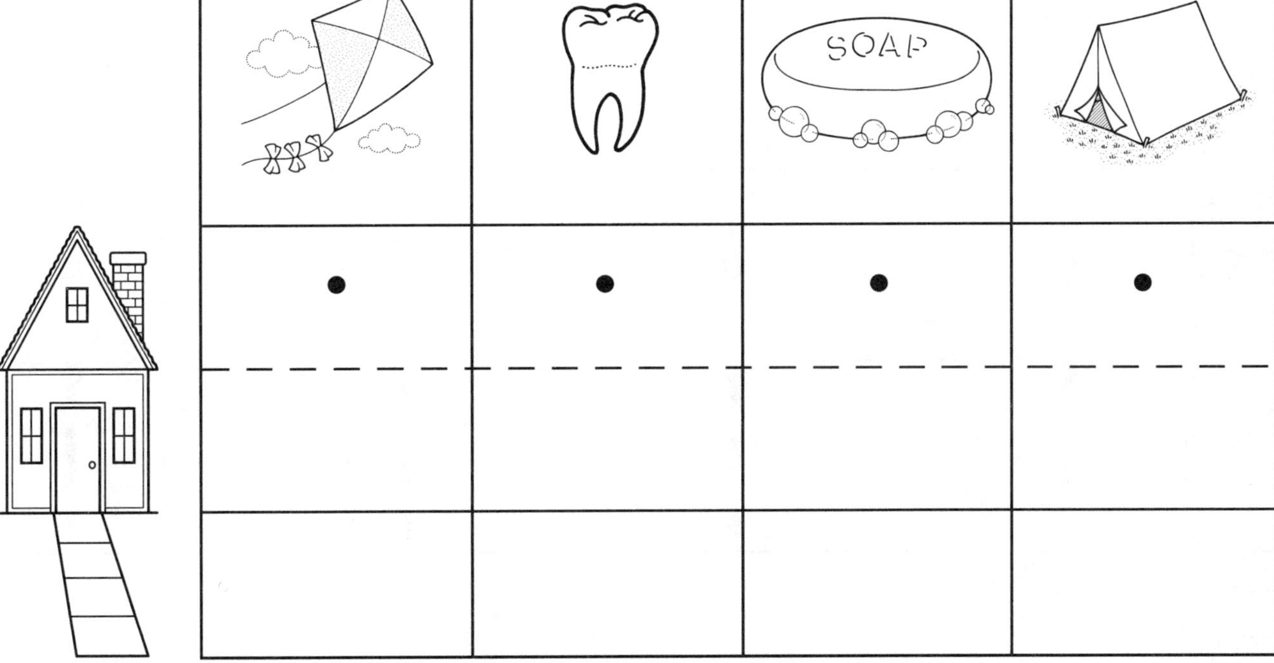

Identify the pictures with children. Direct them to circle each picture that begins with /t/ as in *turtle* and print the letter *t* under it, starting at the dot.

Lesson 10

i /ĭ/ igloo

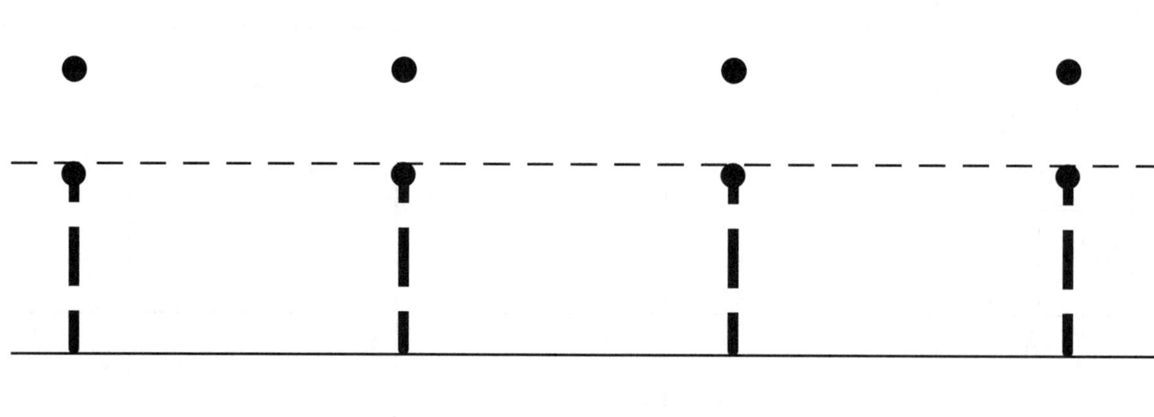

Have children trace all of the *i*'s on this page. Tell them to start at the dot and say /ĭ/ as in *igloo* as they trace each *i*.

i / ĭ / igloo

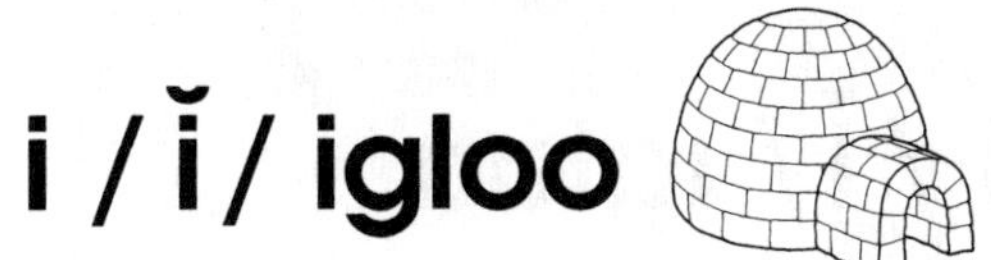

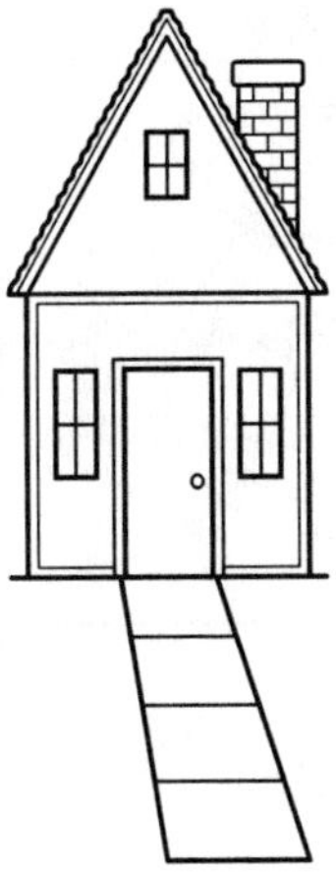

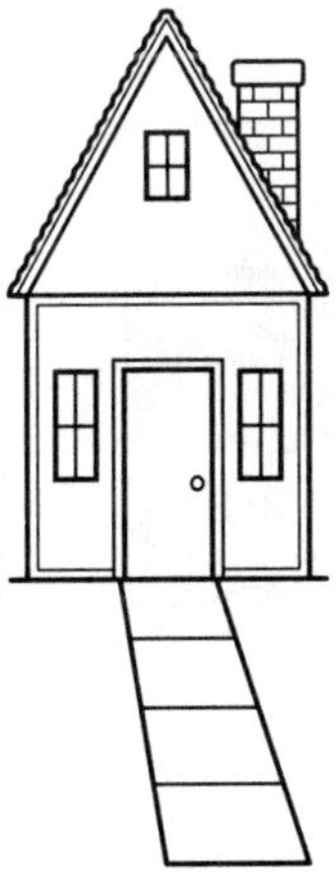

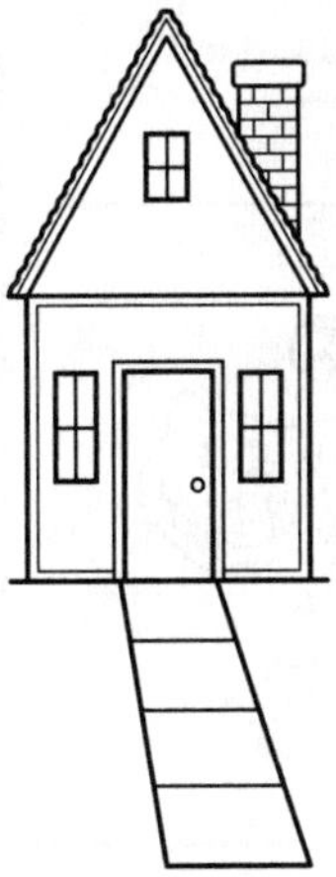

Direct children to trace the *i*'s and say /ĭ/ as in *igloo* as they trace each letter.

i /ĭ/ igloo 

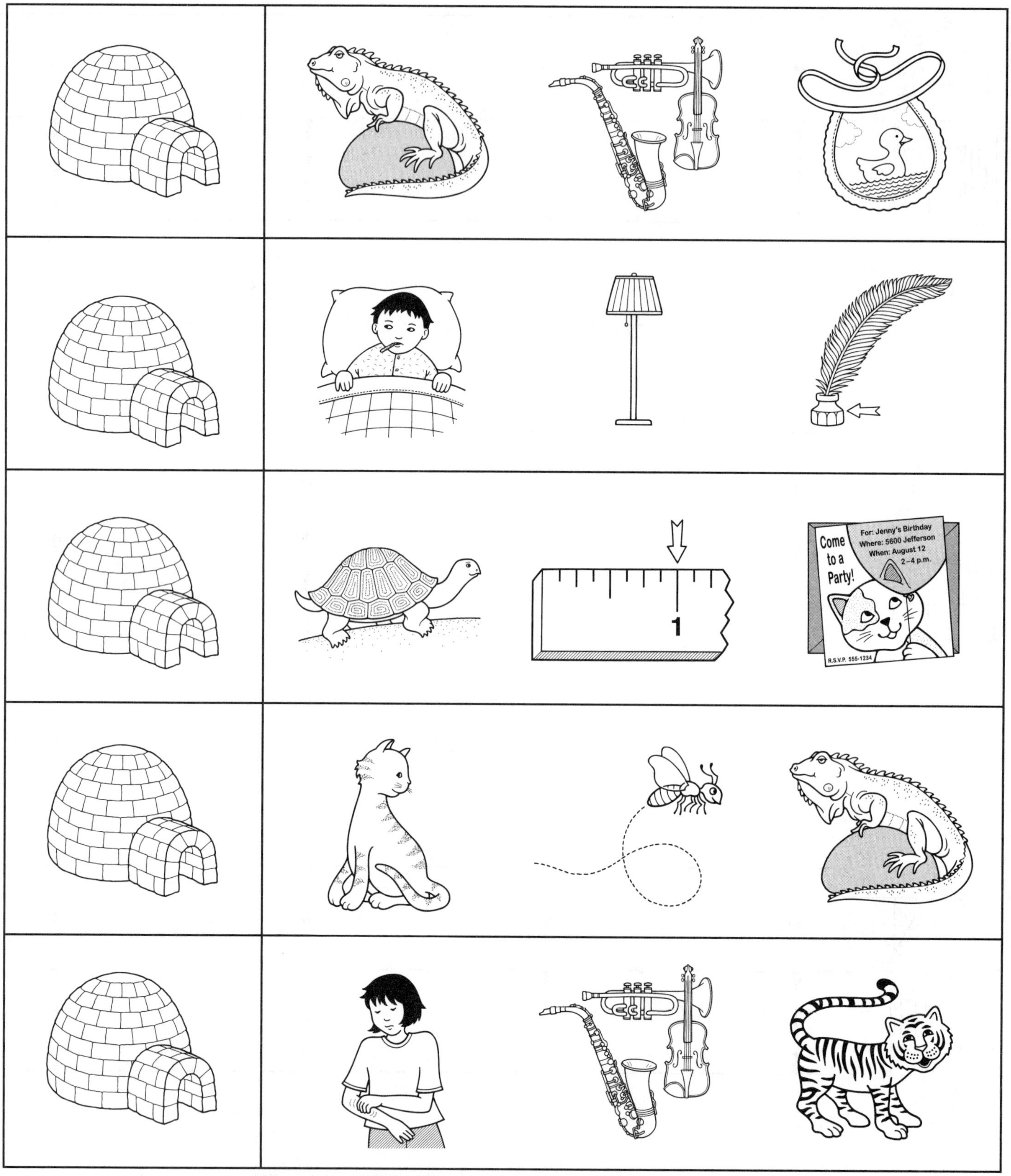

Identify the pictures with children. Have them circle the pictures in each row that begin with /ĭ/ as in *igloo*.

i / ĭ / igloo

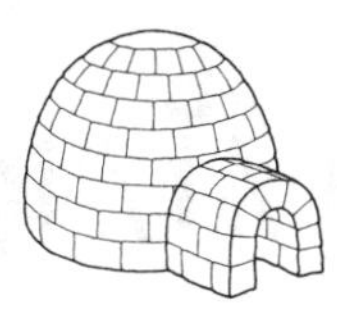

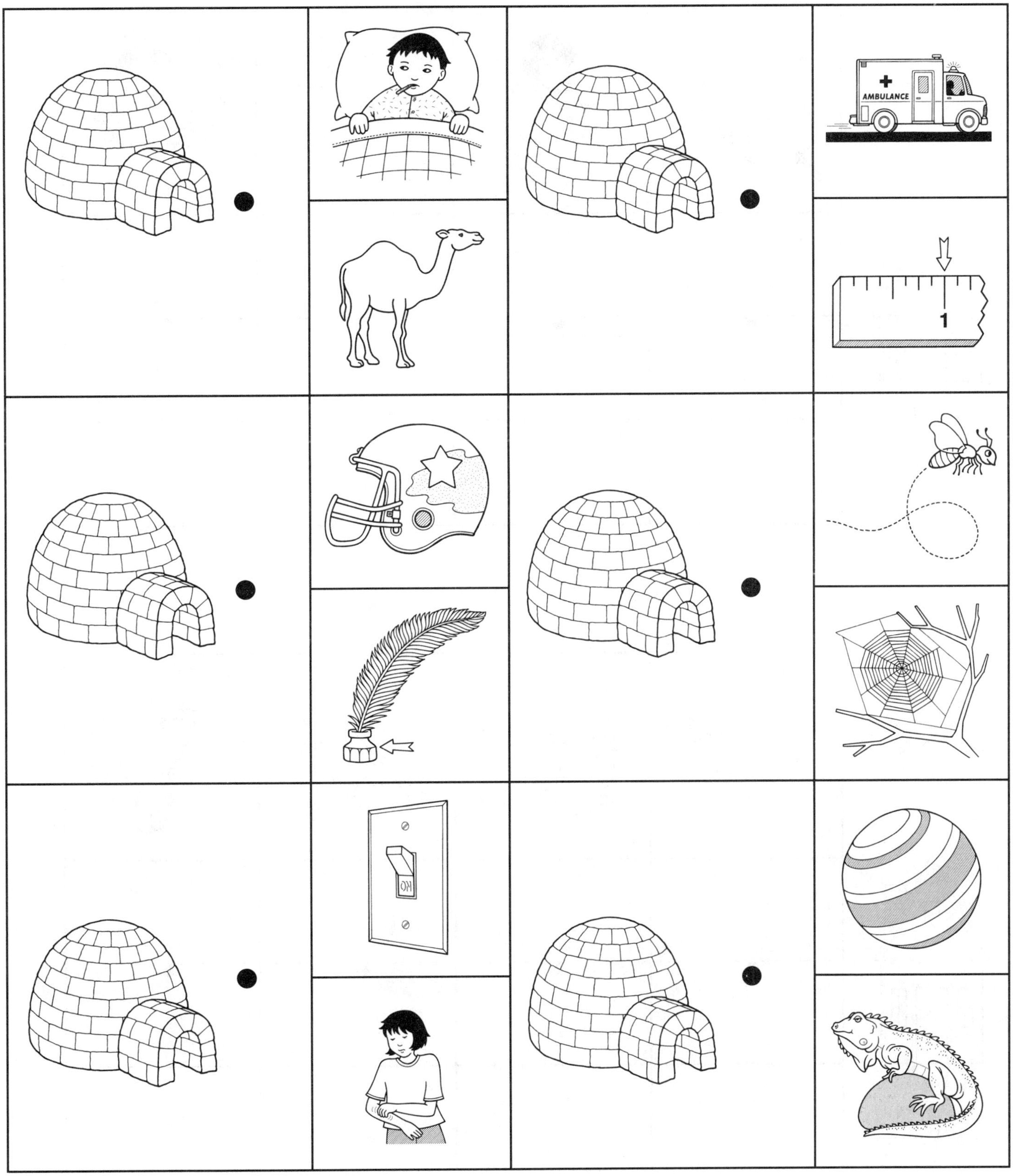

Identify the pictures with children. Tell them to start at the dot next to the igloo and draw a line to the picture that begins with /ĭ/ as in *igloo.*

i /ĭ/ igloo

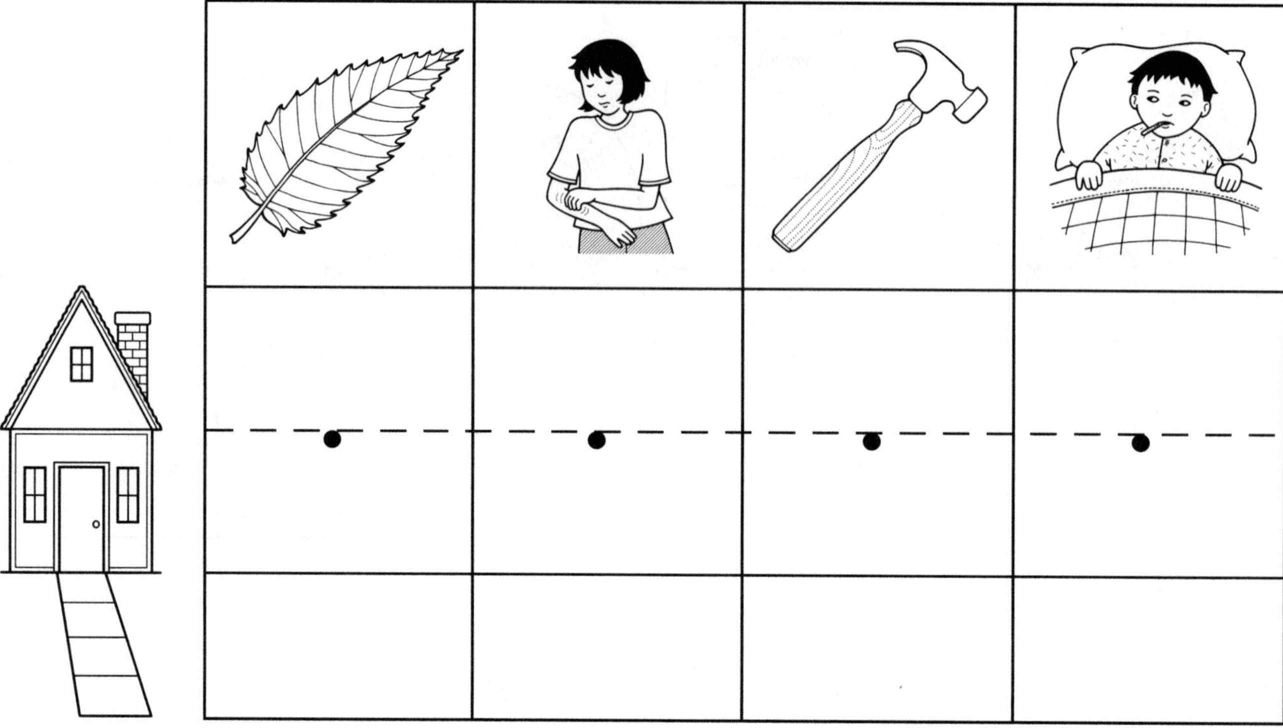

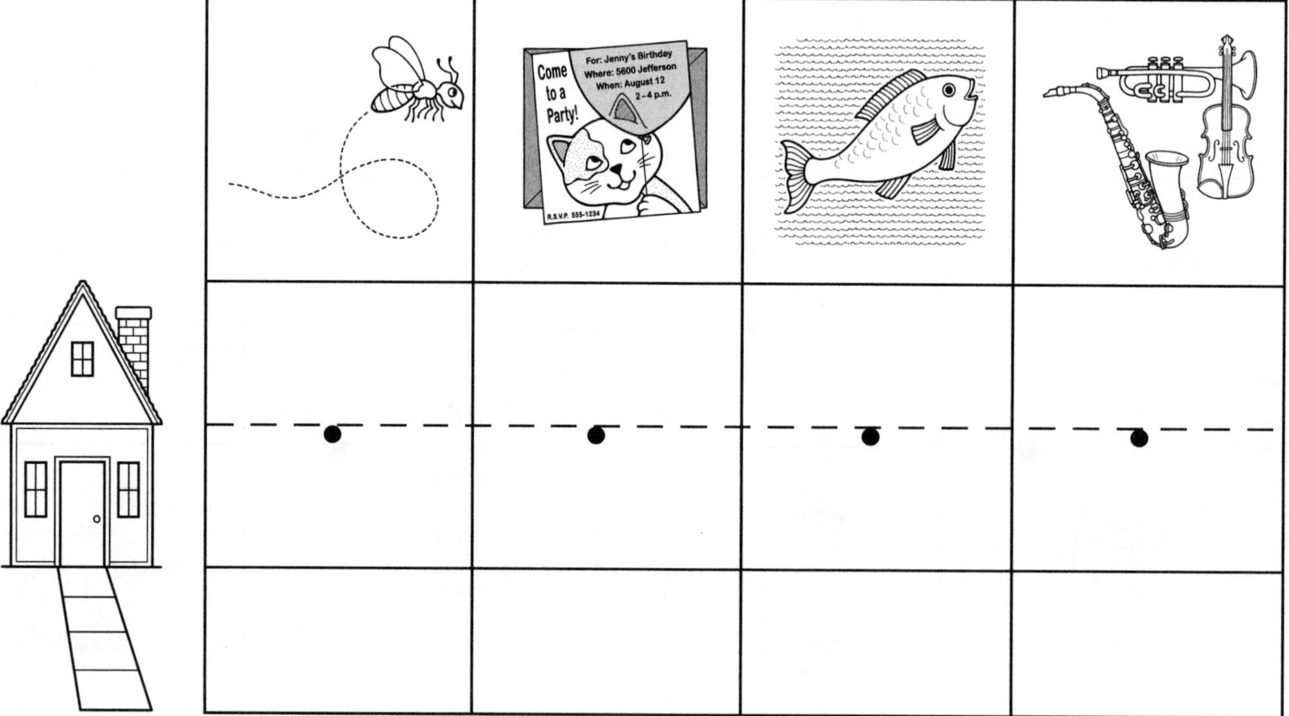

Identify the pictures with children. Direct them to circle each picture that begins with /ĭ/ as in *igloo* and print the letter *i* under it, starting at the dot.

Lesson 11

j /j/ jug

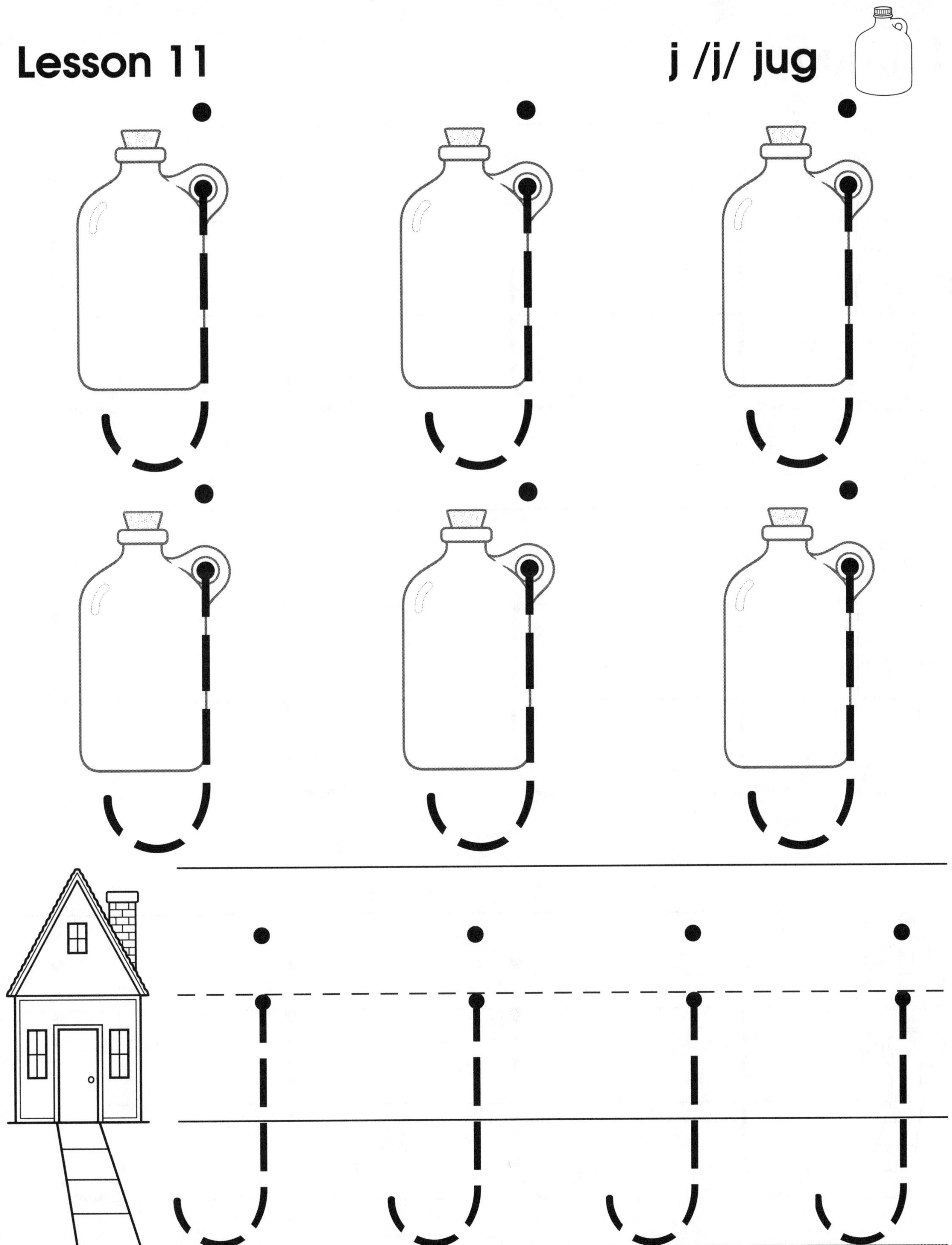

Have children trace all of the *j*'s on this page. Tell them to start at the dot and say /j/ as in *jug* as they trace each *j*.

j /j/ jug

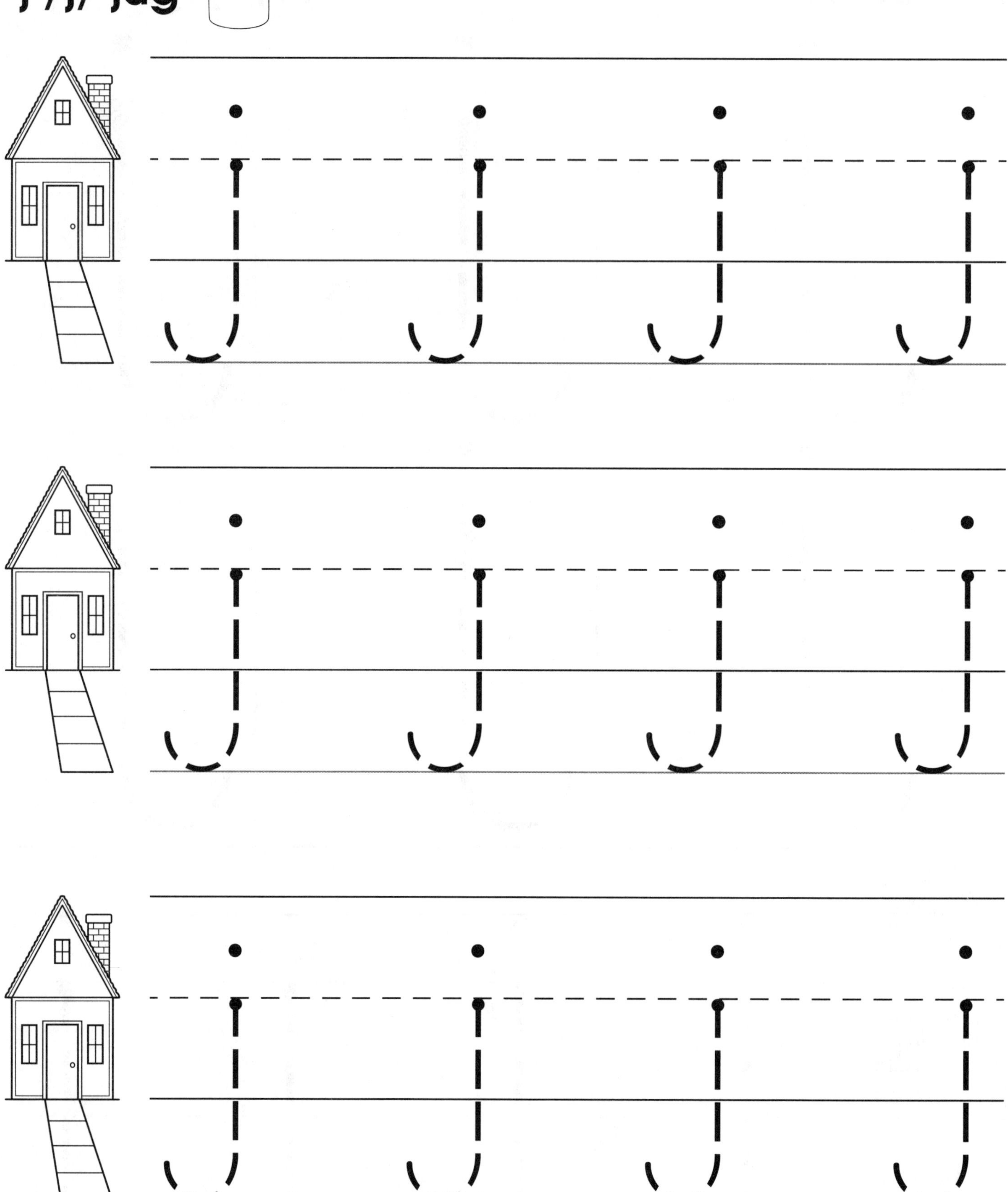

Direct children to trace the *j*'s and say /j/ as in *jug* as they trace each letter.

j /j/ jug

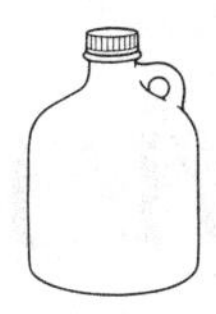

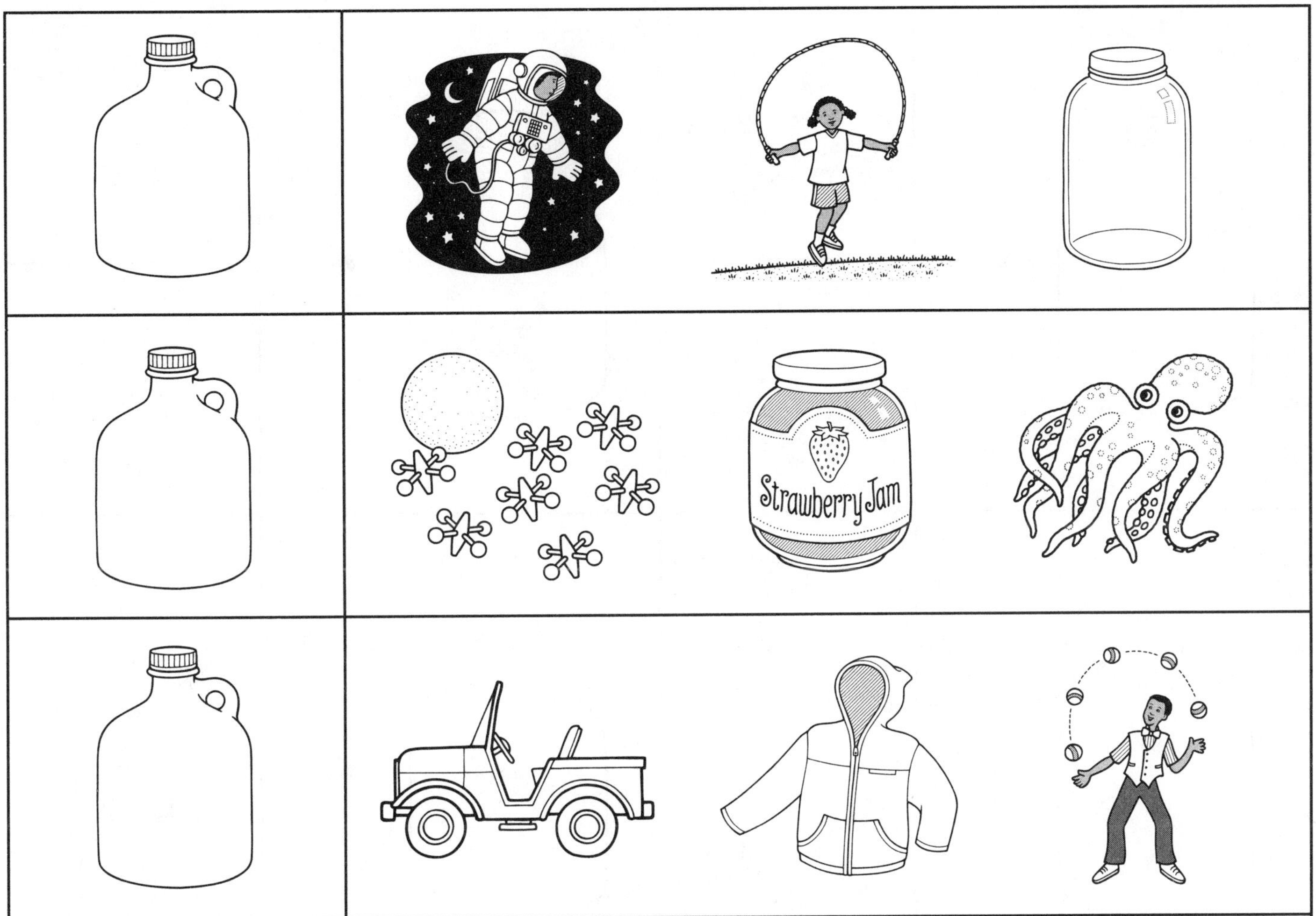
Strawberry Jam
a b c d e f g
h i j k l m
n o p q r s
t u v w x y z

Identify the pictures with children. Have them circle the pictures in each row that begin with /j/ as in *jug*.

j /j/ jug 

Identify the pictures with children. Tell them to start at the dot next to the jug and draw a line to the picture that begins with /j/ as in *jug*.

j /j/ jug 

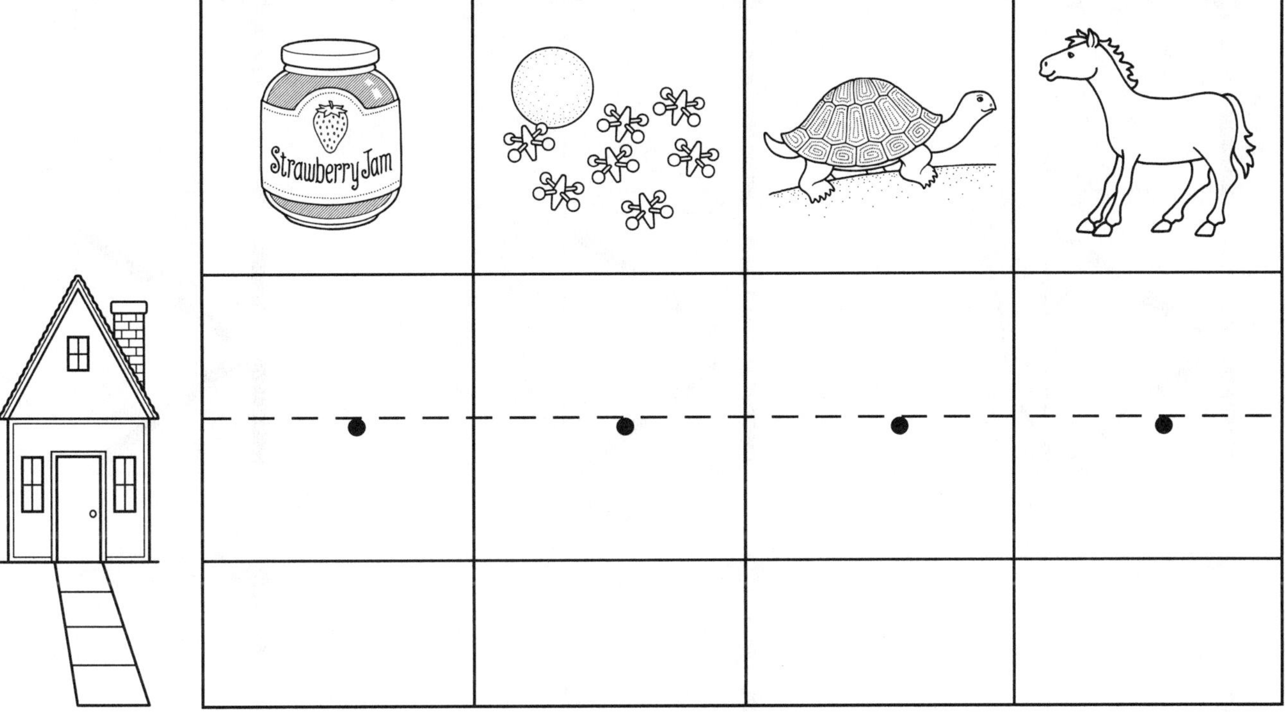

Identify the pictures with children. Direct them to circle each picture that begins with /j/ as in *jug* and print the letter *j* under it, starting at the dot.

Lesson 12

k /k/ kettle

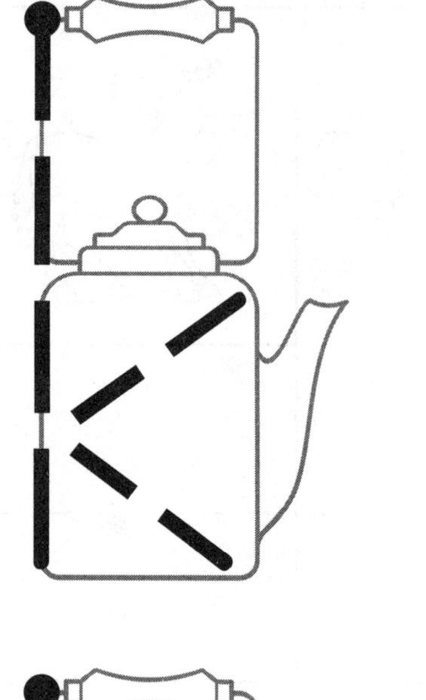

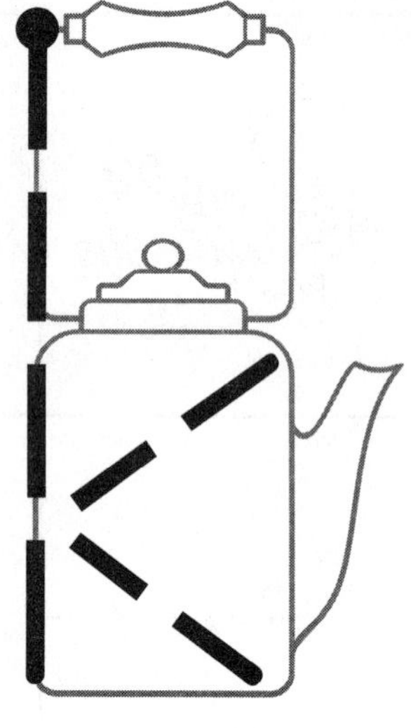

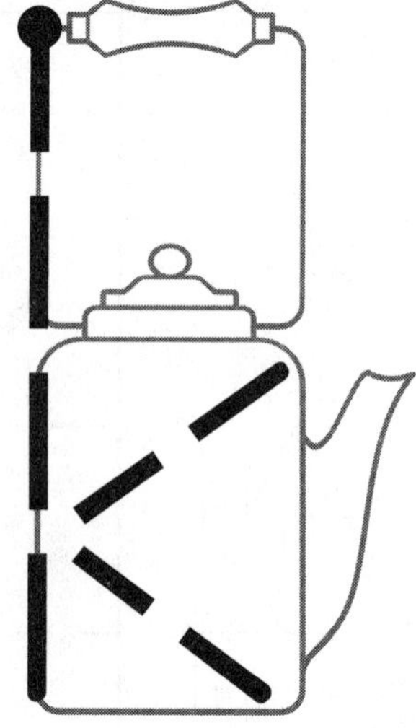

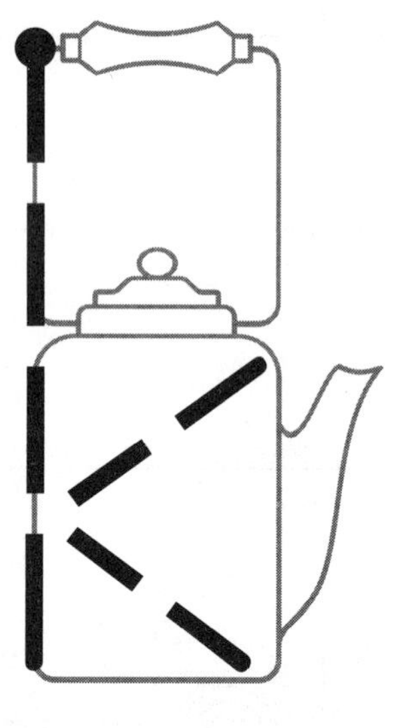

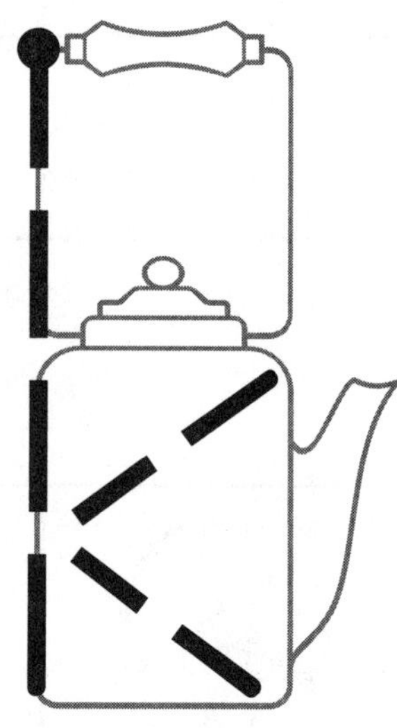

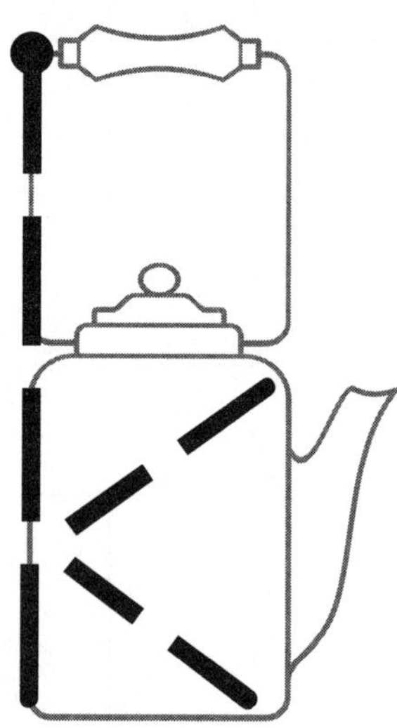

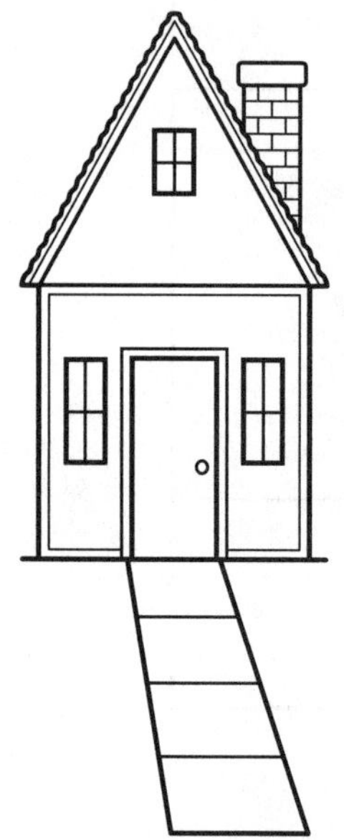

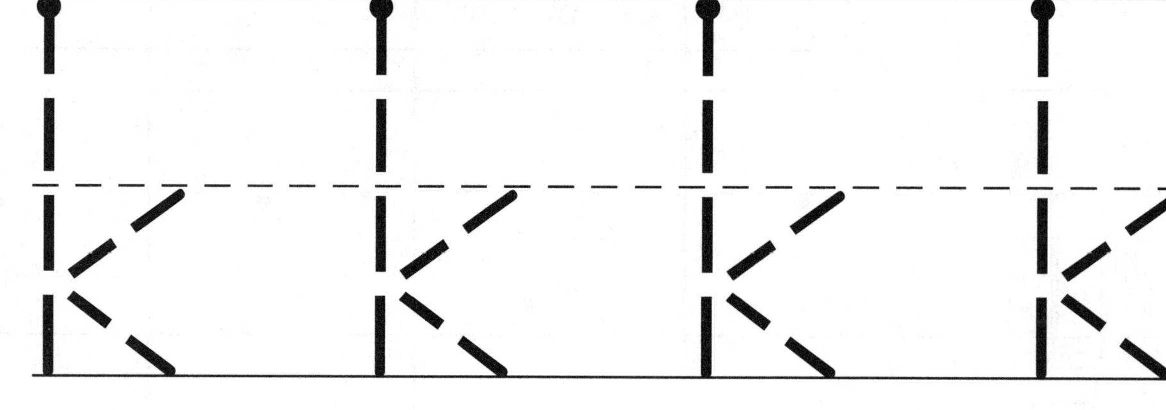

Have children trace all of the *k*'s on this page. Tell them to start at the dot and say /k/ as in *kettle* as they trace each *k*.

k /k/ kettle 

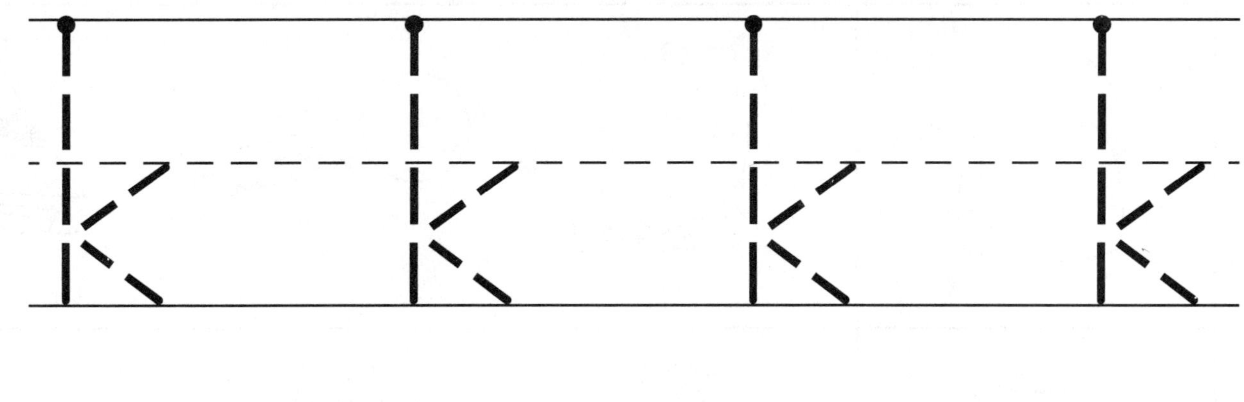

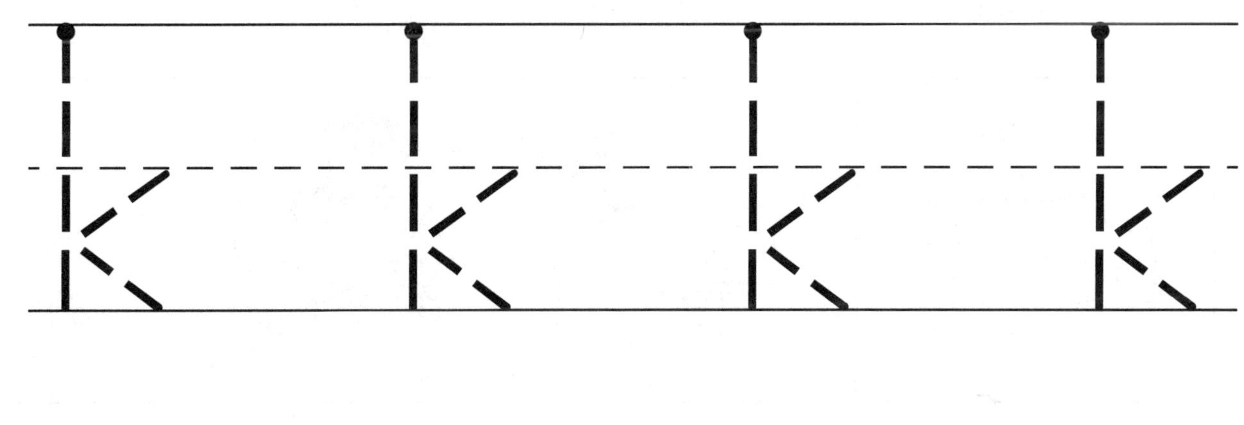

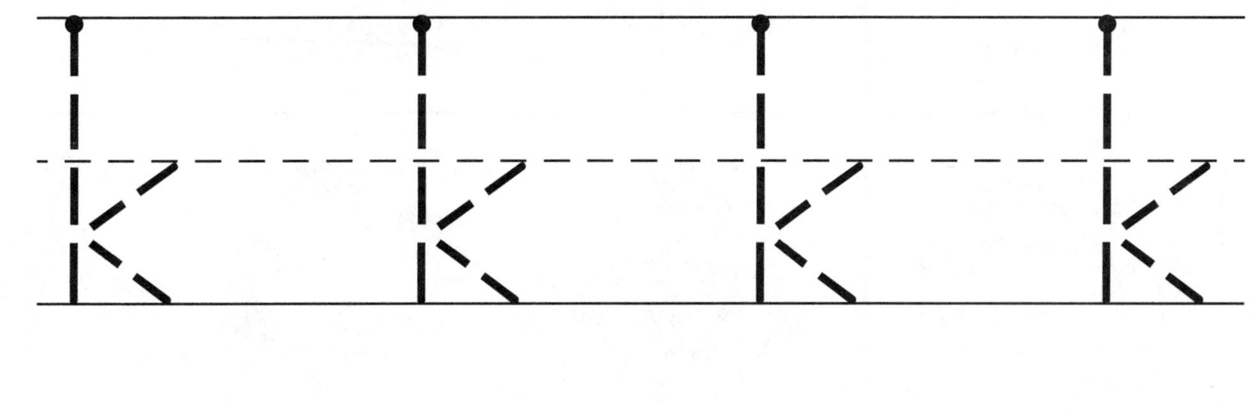

Direct children to trace the *k*'s and say /k/ as in *kettle* as they trace each letter.

k /k/ kettle 

Identify the pictures with children. Have them circle the pictures in each row that begin with /k/ as in *kettle*.

k /k/ kettle 

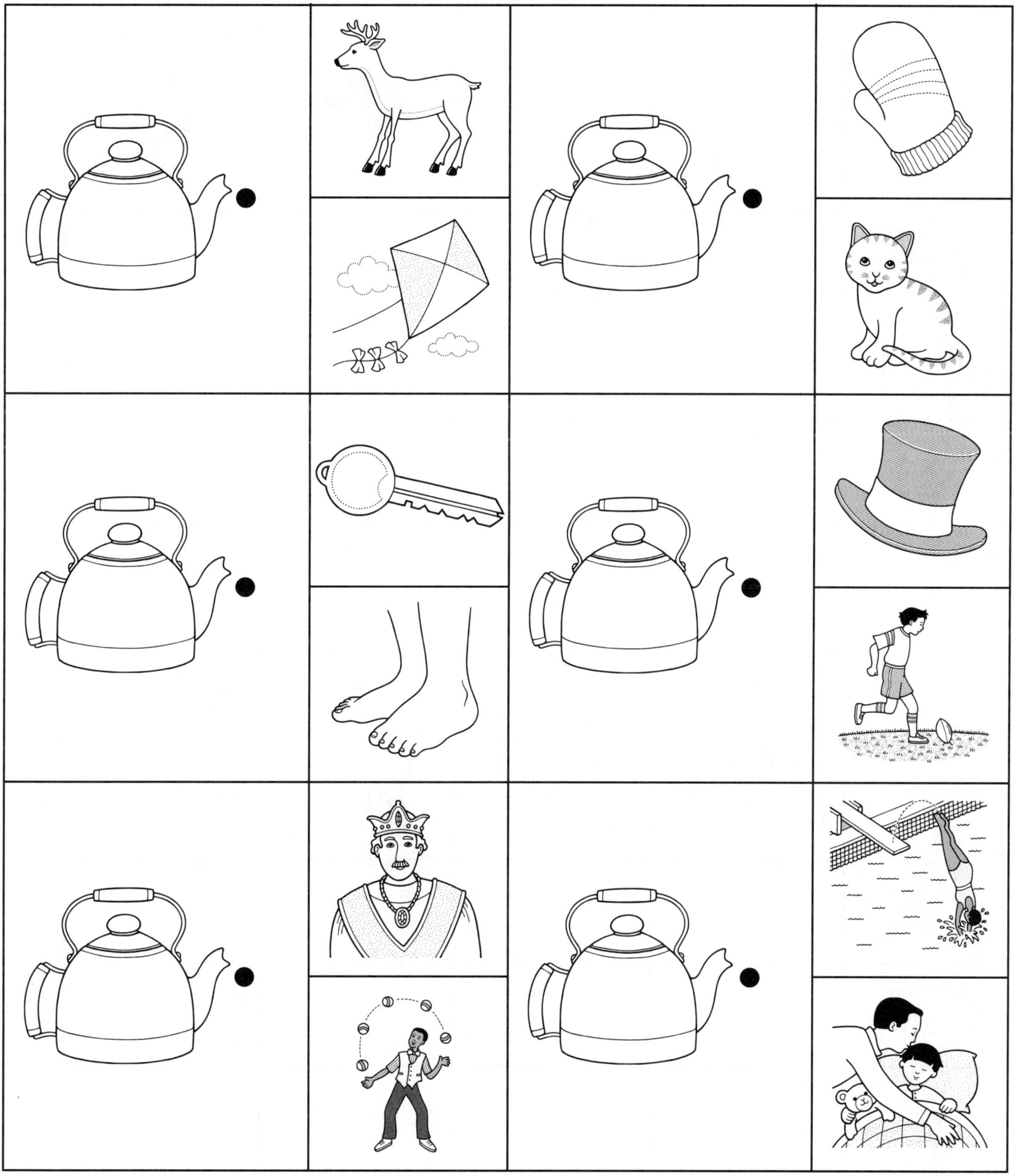

Identify the pictures with children. Tell them to start at the dot next to the kettle and draw a line to the picture that begins with /k/ as in *kettle*.

k /k/ kettle 

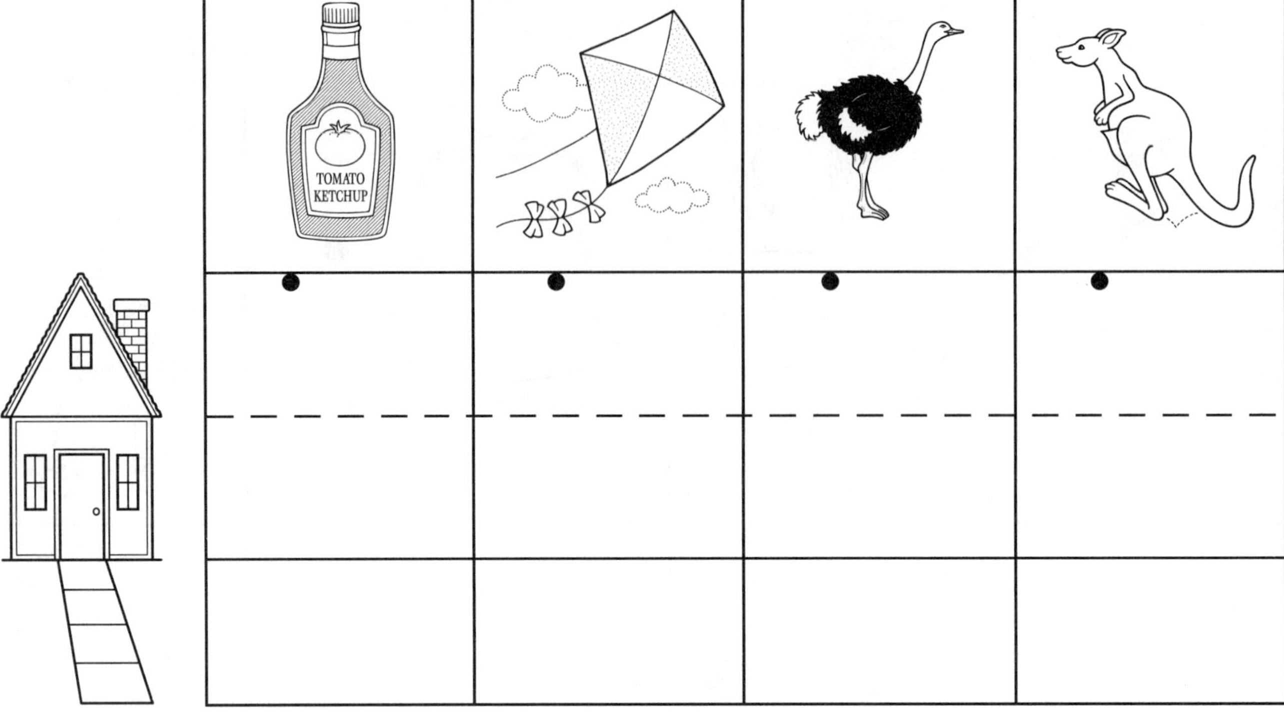

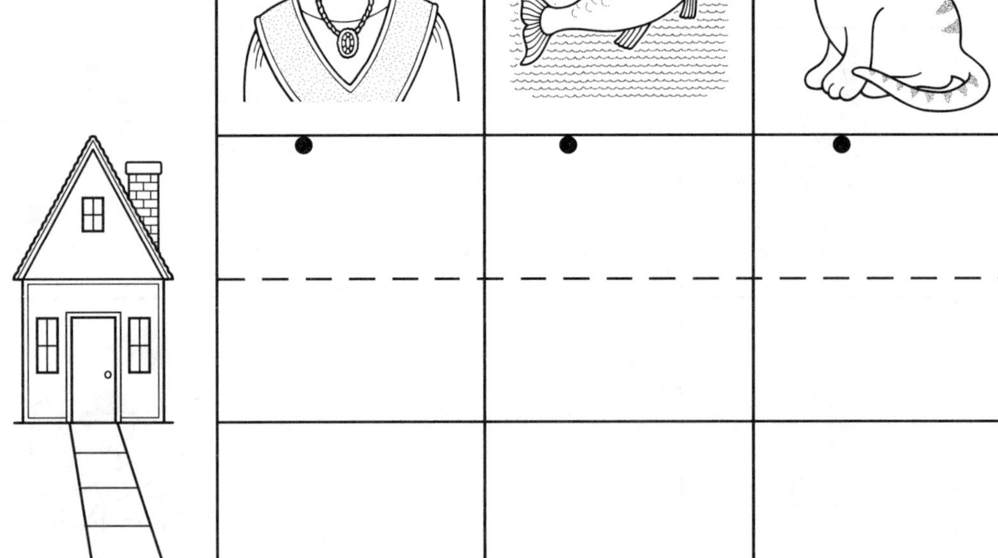

Identify the pictures with children. Direct them to circle each picture that begins with /k/ as in *kettle* and print the letter *k* under it, starting at the dot.

Lesson 13

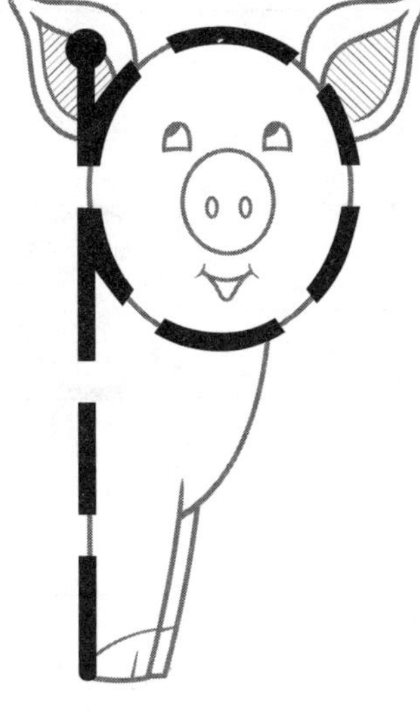

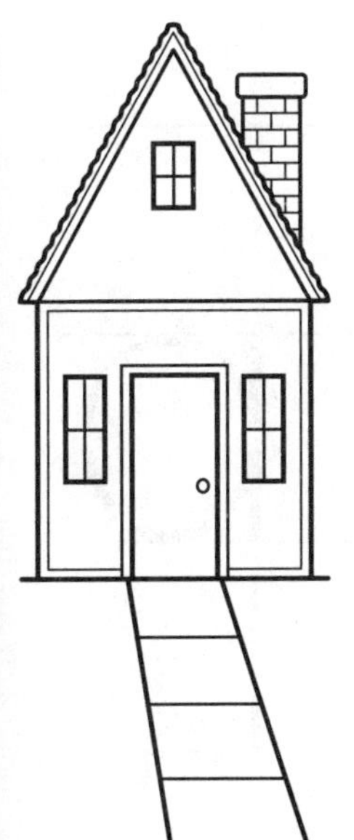
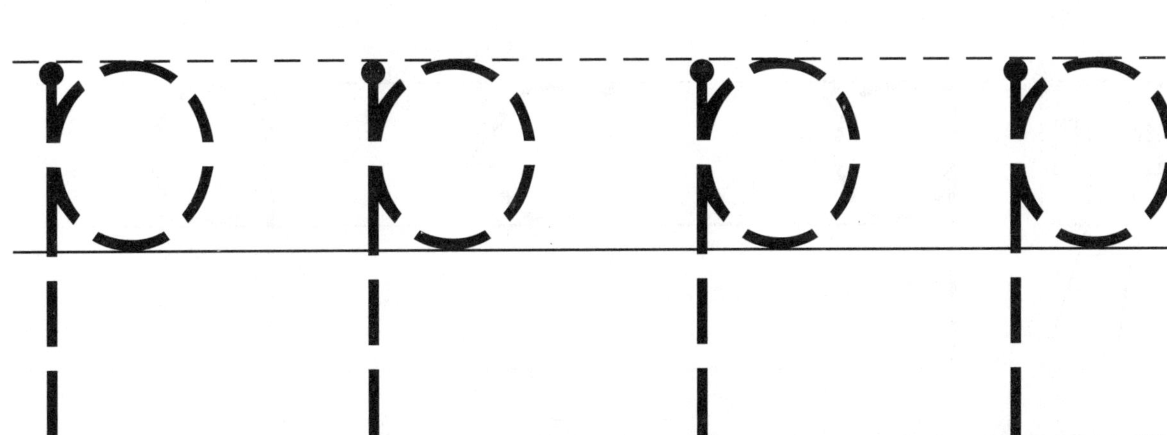

Have children trace all of the *p*'s on this page. Tell them to start at the dot and say /p/ as in *pig* as they trace each *p*.

p /p/ pig

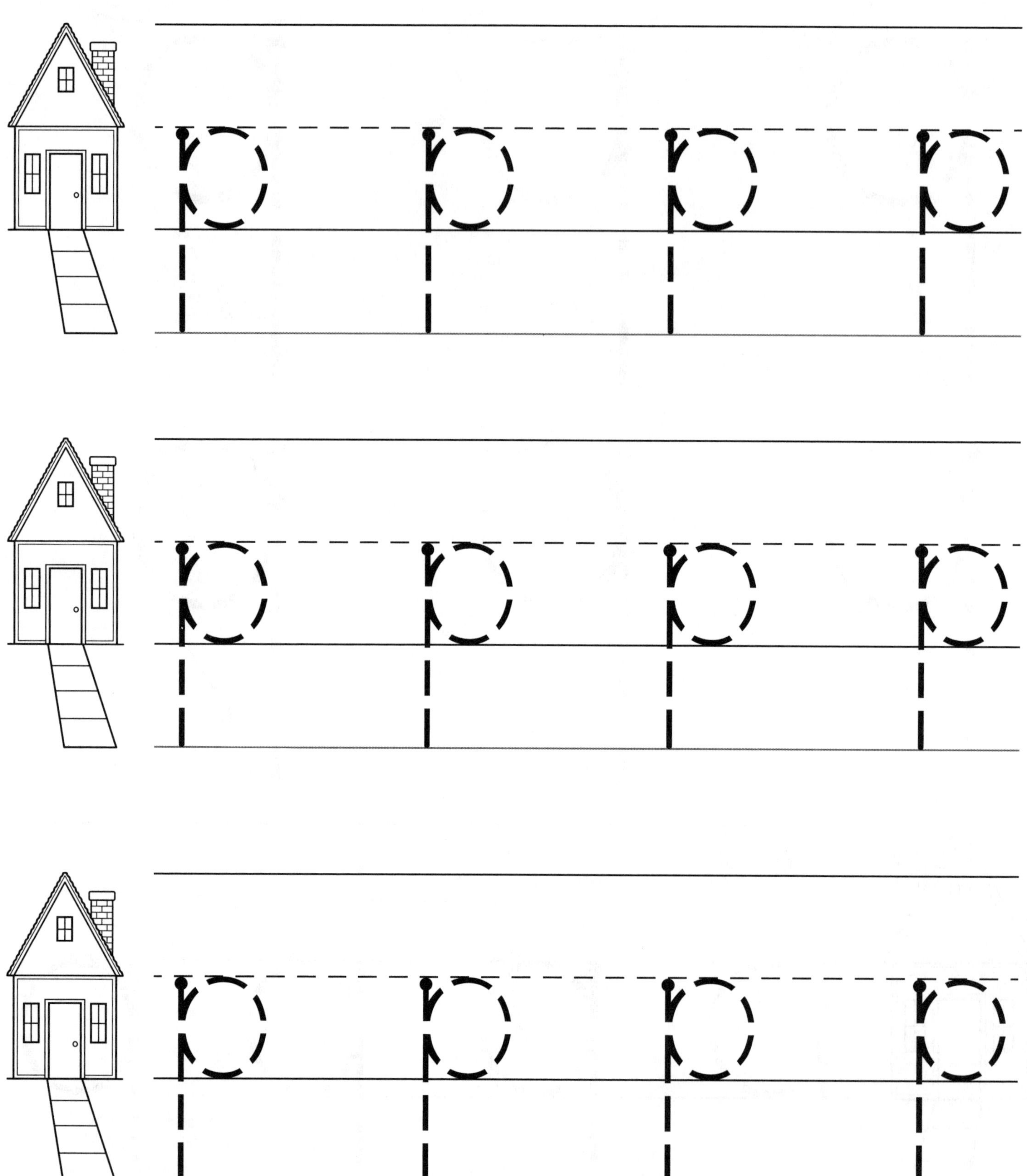

Direct children to trace the *p*'s and say /p/ as in *pig* as they trace each letter.

p /p/ pig

Identify the pictures with children. Have them circle the pictures in each row that begin with /p/ as in *pig*.

p /p/ pig 

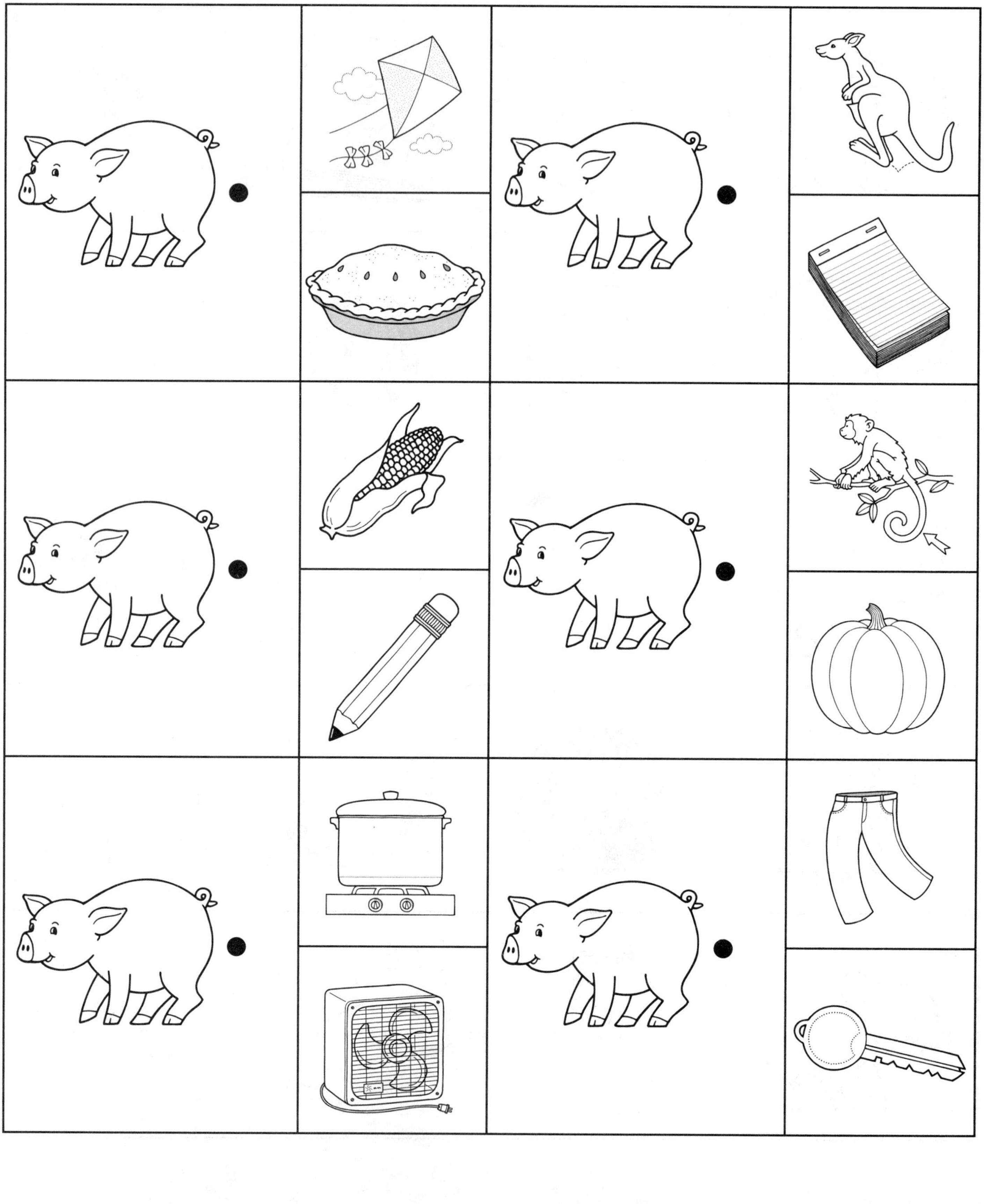

Identify the pictures with children. Tell them to start at the dot next to the pig and draw a line to the picture that begins with /p/ as in *pig*.

p /p/ pig

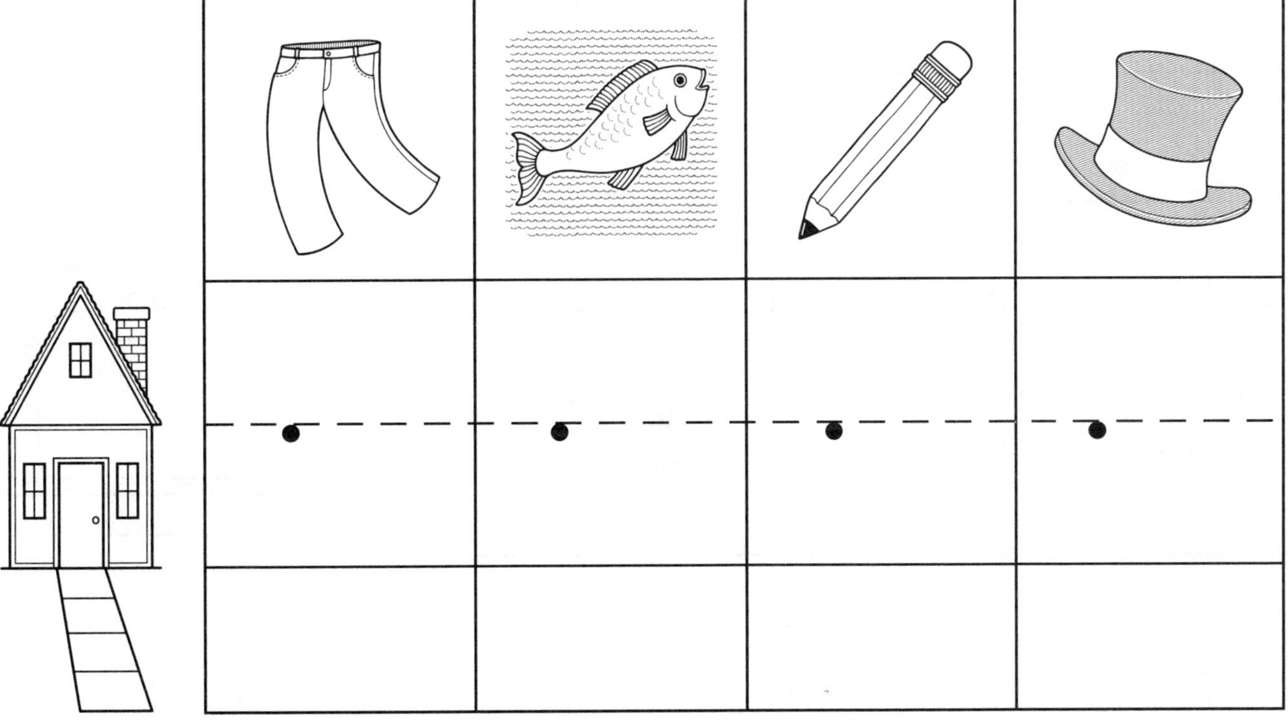

Identify the pictures with children. Direct them to circle each picture that begins with /p/ as in *pig* and print the letter *p* under it, starting at the dot.

p /p/ pig 

Identify the pictures in row 1 with children. Have them say the beginning sound of each. Then help children blend those sounds together to make a new word and draw a line to the picture of that word. Follow the same procedure with rows 2 and 3.

Lesson 14

u /ŭ/ umbrella

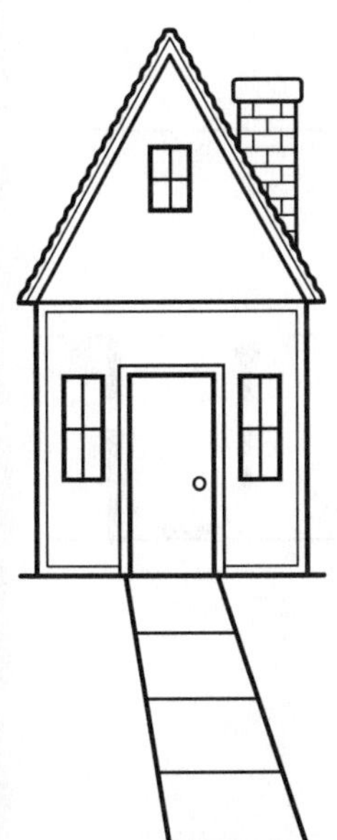

Have children trace all of the *u*'s on this page. Tell them to start at the dot and say /ŭ/ as in *umbrella* as they trace each *u*.

u /ŭ/ umbrella 

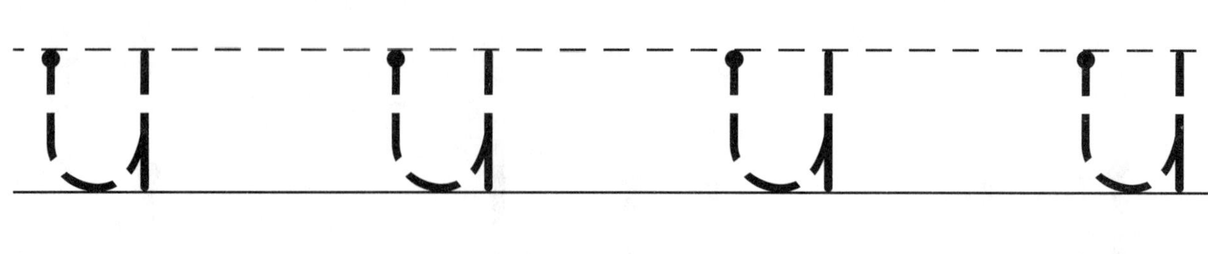

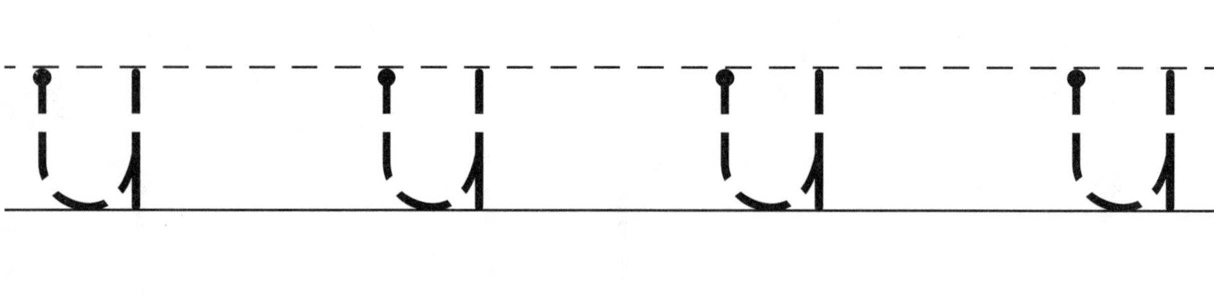

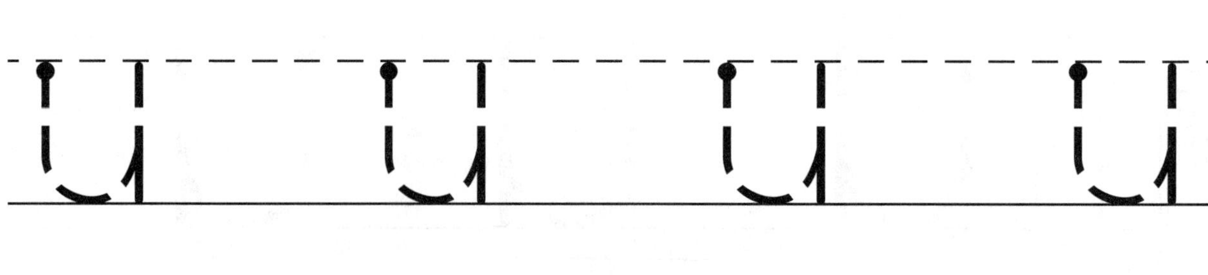

Direct children to trace the *u*'s and say /ŭ/ as in *umbrella* as they trace each letter.

u /ŭ/ umbrella

Identify the pictures with children. Have them circle the pictures in each row that begin with /ŭ/ as in *umbrella*.

u /ŭ/ umbrella 

Identify the pictures with children. Tell them to start at the dot next to the umbrella and draw a line to the picture that begins with /ŭ/ as in *umbrella*.

u /ŭ/ umbrella

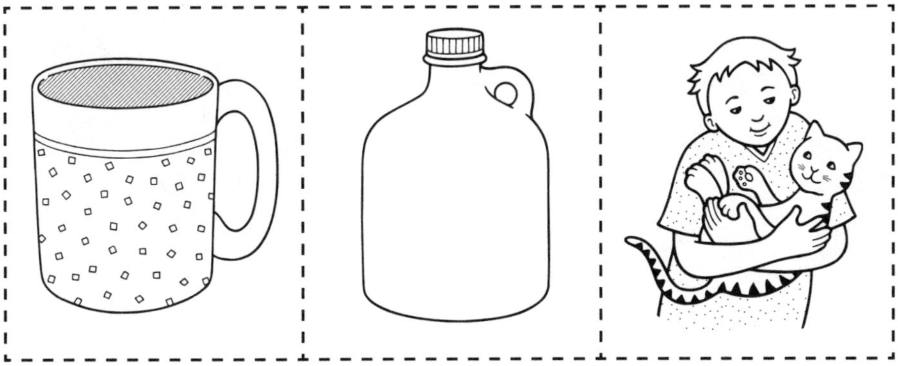

Identify the pictures in row 1 with children. Have them say the beginning sounds and blend them together to make a new word. Follow the same procedure with rows 2 and 3. Help children cut out the pictures at the bottom of the page and paste each next to the blended word it matches.

u /ŭ/ umbrella

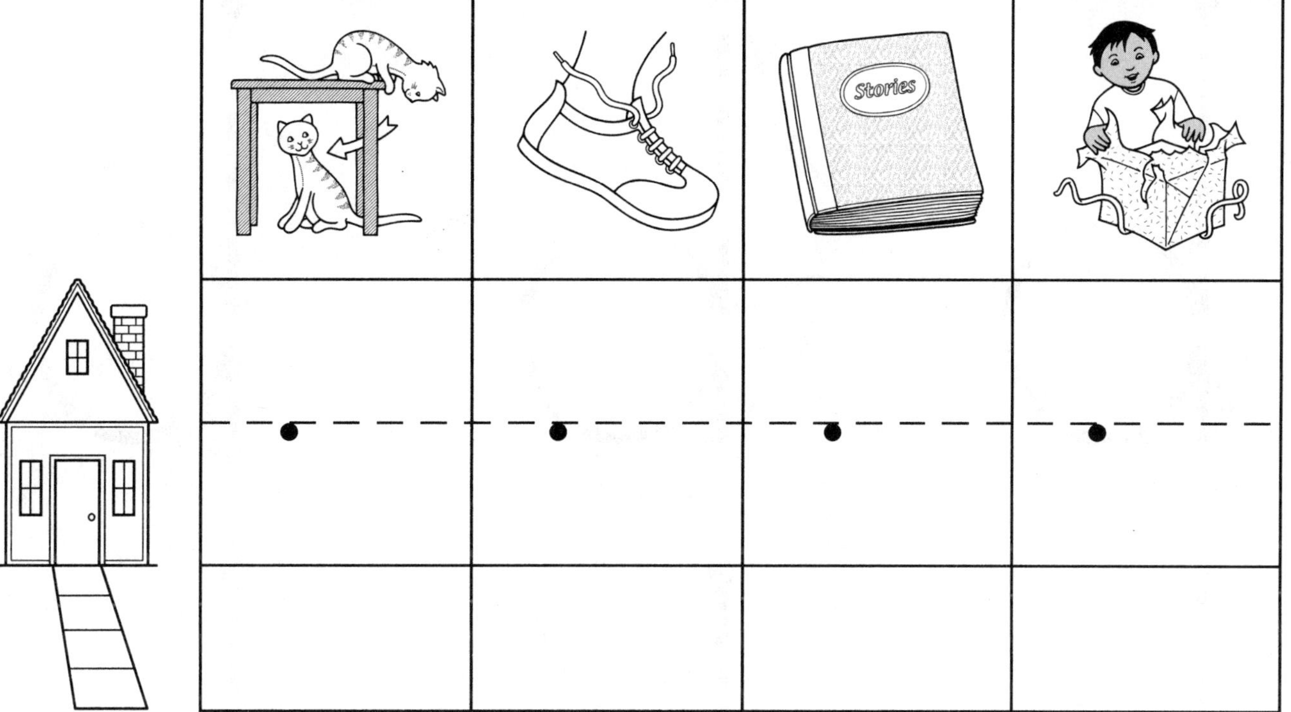

Identify the pictures with children. Direct them to circle each picture that begins with /ŭ/ as in *umbrella* and print the letter *u* under it, starting at the dot.

Lesson 15

b /b/ bat

Have children trace all of the *b*'s on this page. Tell them to start at the dot and say /b/ as in *bat* as they trace each *b*.

b /b/ bat

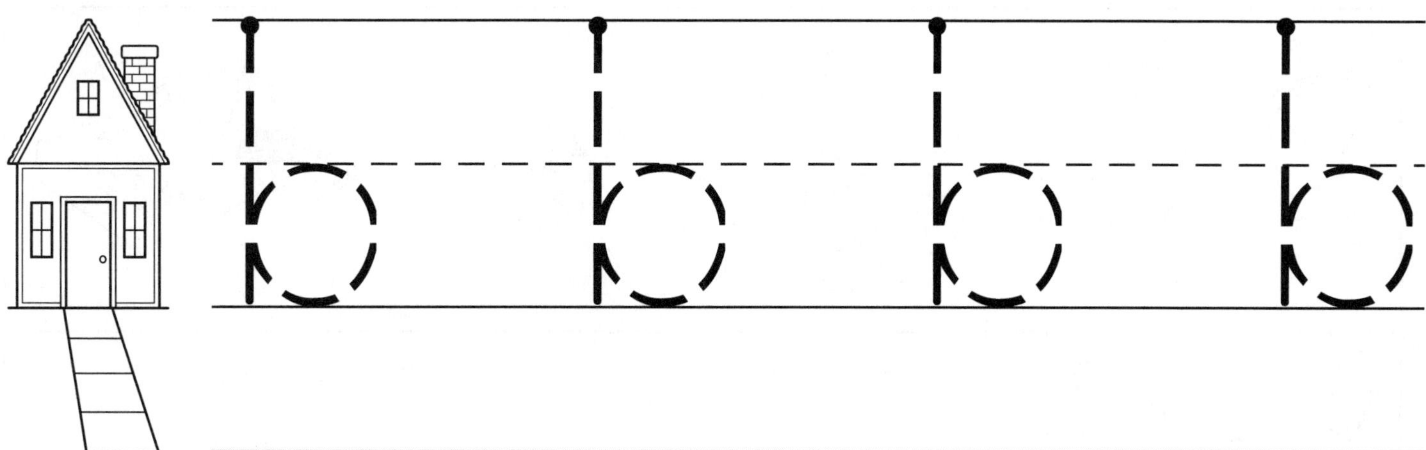

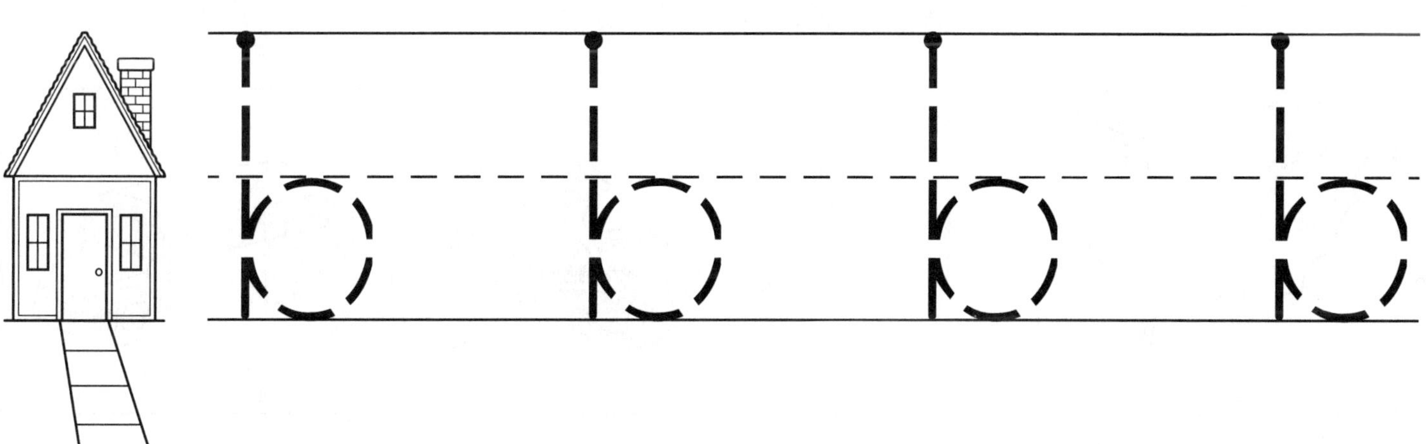

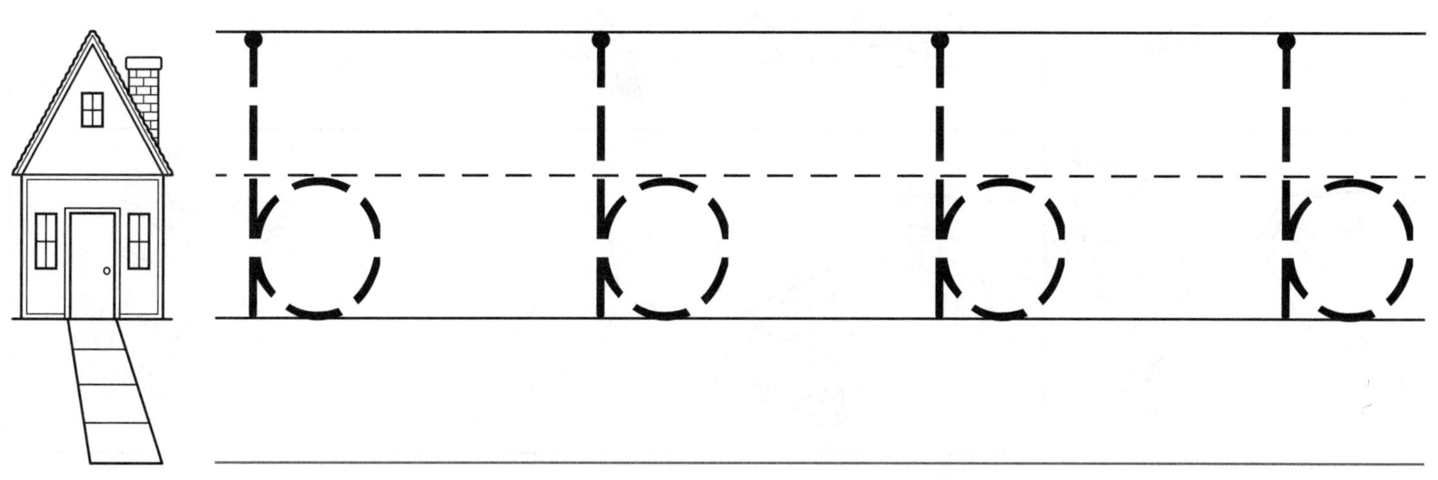

Direct children to trace the *b*'s and say /b/ as in *bat* as they trace each letter.

b /b/ bat 

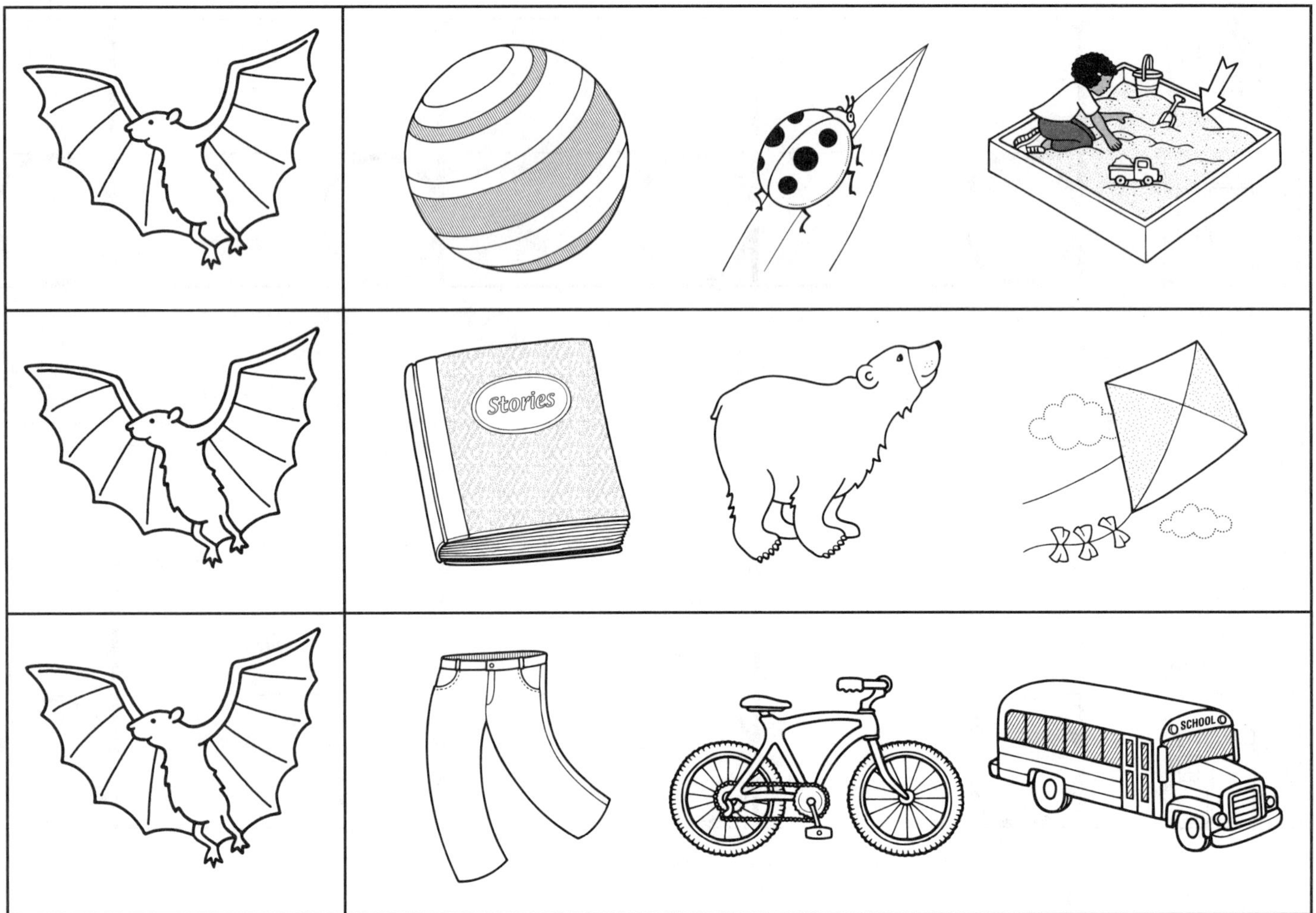

Identify the pictures with children. Have them circle the pictures in each row that begin with /b/ as in *bat*.

b /b/ bat

Identify the pictures with children. Tell them to start at the dot next to the bat and draw a line to the picture that begins with /b/ as in *bat*.

b /b/ bat 

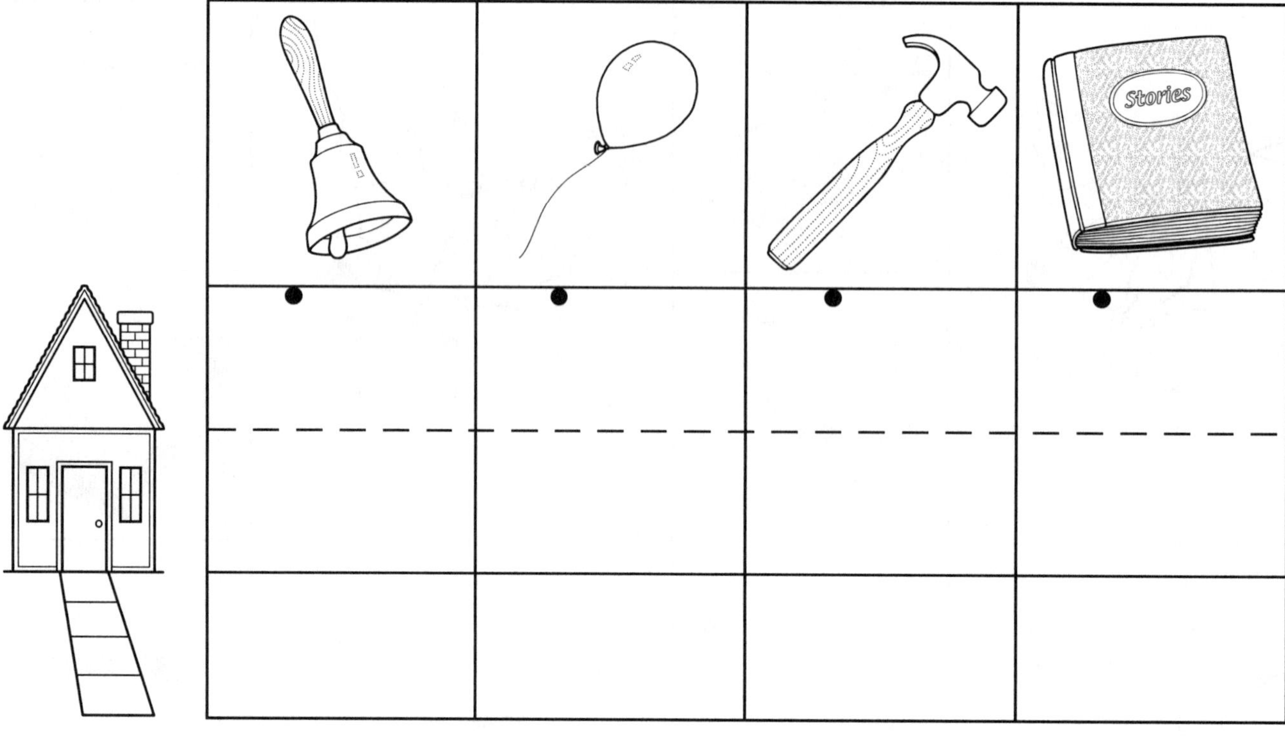

Identify the pictures with children. Direct them to circle each picture that begins with /b/ as in b*at* and print the letter *b* under it, starting at the dot.

b /b/ bat 

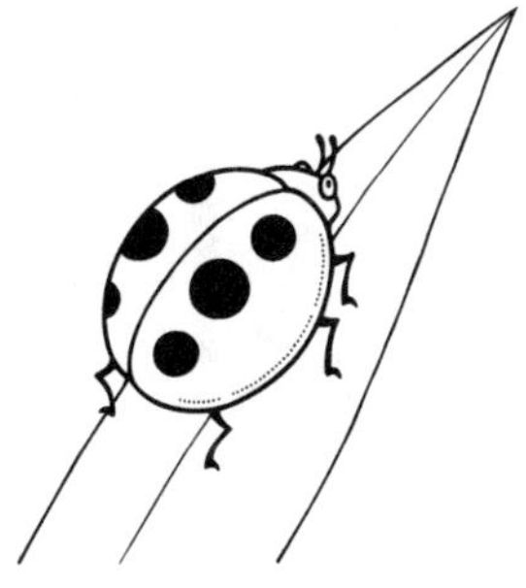

Identify the pictures in row 1 with children. Have them say the beginning sound of each. Then help children blend those sounds together to make a new word and draw a line to the picture of that word. Follow the same procedure with rows 2 and 3.

r /r/ rabbit

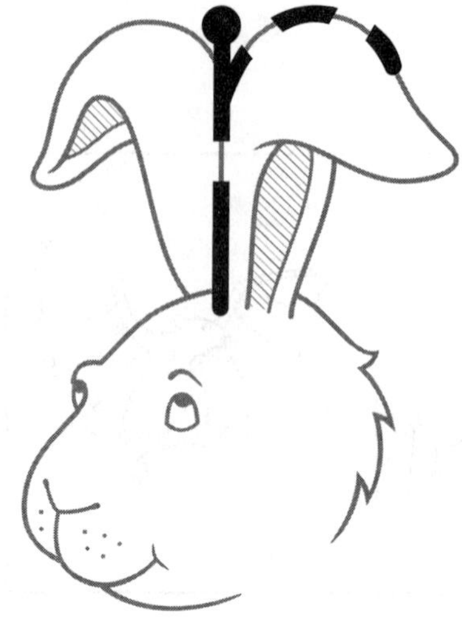
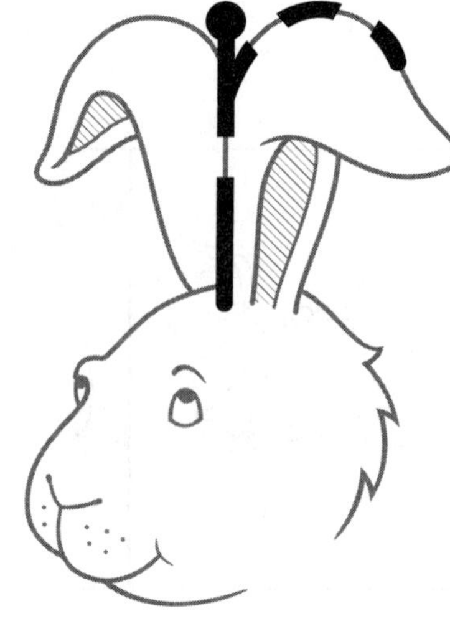

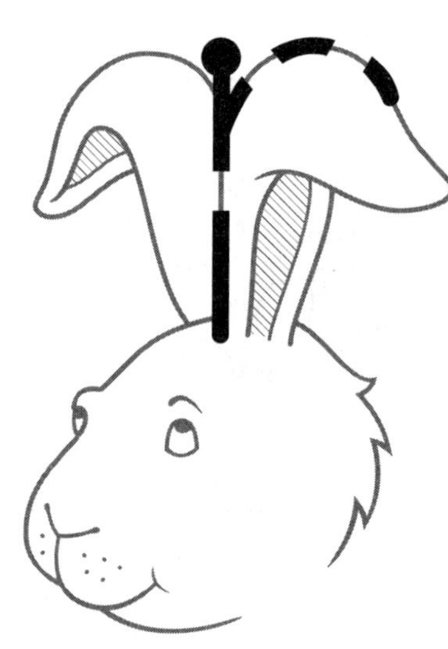

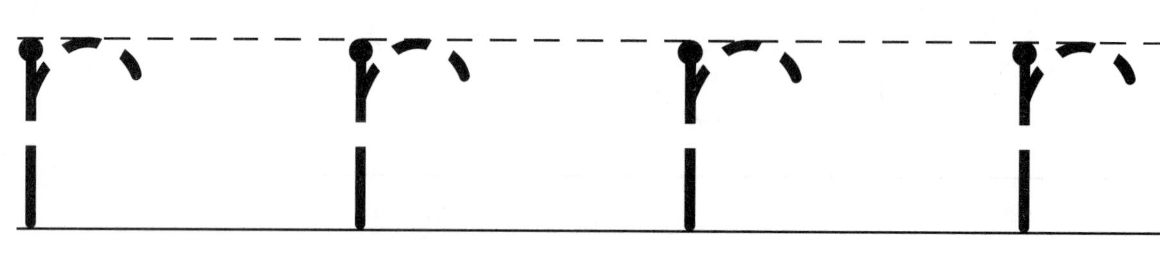

Have children trace all of the *r*'s on this page. Tell them to start at the dot and say /r/ as in *rabbit* as they trace each *r*.

r /r/ rabbit

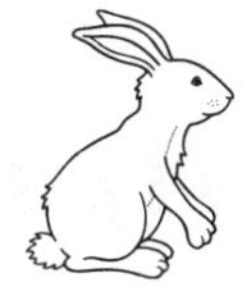

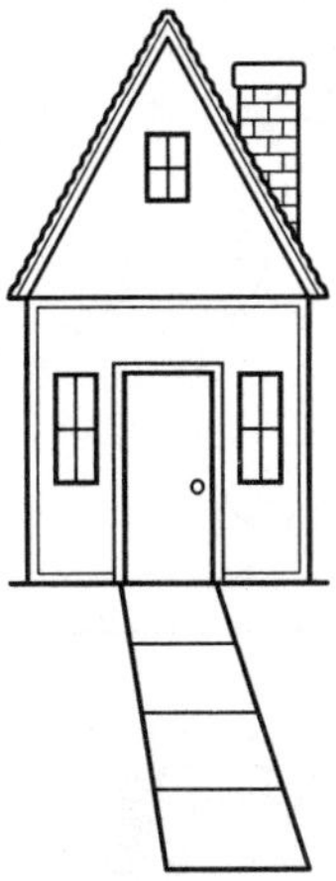

r r r r

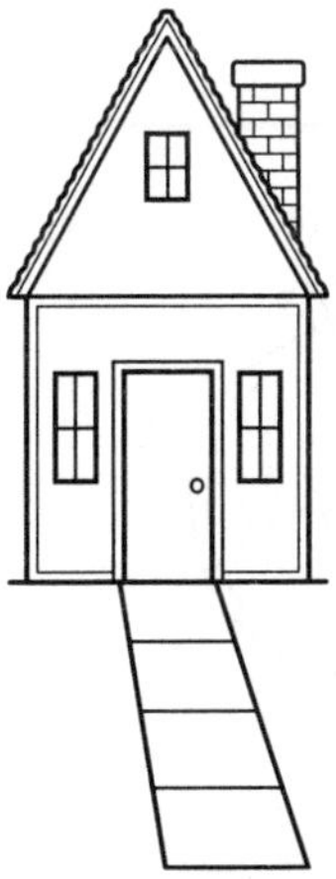

r r r r

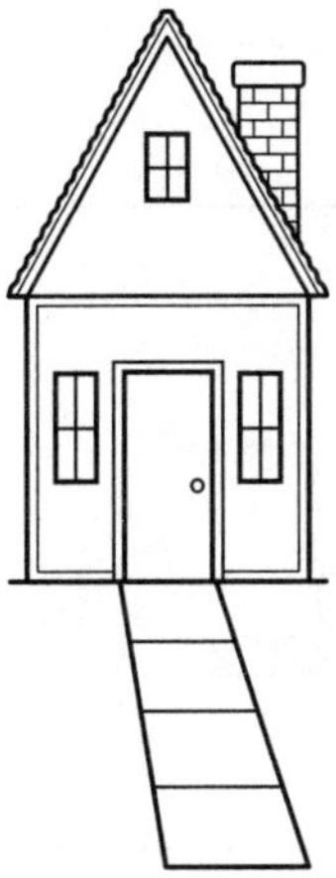

r r r r

Direct children to trace the *r*'s and say /r/ as in *rabbit* as they trace each letter.

r /r/ rabbit 

Identify the pictures with children. Have them circle the pictures in each row that begin with /r/ as in *rabbit*.

r /r/ rabbit

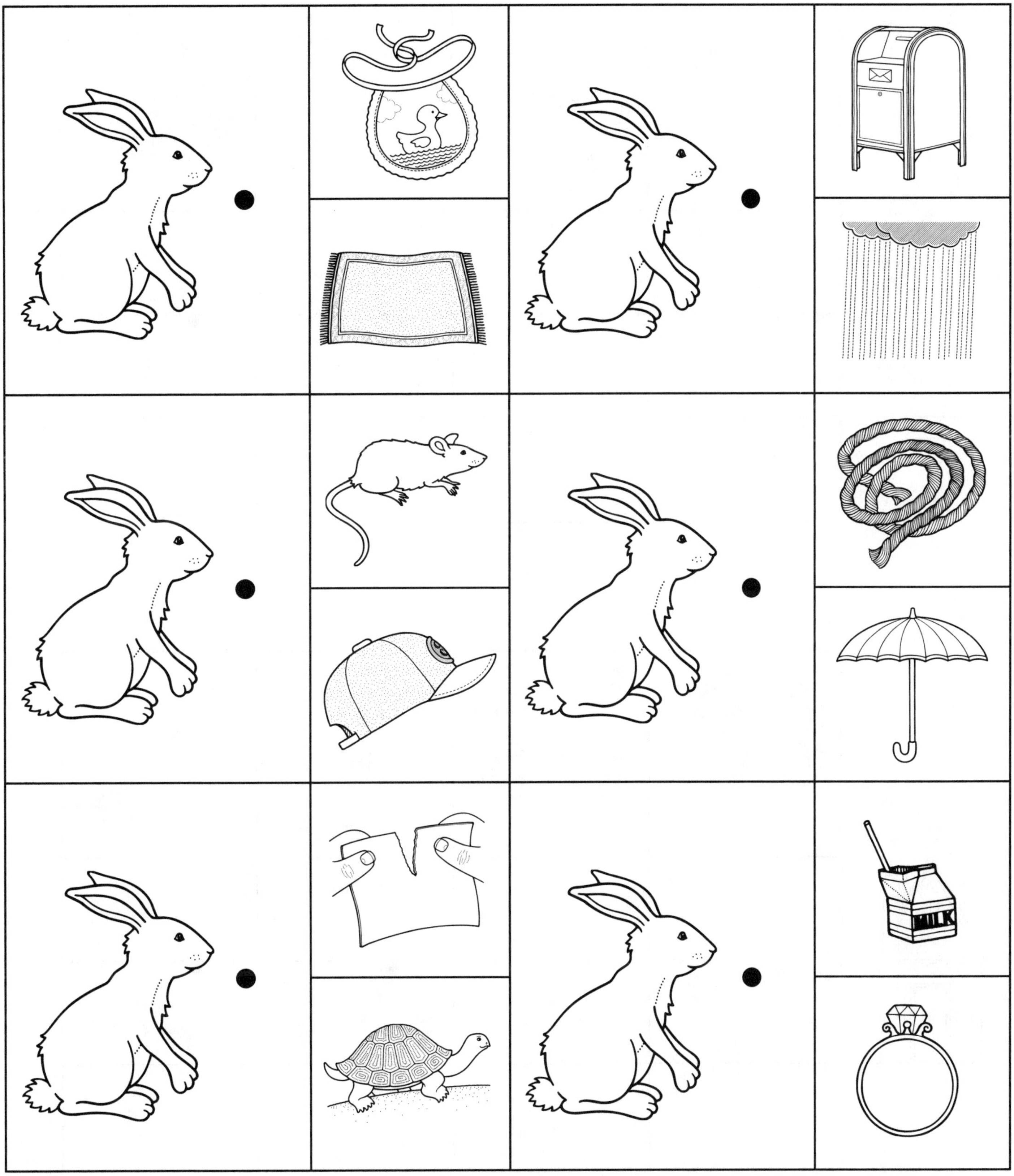

Identify the pictures with children. Tell them to start at the dot next to the rabbit and draw a line to the picture that begins with /r/ as in *rabbit*.

r /r/ rabbit

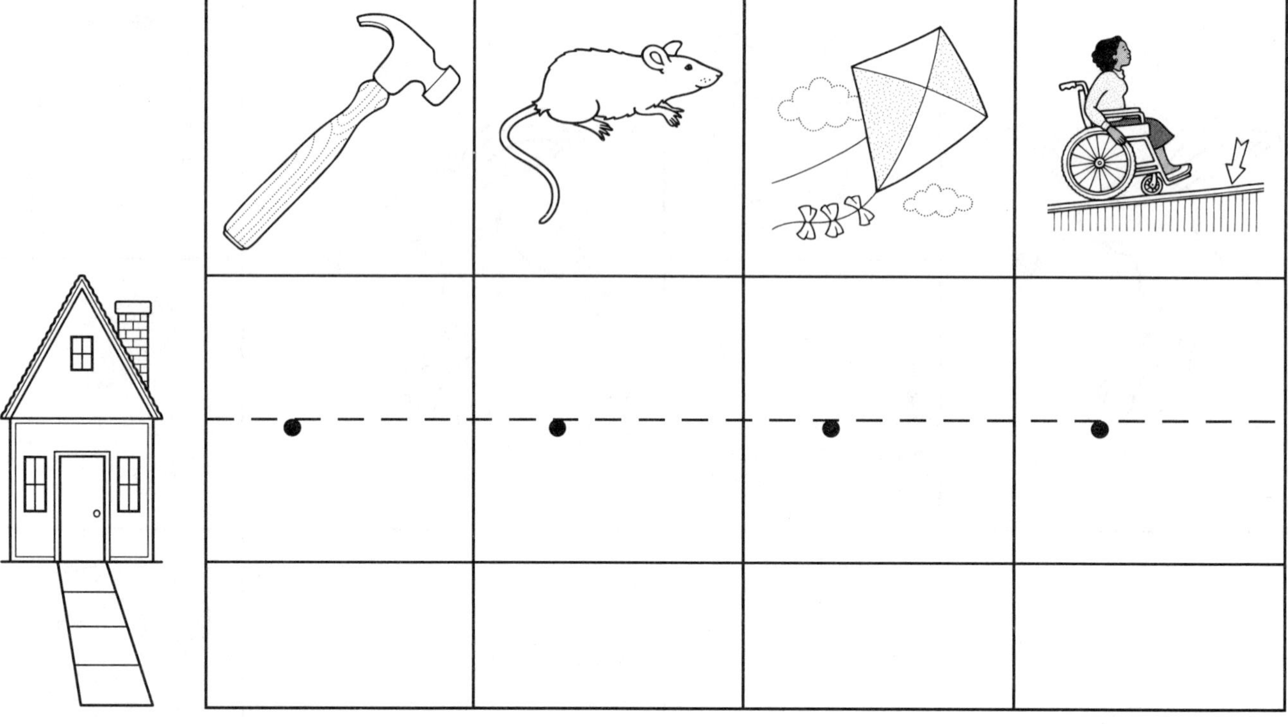

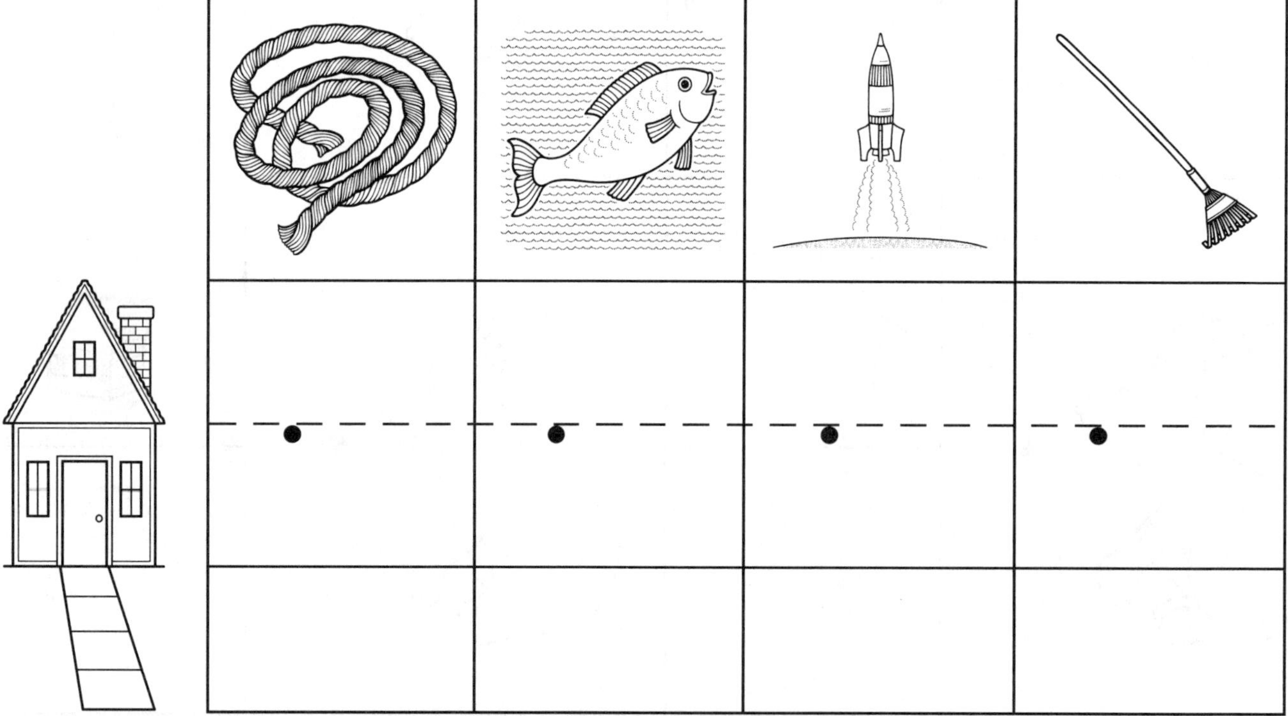

Identify the pictures with children. Direct them to circle each picture that begins with /r/ as in *rabbit* and print the letter *r* under it, starting at the dot.

r /r/ rabbit

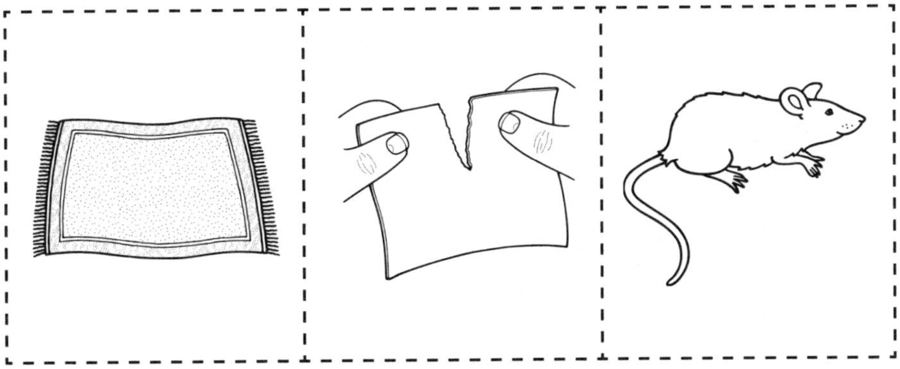

Identify the pictures in row 1 with children. Have them say the beginning sounds and blend them together to make a new word. Follow the same procedure with rows 2 and 3. Help children cut out the pictures at the bottom of the page and paste each next to the blended word it matches.

Lesson 17

f /f/ fish

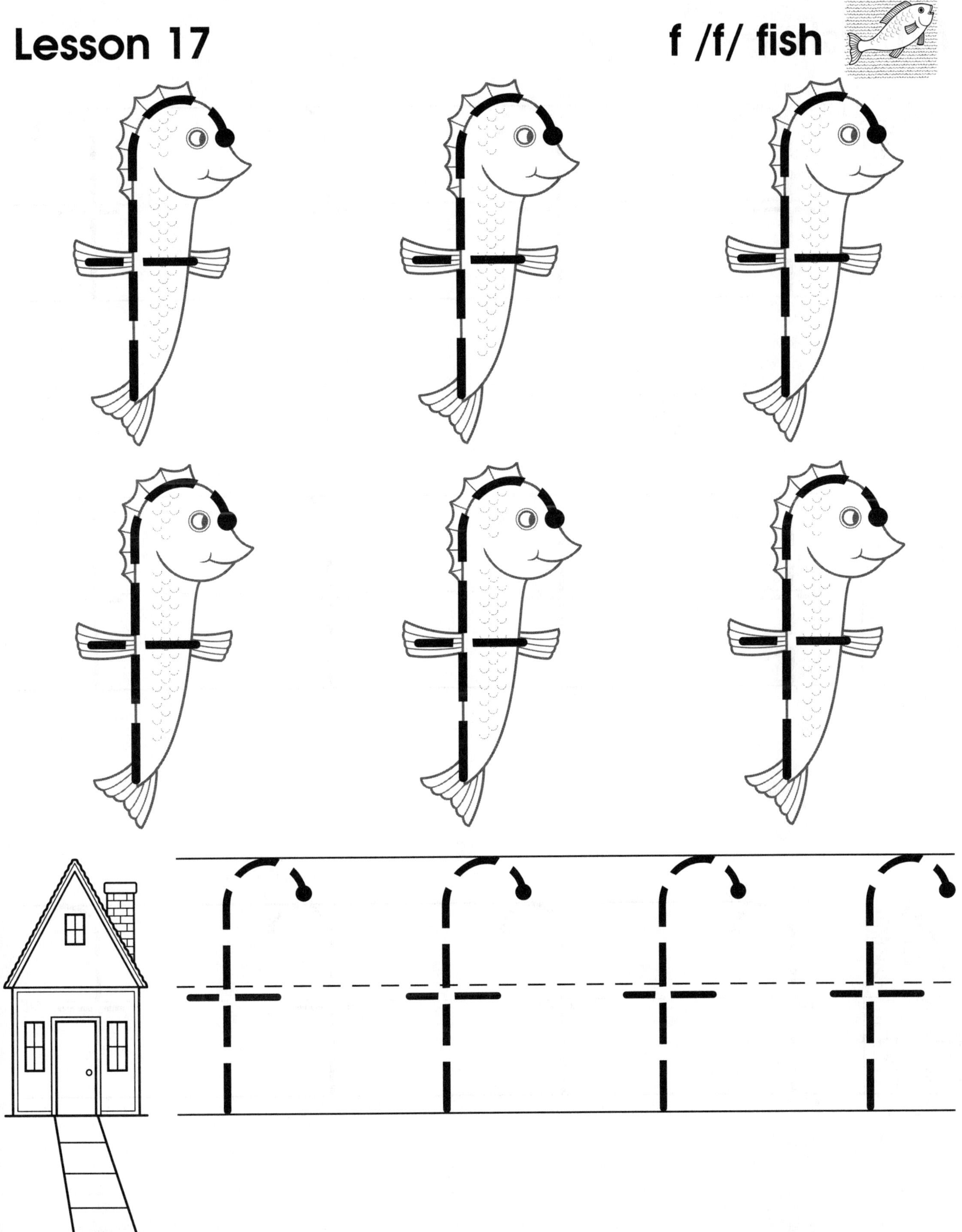

Have children trace all of the *f*'s on this page. Tell them to start at the dot and say /f/ as in *fish* as they trace each *f*.

f /f/ fish 

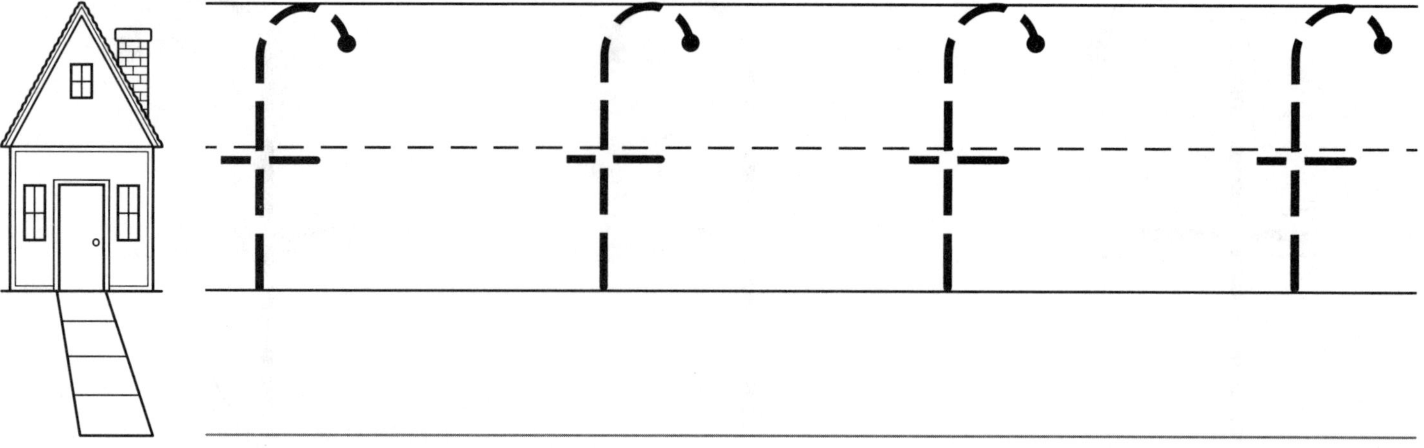

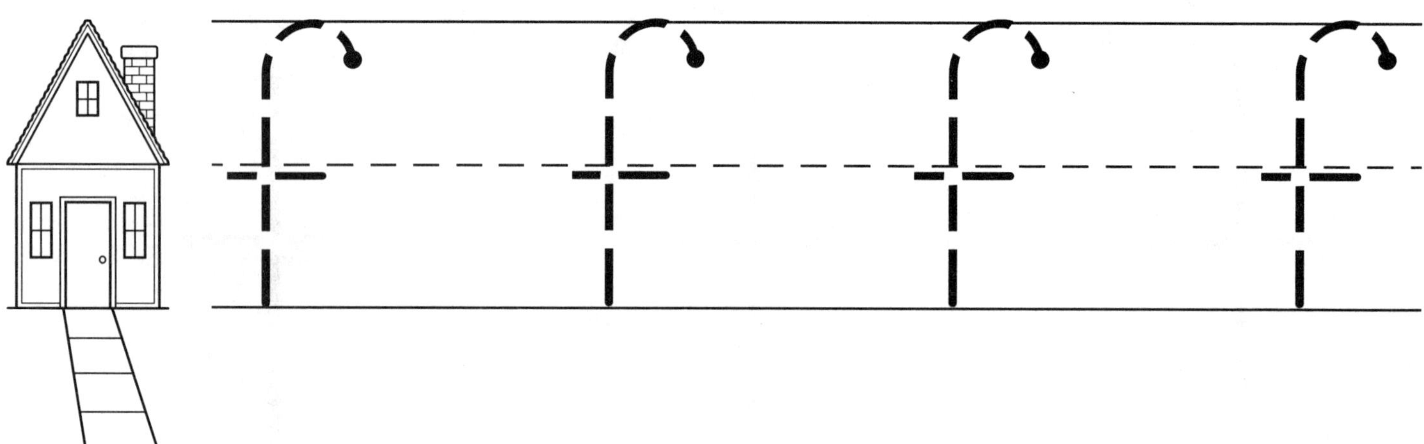

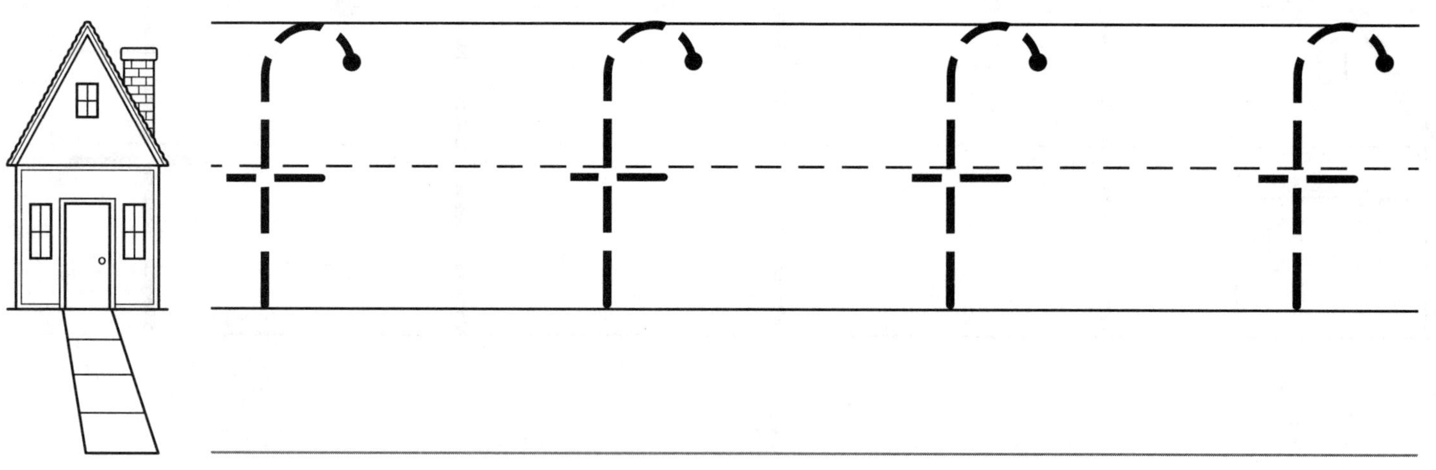

Direct children to trace the *f*'s and say /f/ as in *fish* as they trace each letter.

f /f/ fish 

Identify the pictures with children. Have them circle the pictures in each row that begin with /f/ as in *fish*.

f /f/ fish 

Identify the pictures with children. Tell them to start at the dot next to the fish and draw a line to the picture that begins with /f/ as in *fish*.

f /f/ fish 

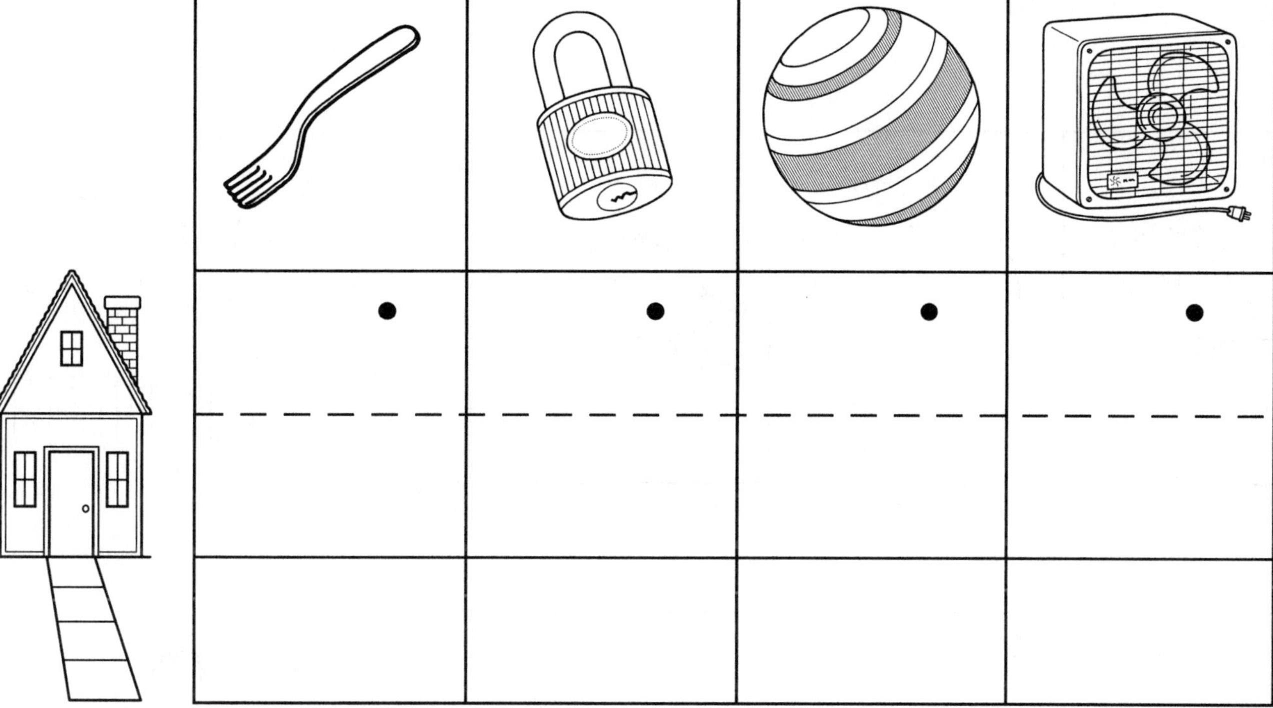

Identify the pictures with children. Direct them to circle each picture that begins with /f/ as in *fish* and print the letter *f* under it, starting at the dot.

f /f/ fish 

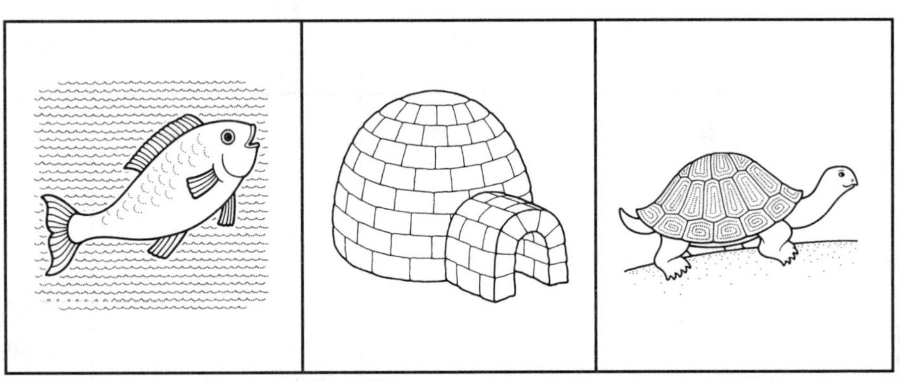

Identify the pictures in row 1 with children. Have them say the beginning sound of each. Then help children blend those sounds together to make a new word and draw a line to the picture of that word. Follow the same procedure with rows 2 and 3.

Lesson 18

n /n/ nail

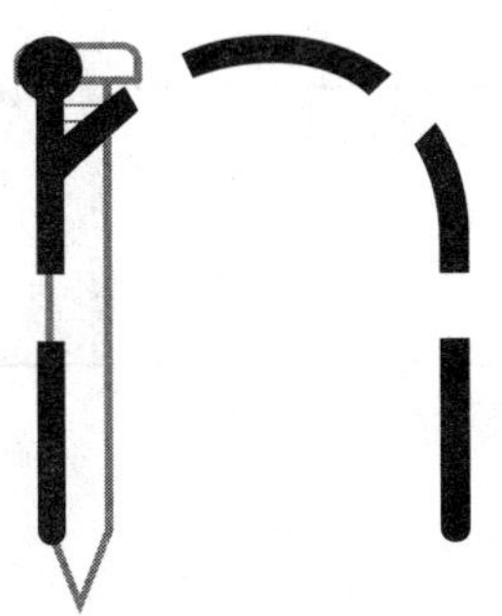
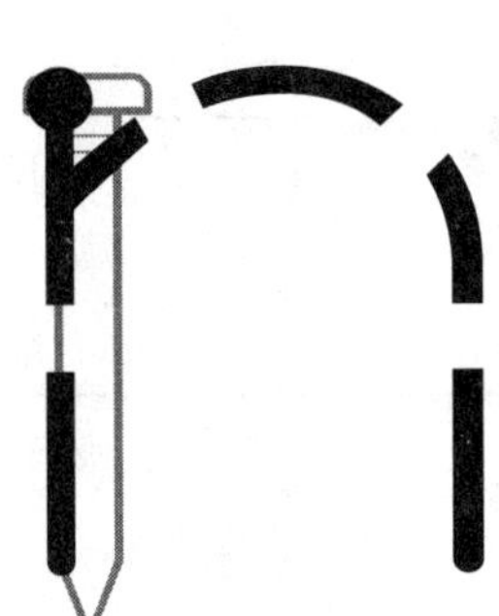
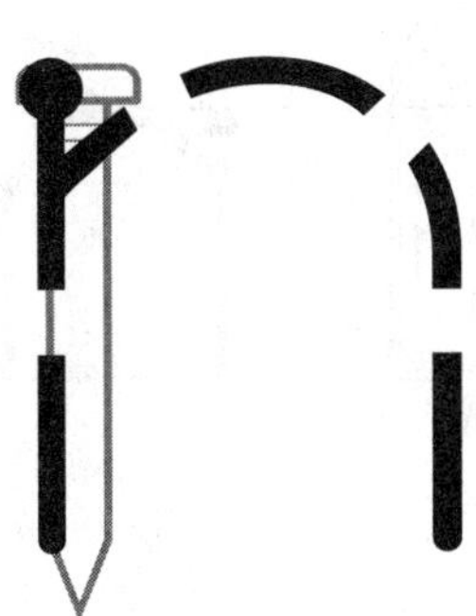

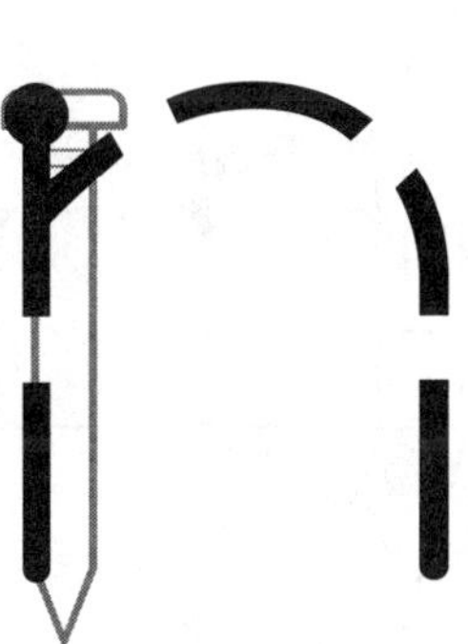

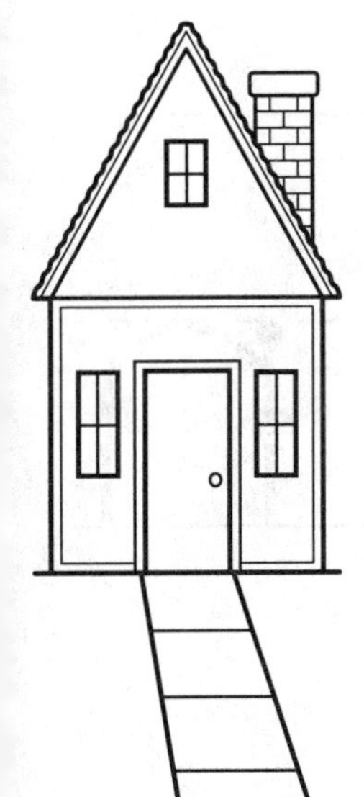
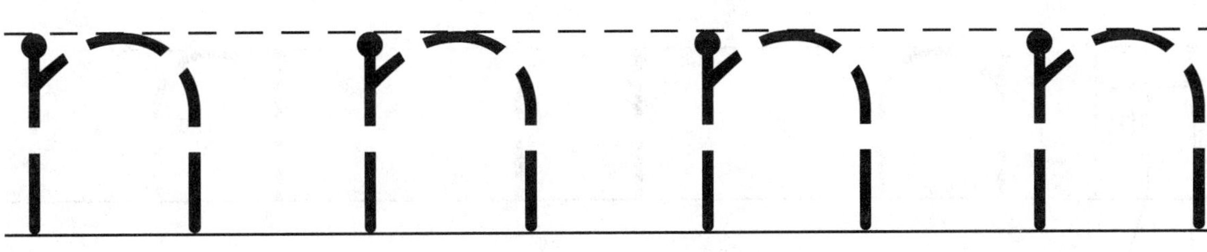

Have children trace all of the *n*'s on this page. Tell them to start at the dot and say /n/ as in *nail* as they trace each *n*.

n /n/ nail

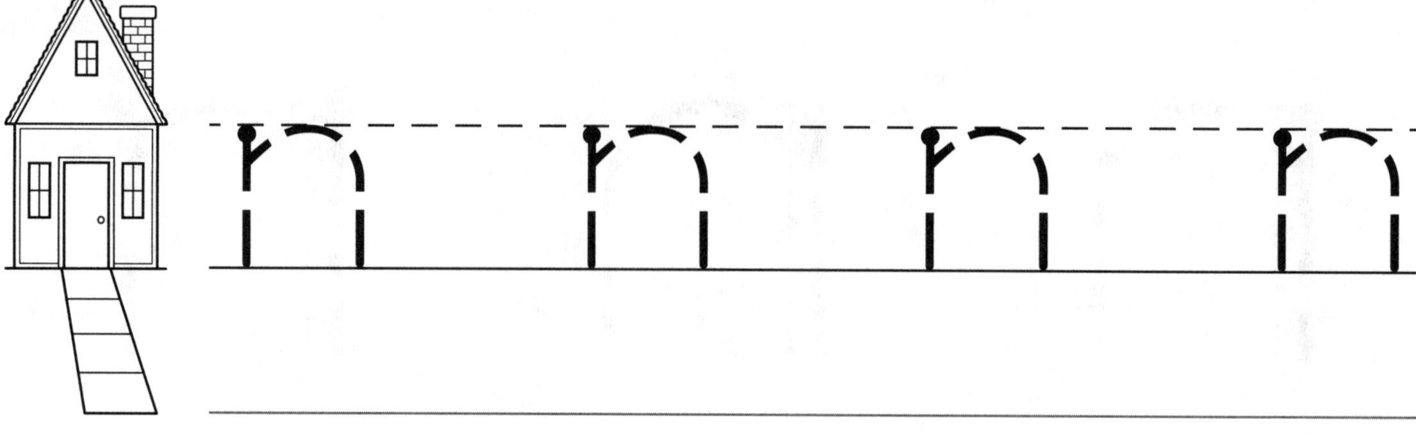

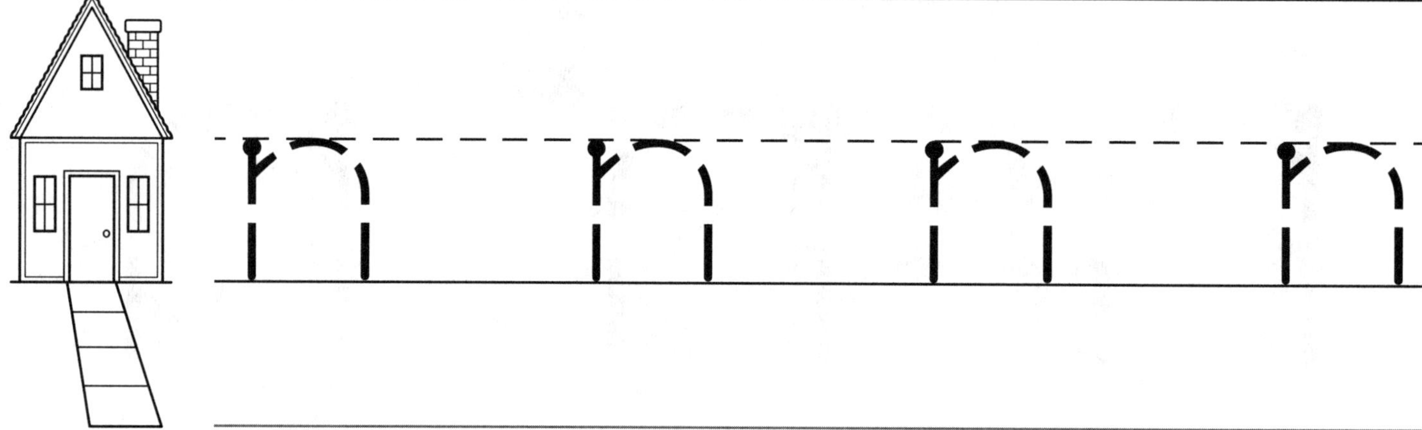

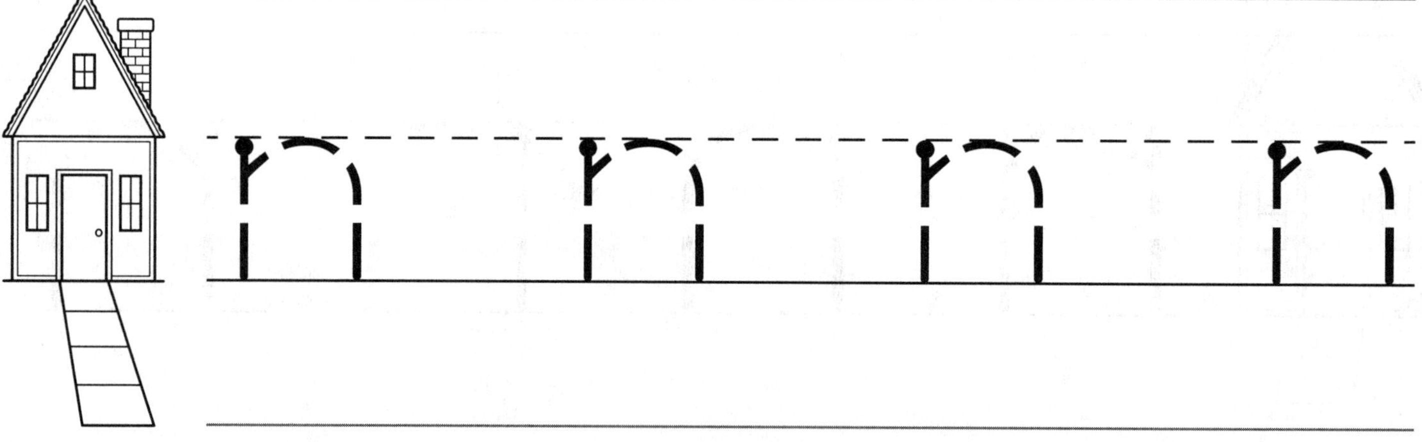

Direct children to trace the *n*'s and say /n/ as in *nail* as they trace each letter.

n /n/ nail

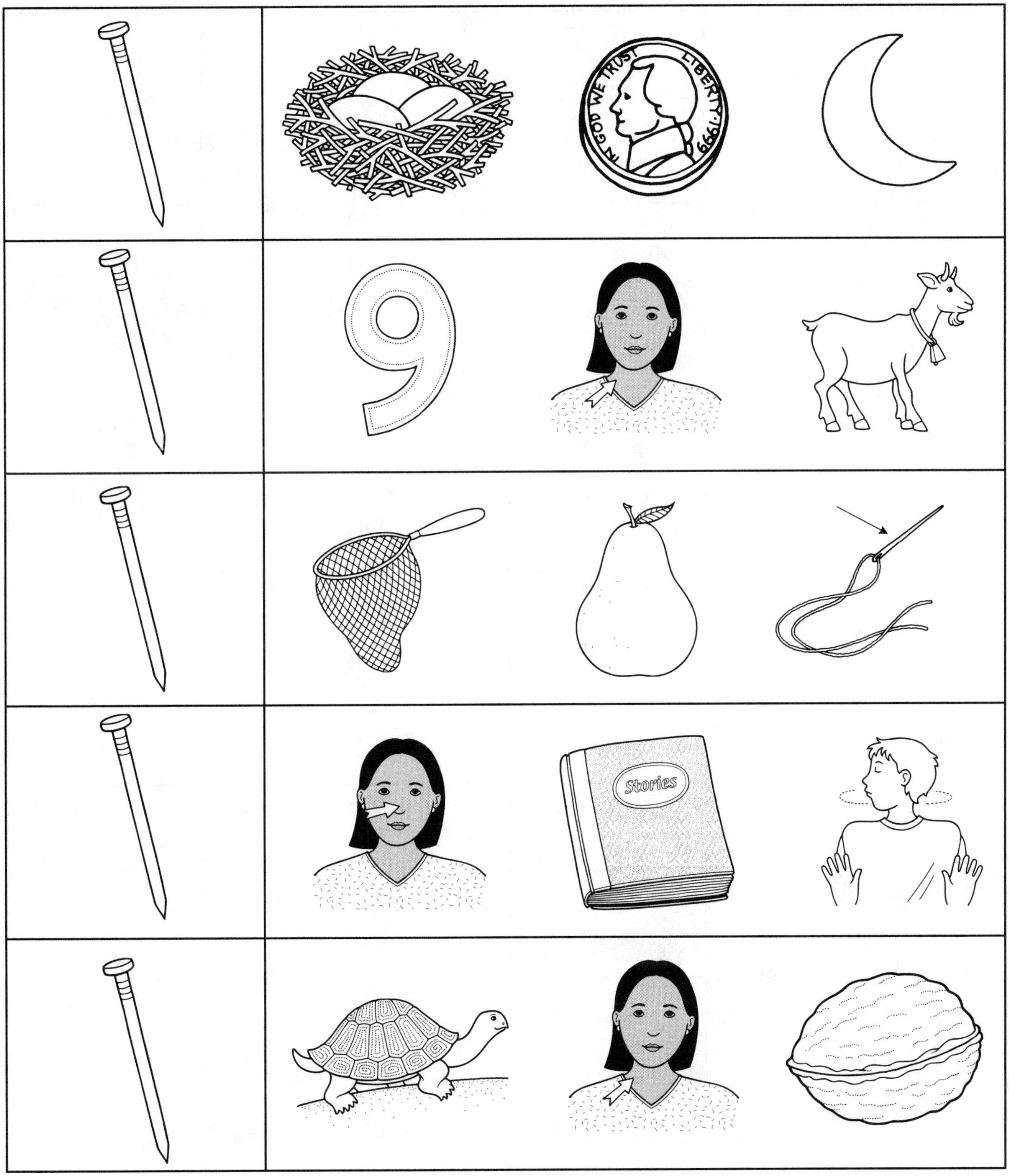

Identify the pictures with children. Have them circle the pictures in each row that begin with /n/ as in *nail*.

n /n/ nail

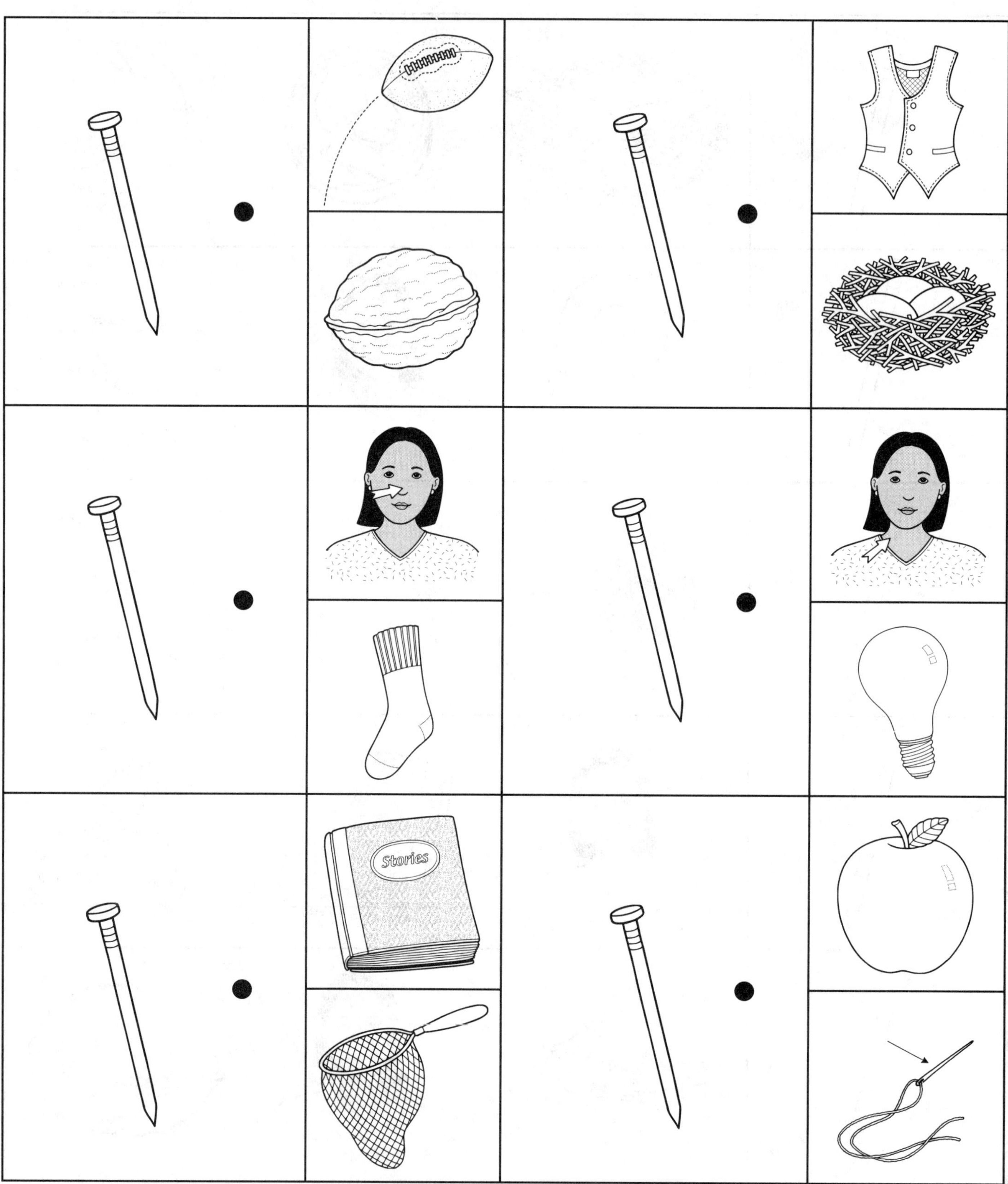

Identify the pictures with children. Tell them to start at the dot next to the nail and draw a line to the picture that begins with /n/ as in *nail*.

n /n/ nail

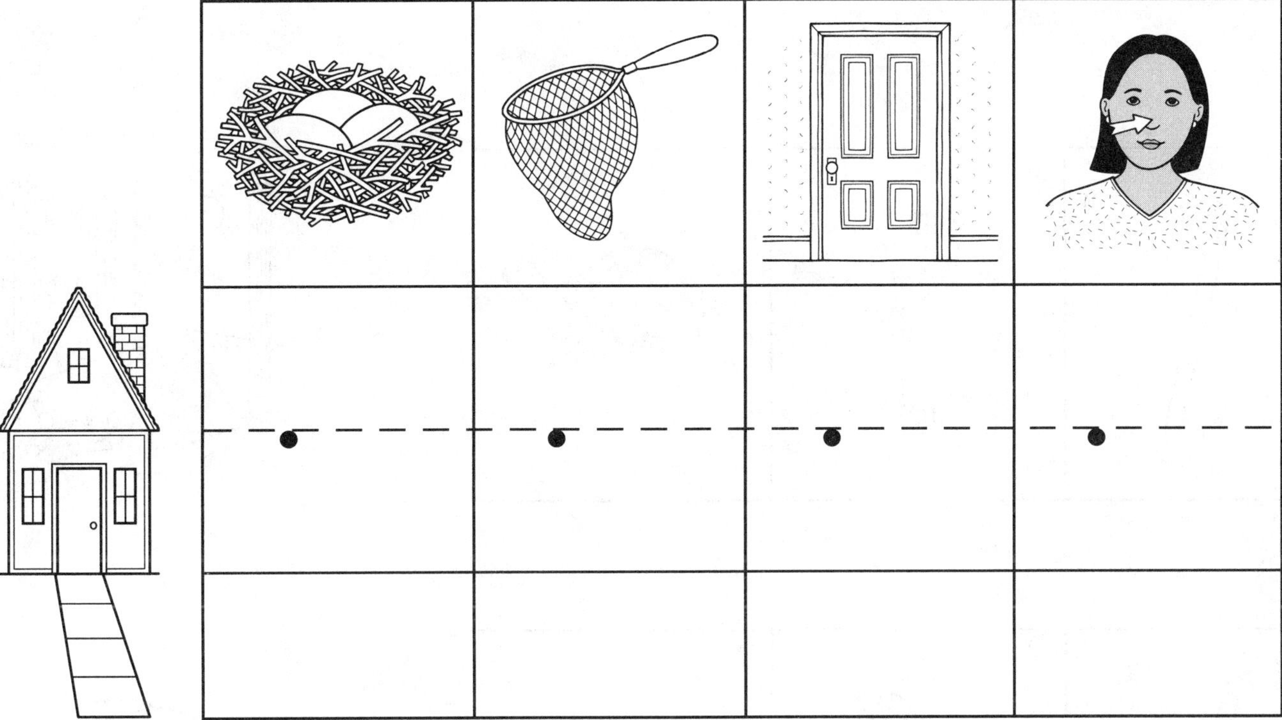

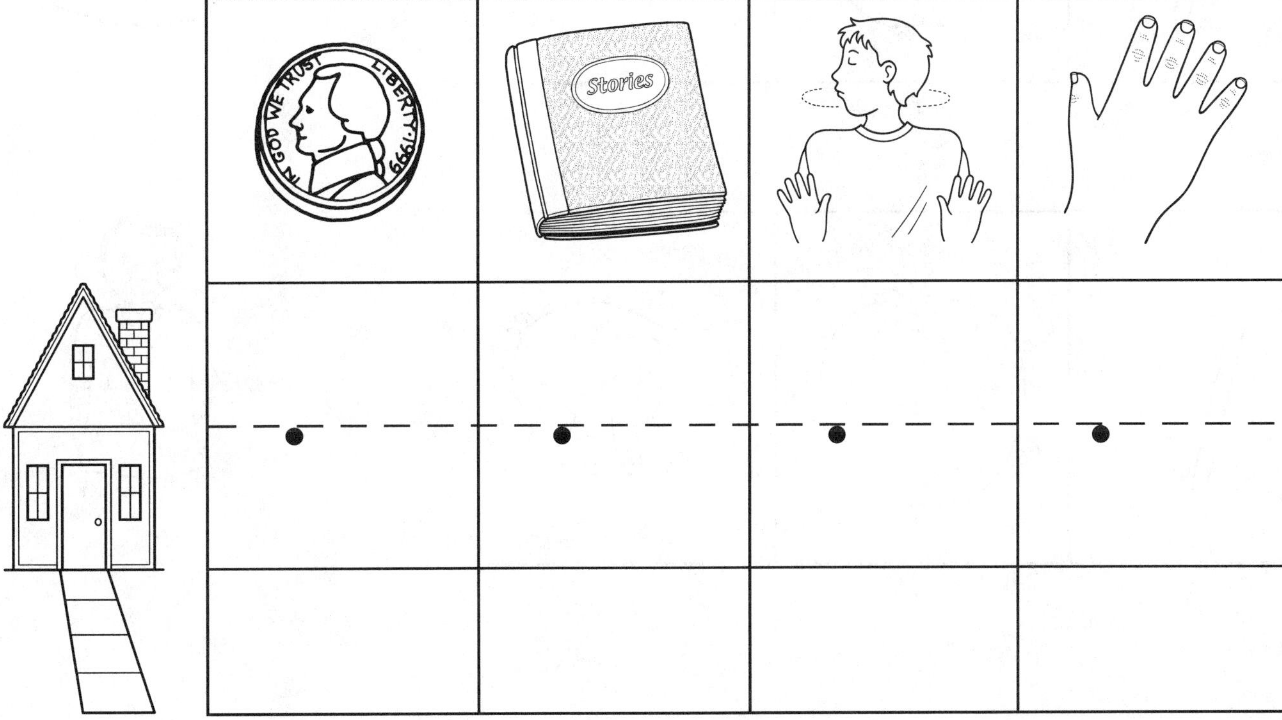

Identify the pictures with children. Direct them to circle each picture that begins with /n/ as in *nail* and print the letter *n* under it, starting at the dot.

n /n/ nail

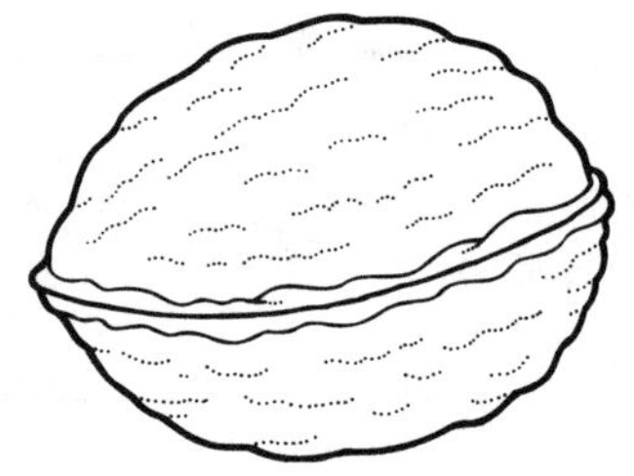

Identify the pictures in row 1 with children. Have them say the beginning sound of each. Then help children blend those sounds together to make a new word and draw a line to the picture of that word. Follow the same procedure with rows 2 and 3.

Lesson 19

e /ĕ/ elephant

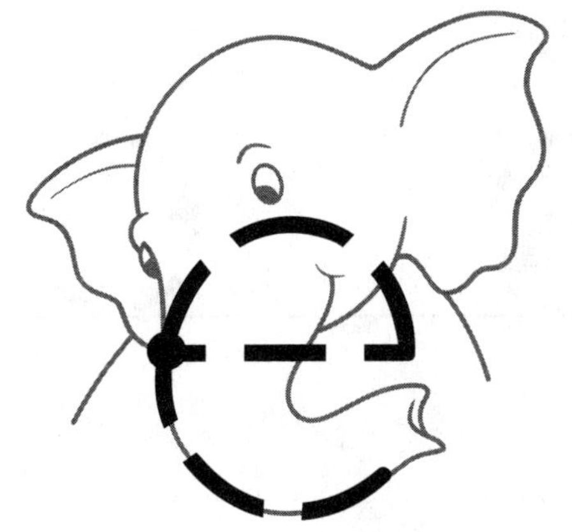
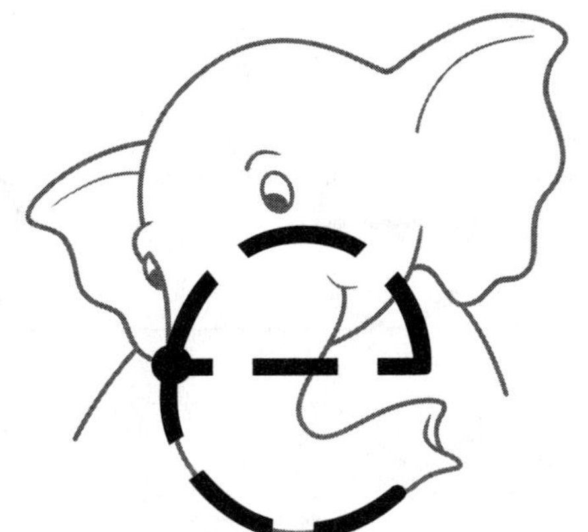
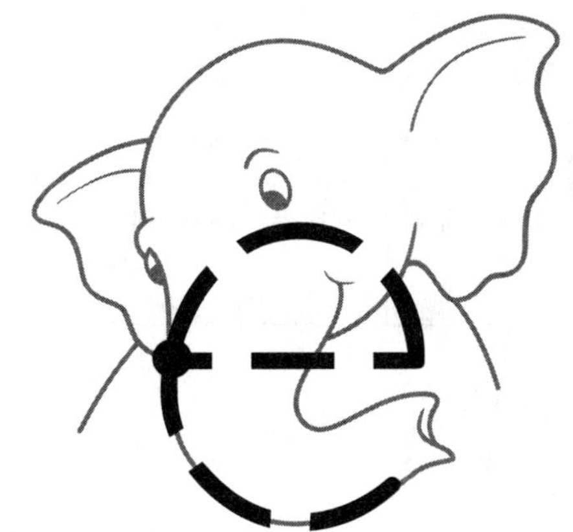
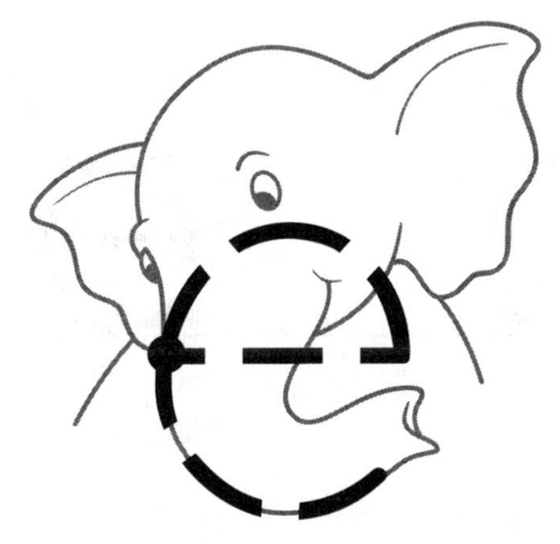
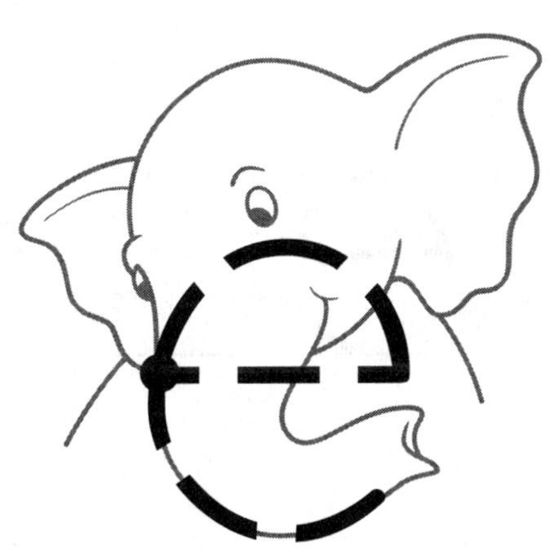
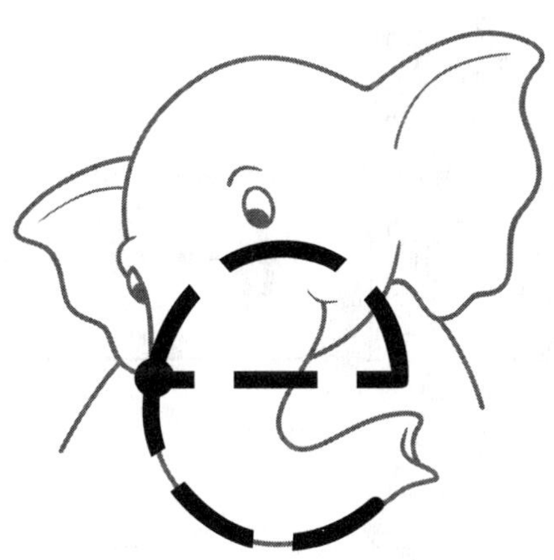

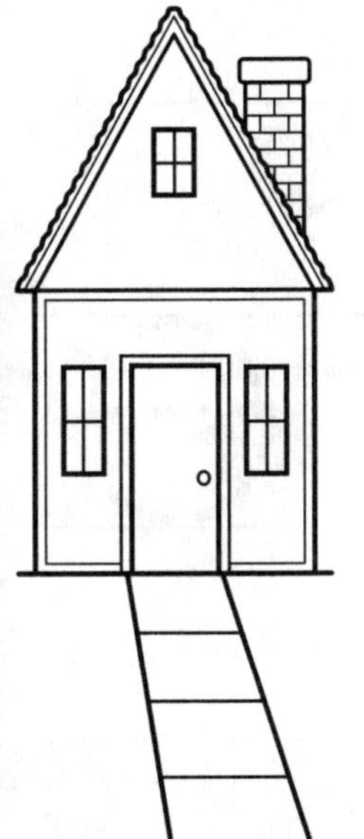
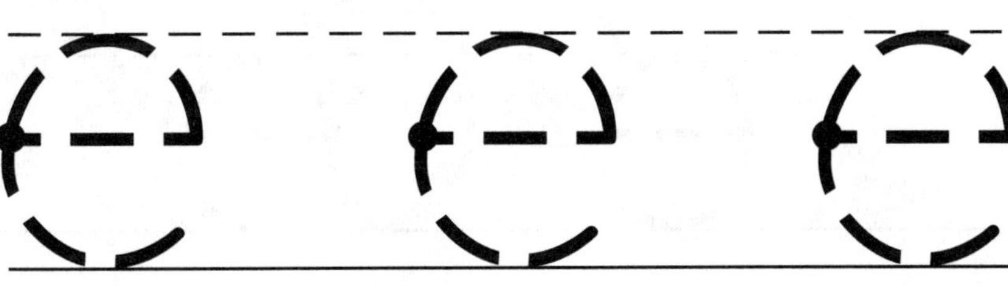

Have children trace all of the *e*'s on this page. Tell them to start at the dot and say /ĕ/ as in *elephant* as they trace each *e*.

e /ĕ/ elephant

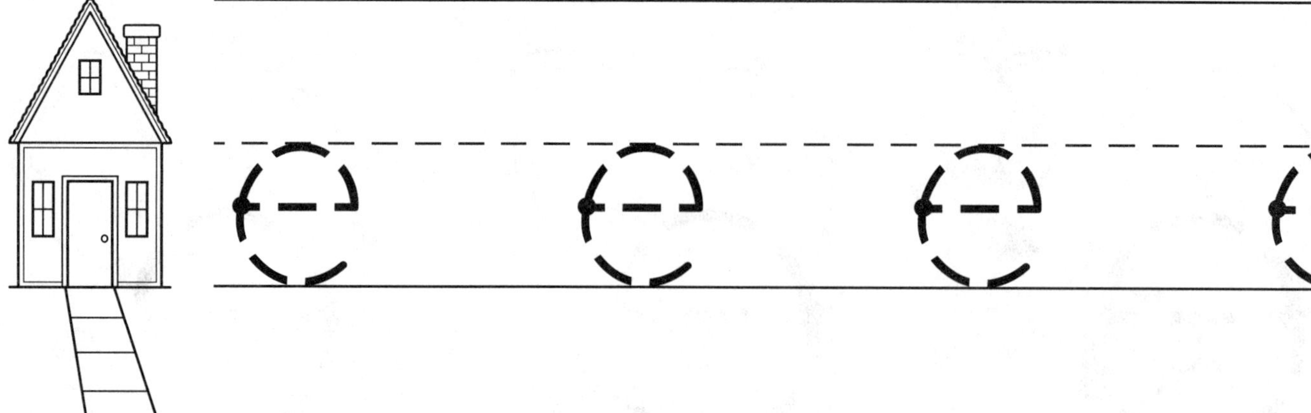

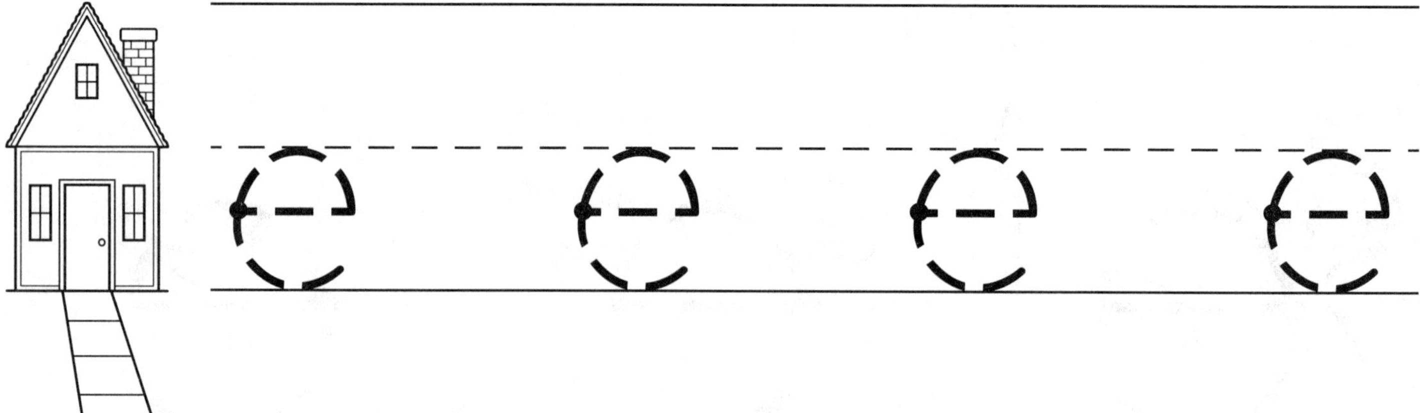

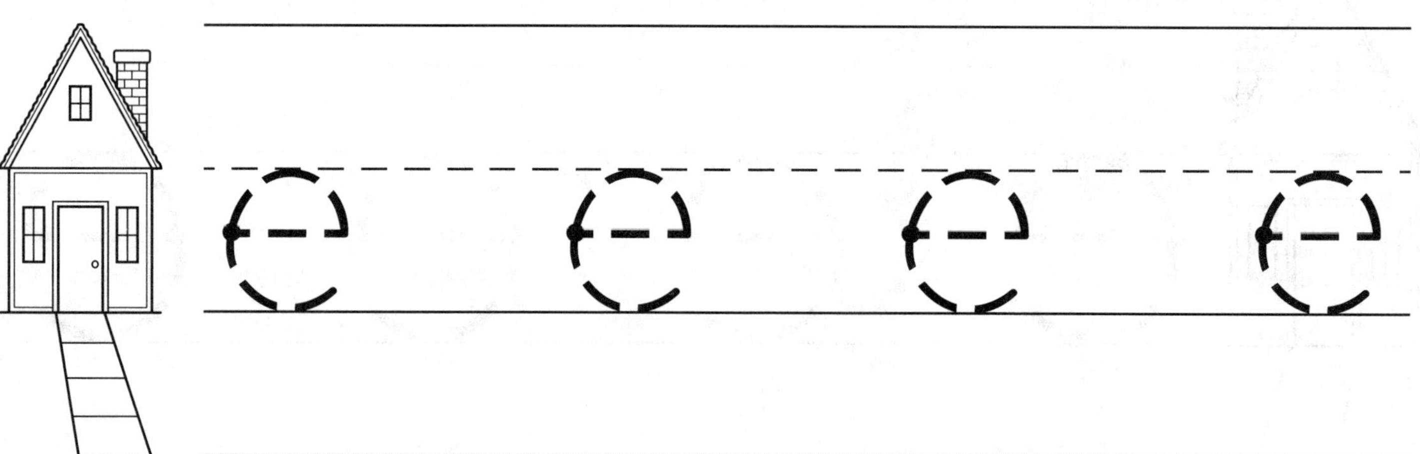

Direct children to trace the *e*'s and say /ĕ/ as in *elephant* as they trace each letter.

e /ĕ/ elephant 

Identify the pictures with children. Have them circle the pictures in each row that begin with /ĕ/ as in *elephant*.

e /ĕ/ elephant 

Identify the pictures with children. Tell them to start at the dot next to the elephant and draw a line to the picture that begins with /ĕ/ as in *elephant*.

e /ĕ/ elephant

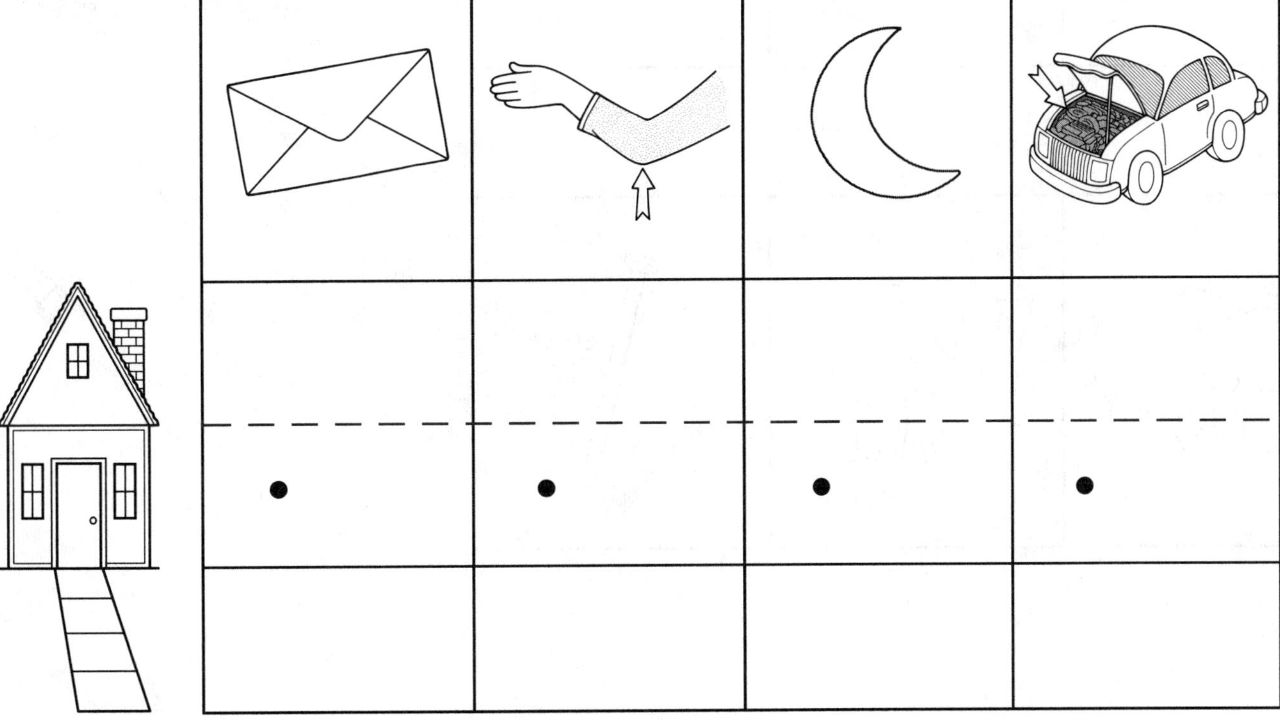

Identify the pictures with children. Direct them to circle each picture that begins with /ĕ/ as in *elephant* and print the letter *e* under it, starting at the dot.

e /ĕ/ elephant 

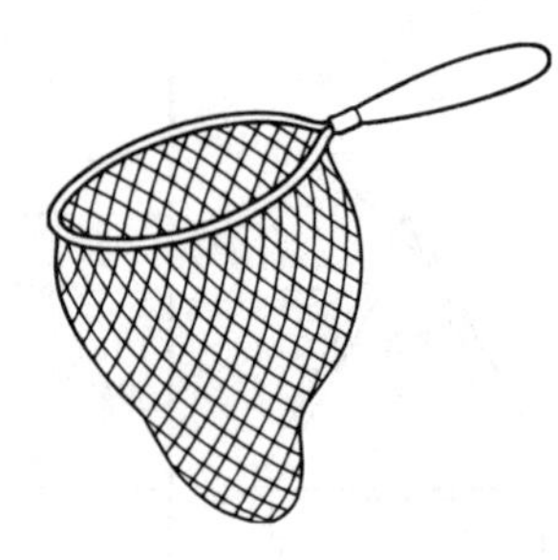

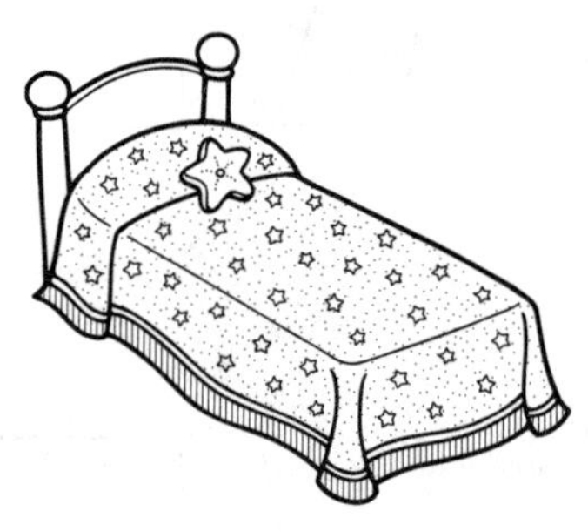

Identify the pictures in row 1 with children. Have them say the beginning sound of each. Then help children blend those sounds together to make a new word and draw a line to the picture of that word. Follow the same procedure with rows 2 and 3.

Lesson 20

s /s/ sun

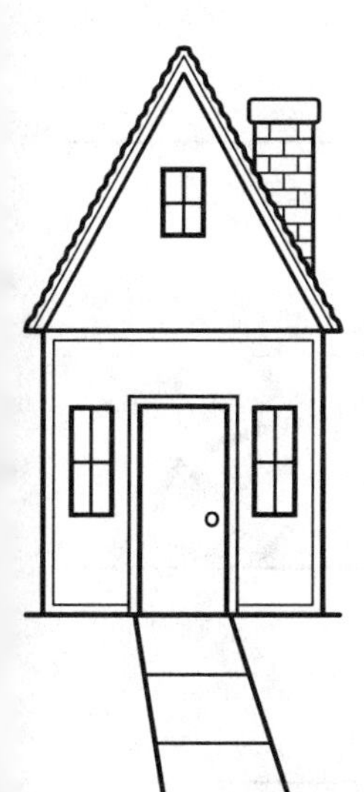

Have children trace all of the *s*'s on this page. Tell them to start at the dot and say /s/ as in *sun* as they trace each *s*.

s /s/ sun

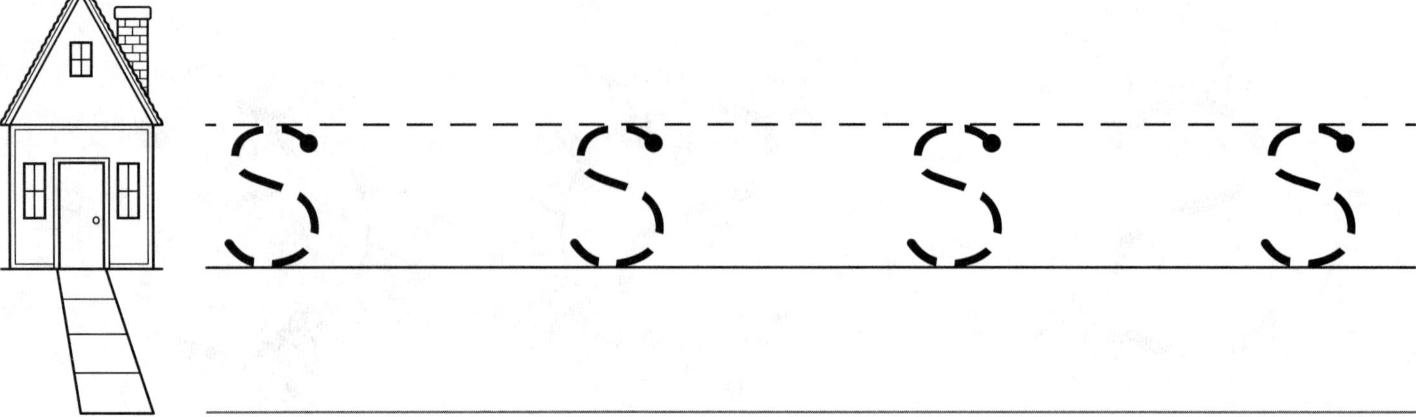

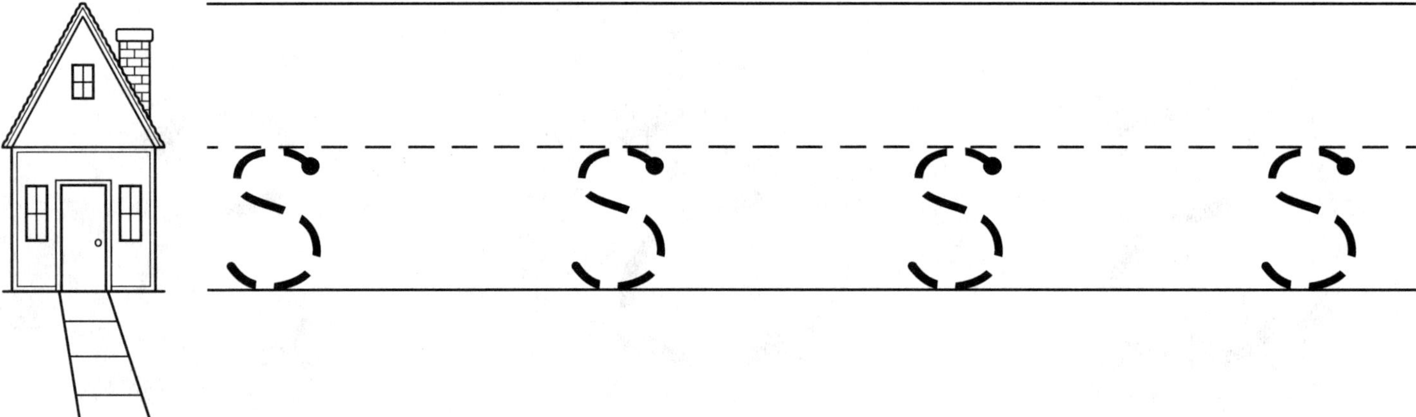

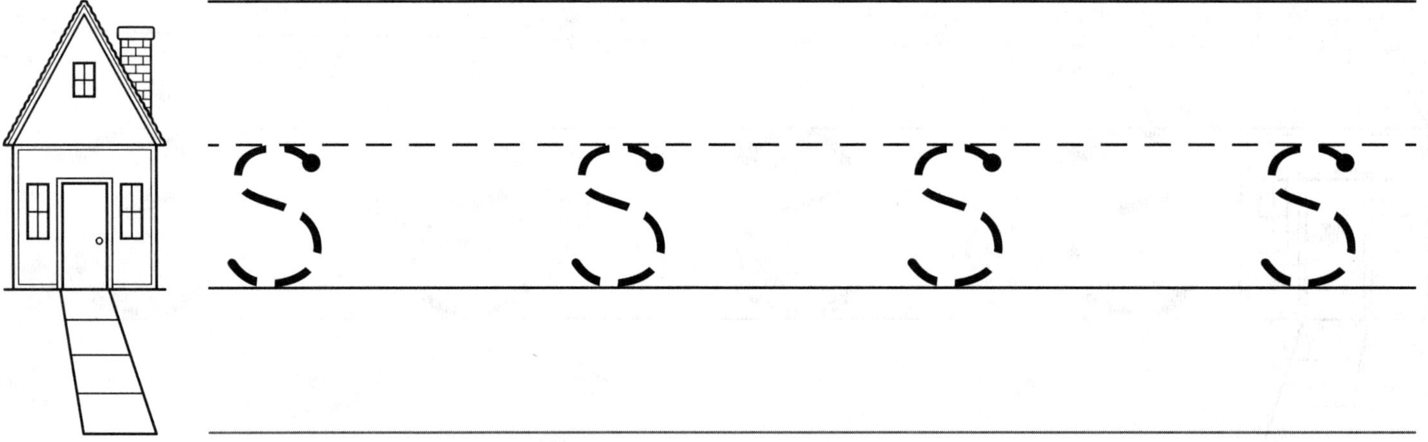

Direct children to trace the *s*'s and say /s/ as in *sun* as they trace each letter.

s /s/ sun 

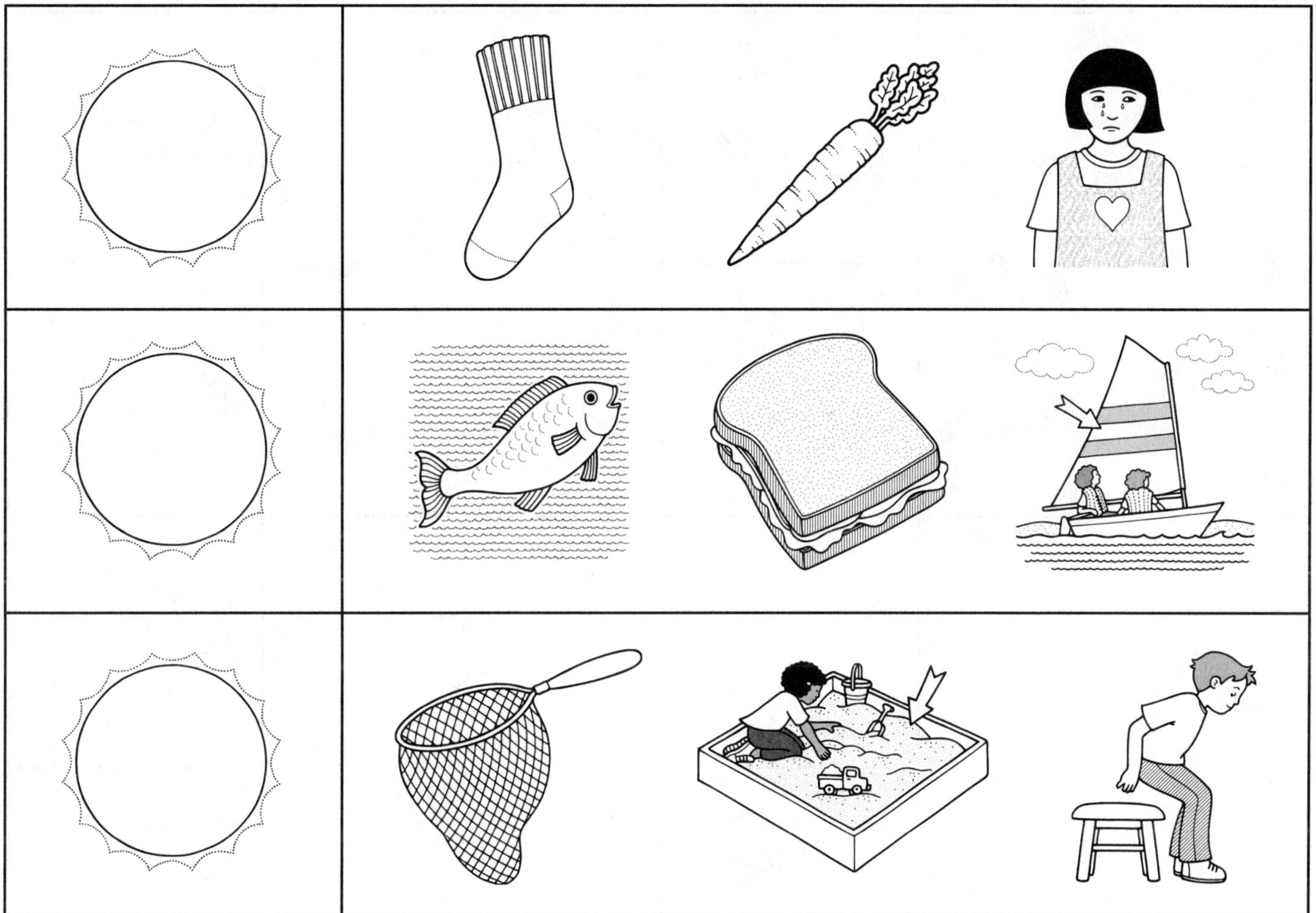

Identify the pictures with children. Have them circle the pictures in each row that begin with /s/ as in *sun*.

s /s/ sun 

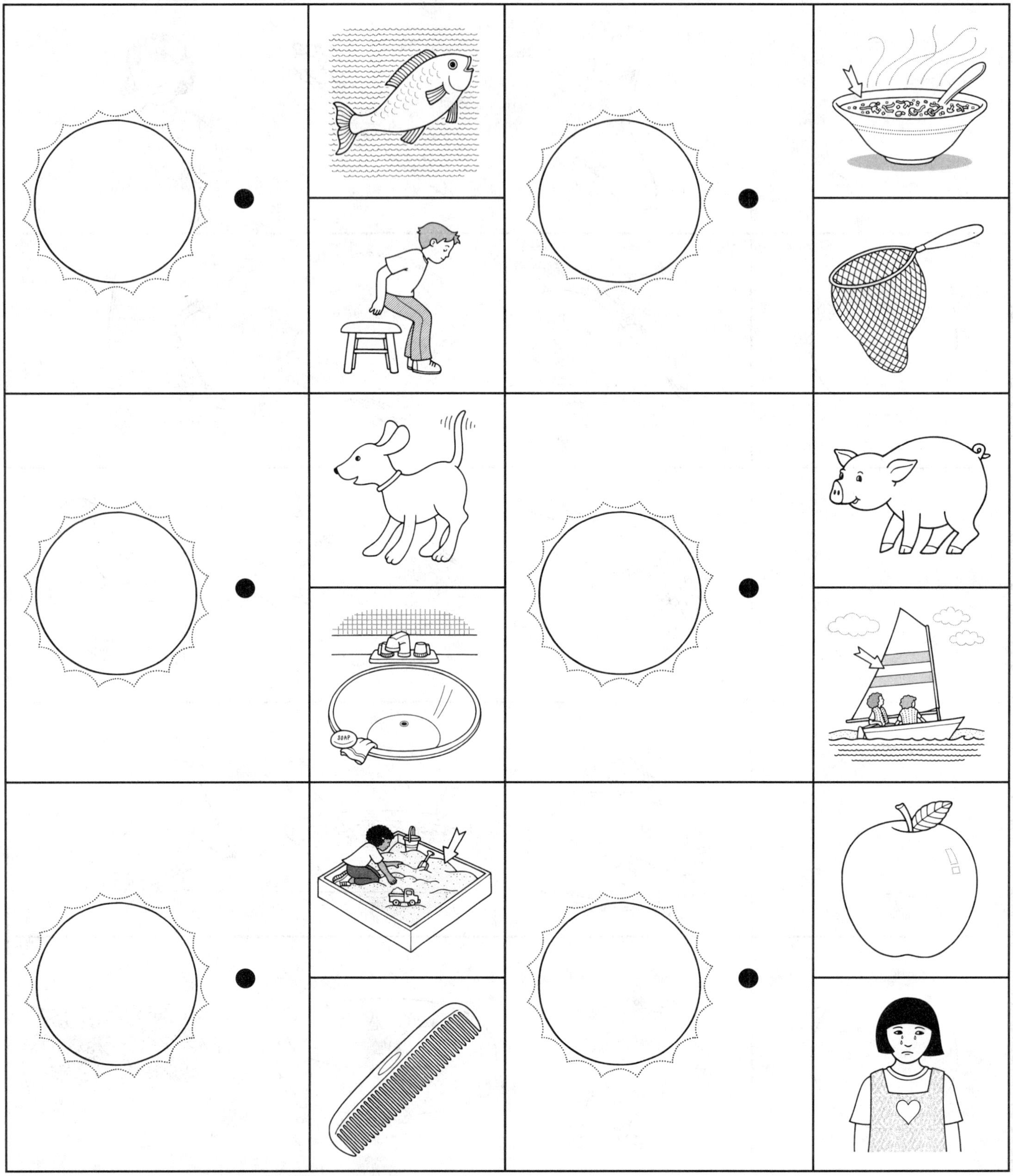

Identify the pictures with children. Tell them to start at the dot next to the sun and draw a line to the picture that begins with /s/ as in *sun*.

s /s/ sun

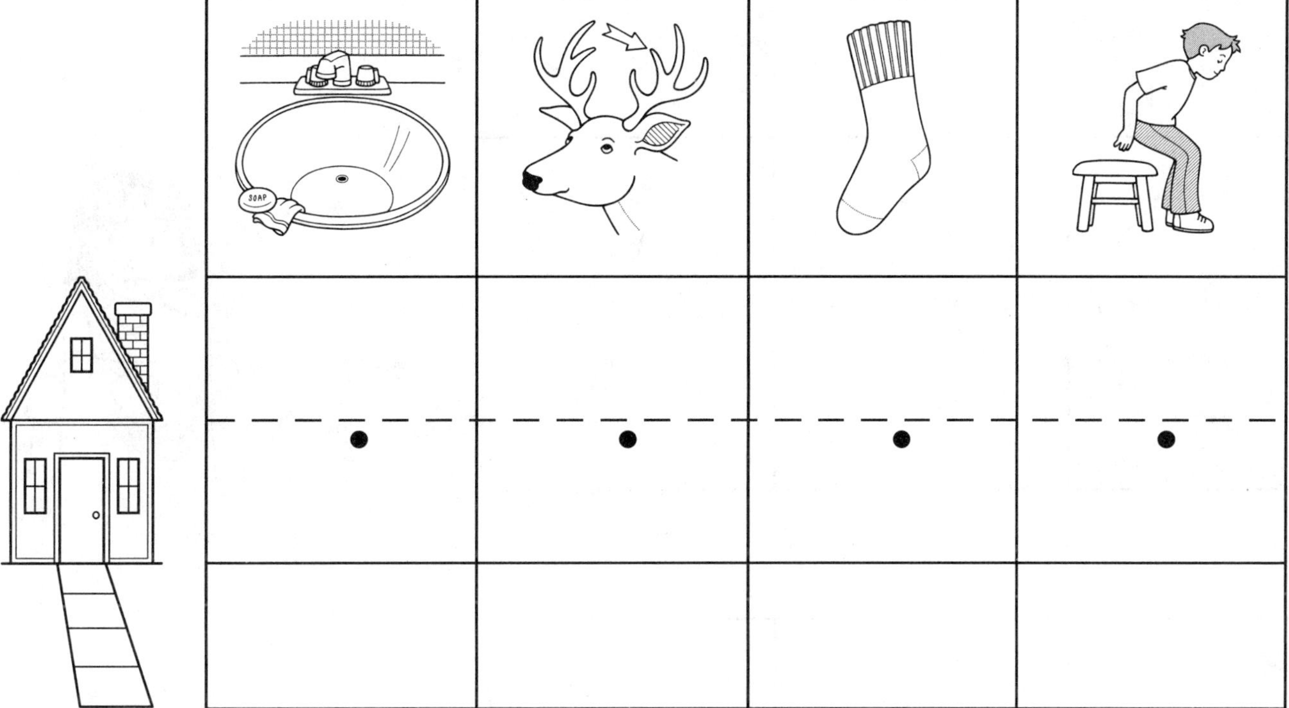

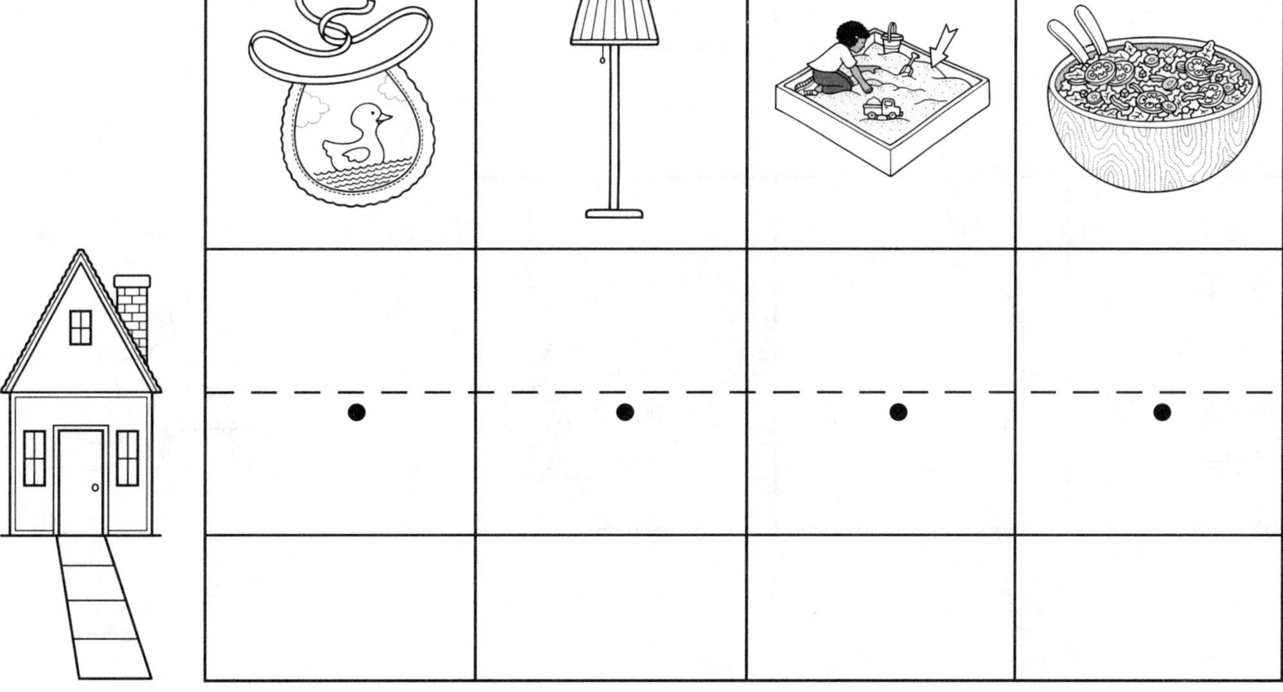

Identify the pictures with children. Direct them to circle each picture that begins with /s/ as in *sun* and print the letter *s* under it, starting at the dot.

s /s/ sun 

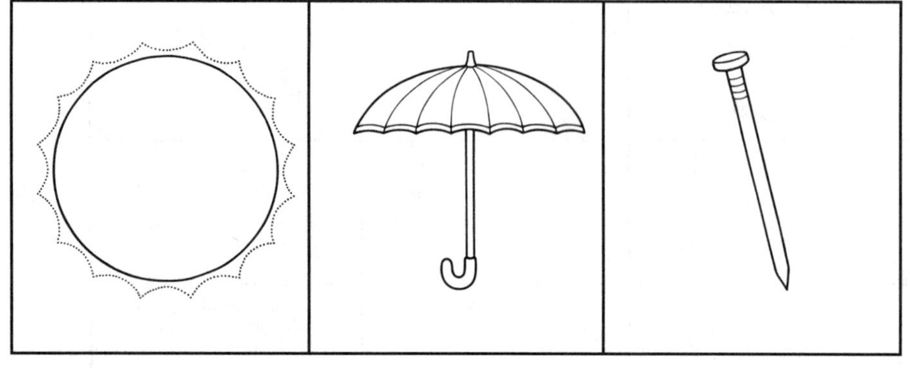

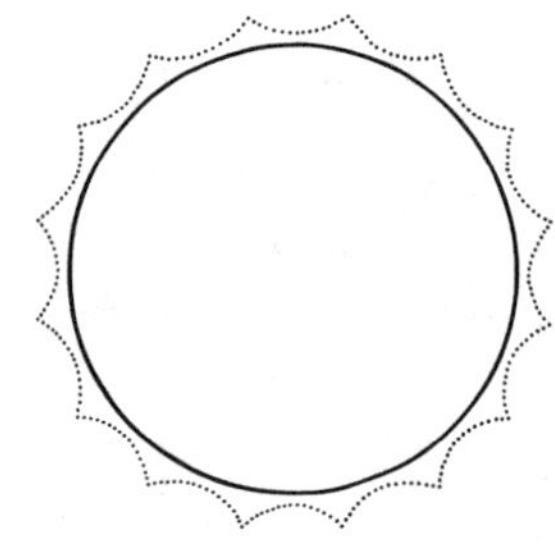

Identify the pictures in row 1 with children. Have them say the beginning sound of each. Then help children blend those sounds together to make a new word and draw a line to the picture of that word. Follow the same procedure with rows 2 and 3.

Lesson 21

w /w/ wag

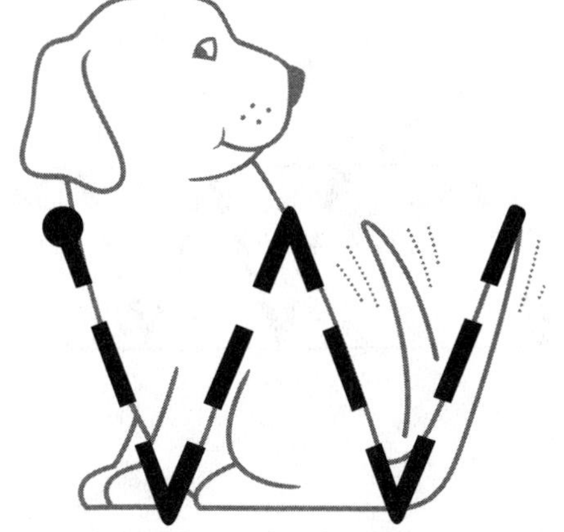

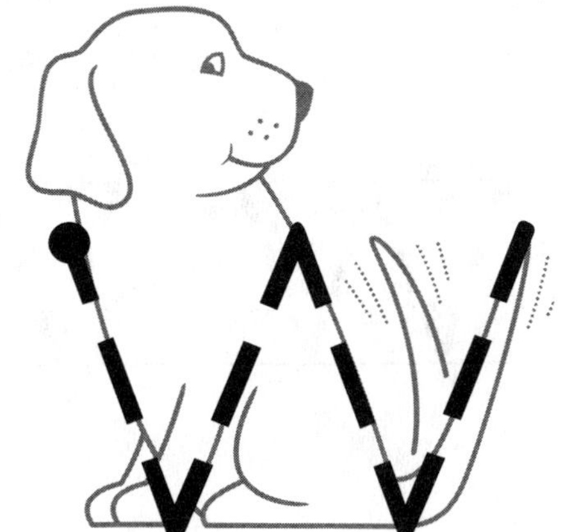

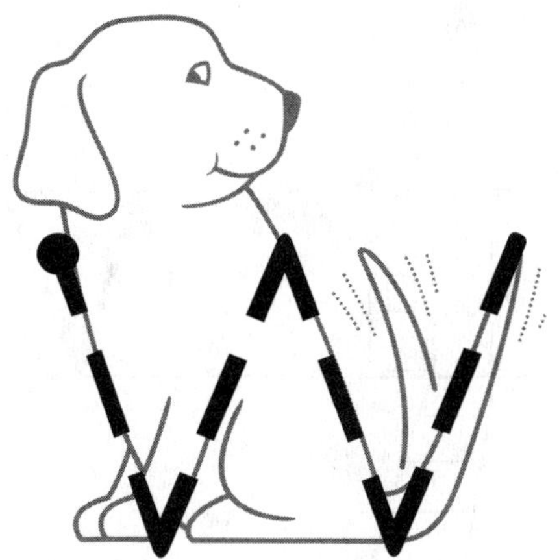

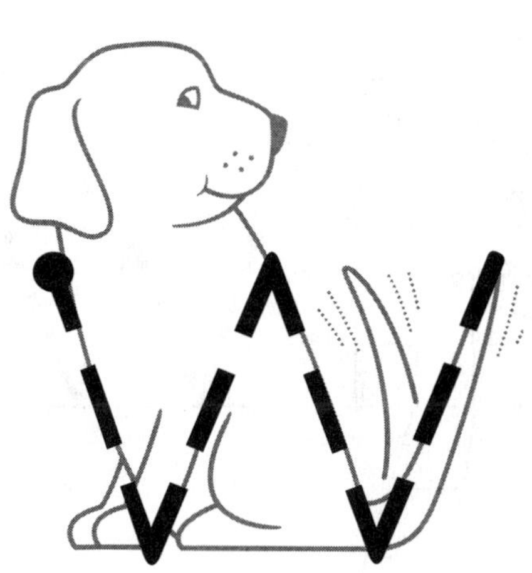

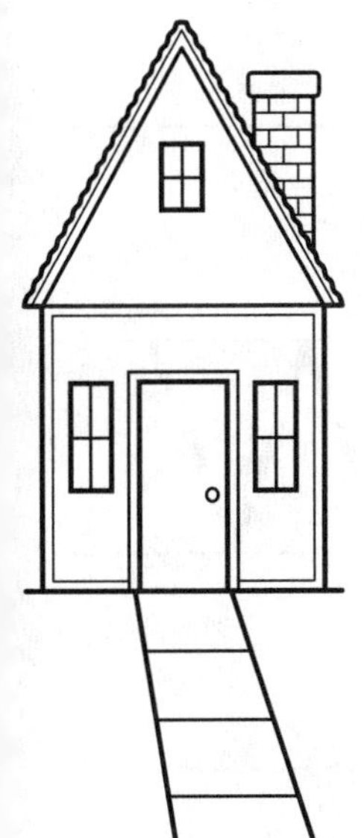

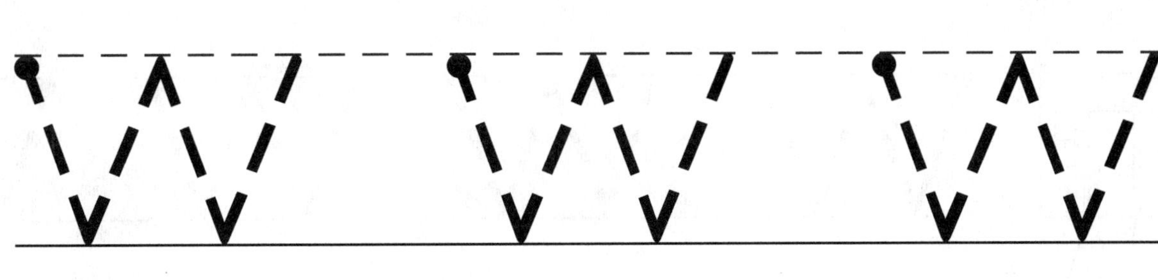

Have children trace all of the *w*'s on this page. Tell them to start at the dot and say /w/ as in *wag* as they trace each *w*.

w /w/ wag

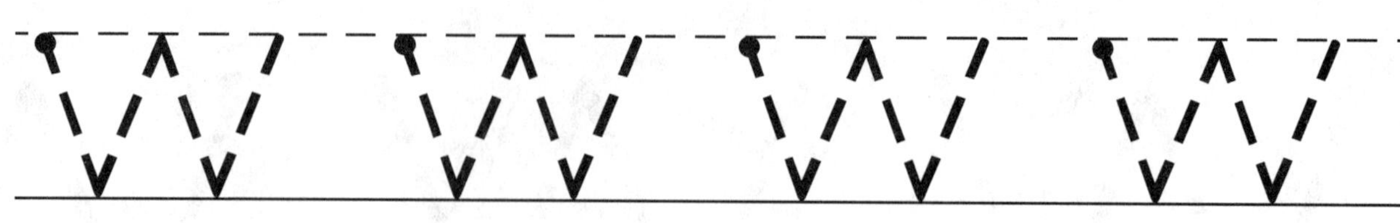

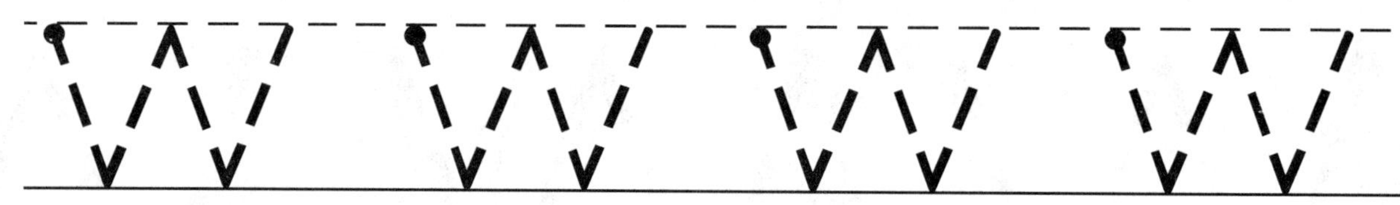

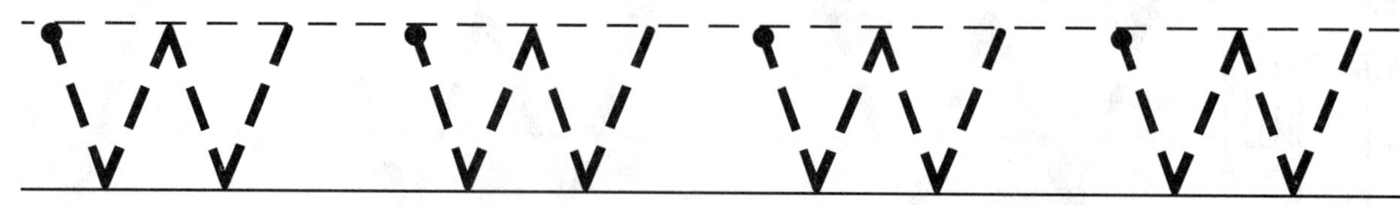

Direct children to trace the *w*'s and say /w/ as in *wag* as they trace each letter.

w /w/ wag

Identify the pictures with children. Have them circle the pictures in each row that begin with /w/ as in *wag*.

w /w/ wag 

Identify the pictures with children. Tell them to start at the dot next to the wag and draw a line to the picture that begins with /w/ as in *wag*.

w /w/ wag

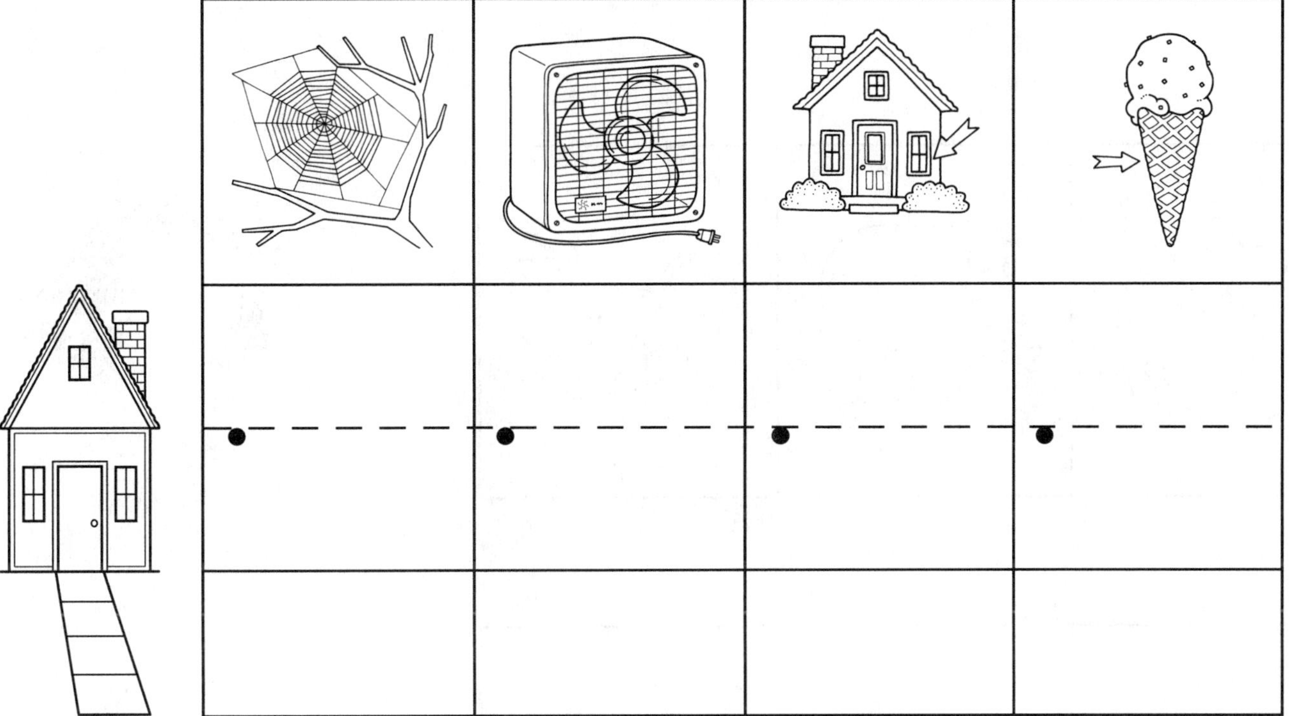

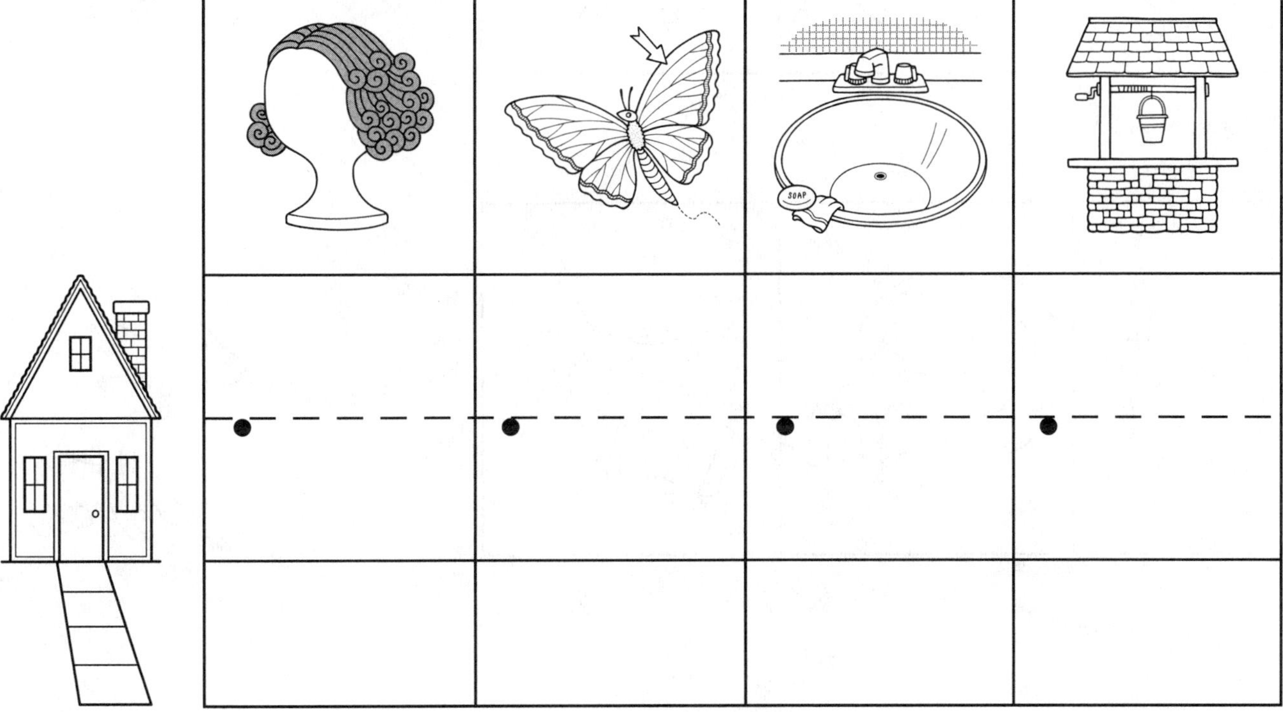

Identify the pictures with children. Direct them to circle each picture that begins with /w/ as in *wag* and print the letter *w* under it, starting at the dot.

w /w/ wag 

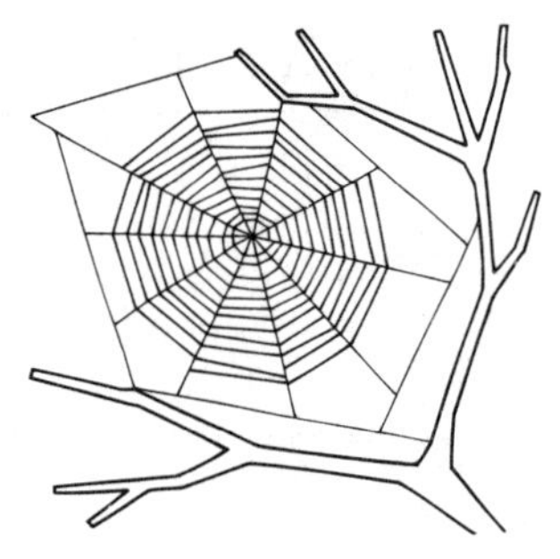

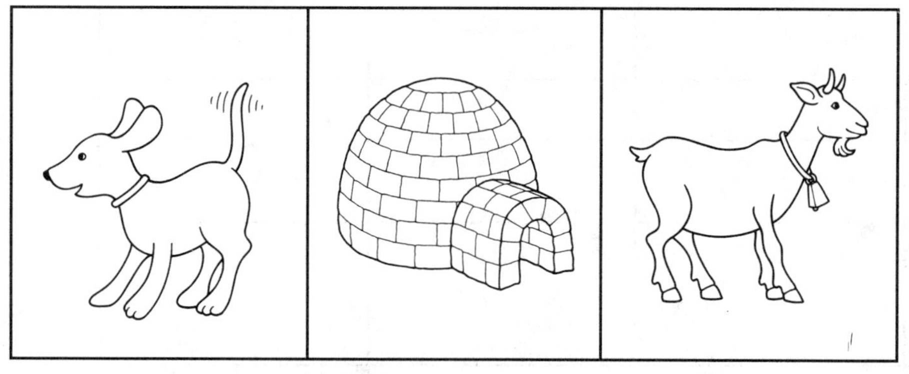

Identify the pictures in row 1 with children. Have them say the beginning sound of each. Then help children blend those sounds together to make a new word and draw a line to the picture of that word. Follow the same procedure with rows 2 and 3.

Lesson 22

y /y/ yarn

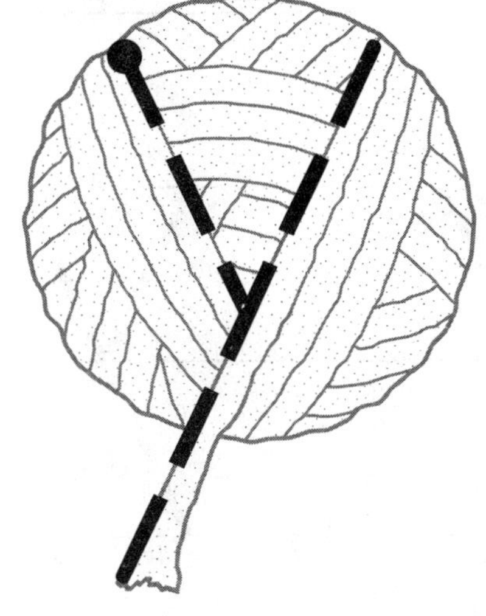

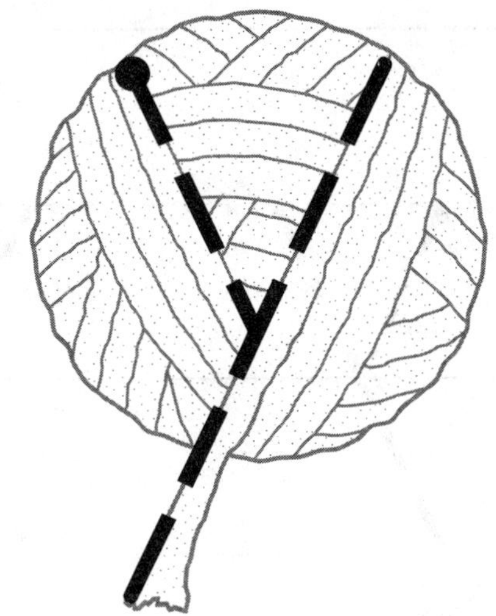

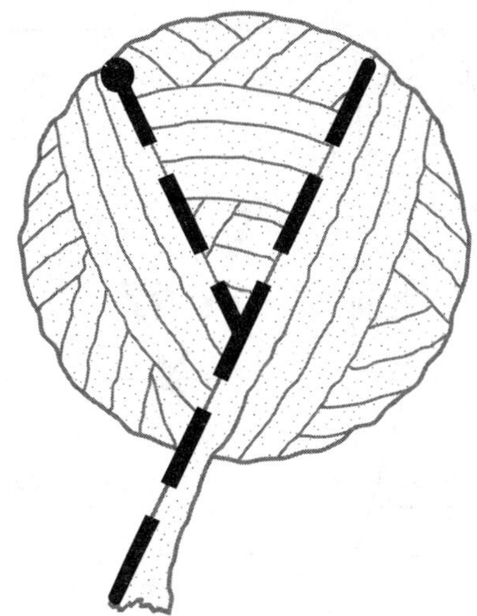

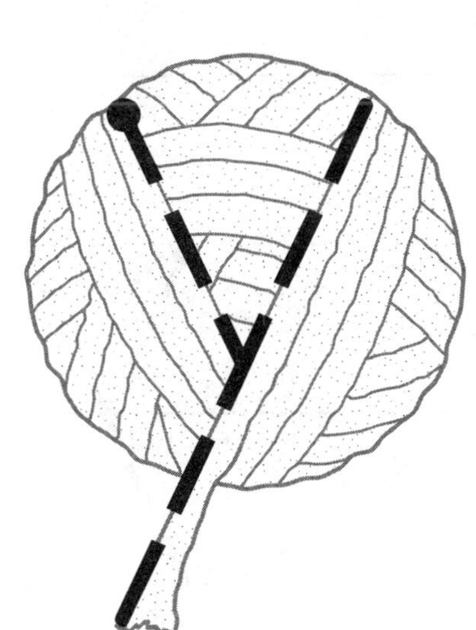

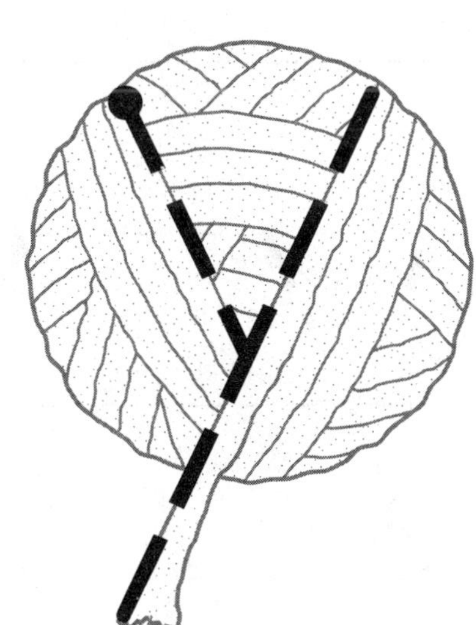

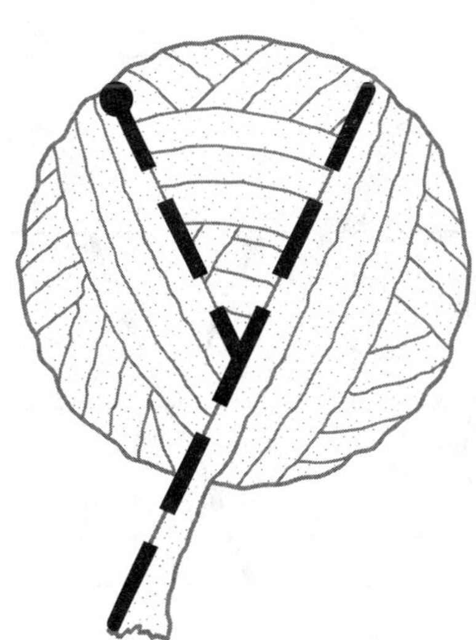

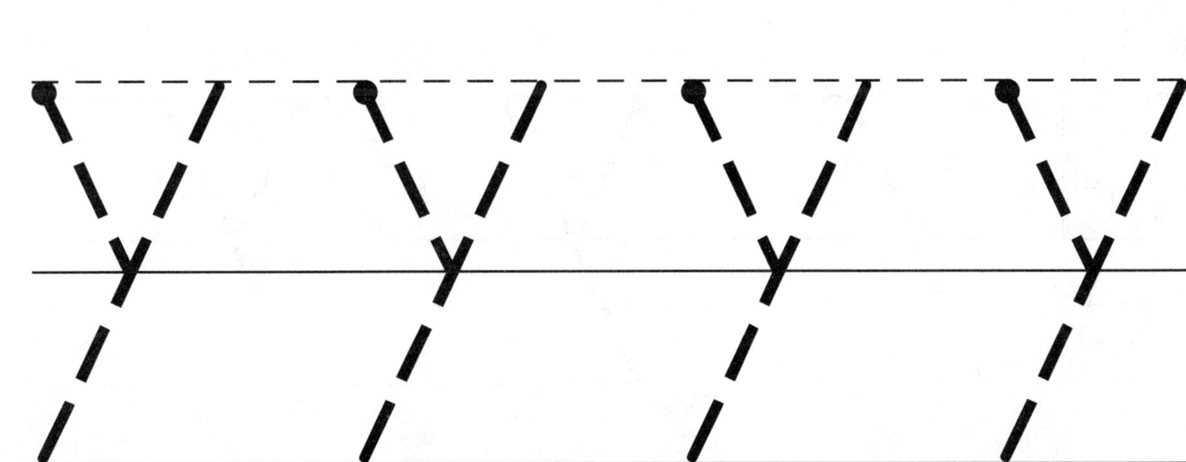

Have children trace all of the *y*'s on this page. Tell them to start at the dot and say /y/ as in *yarn* as they trace each *y*.

y /y/ yarn 

y y y y

y y y y

y y y y

Direct children to trace the *y*'s and say /y/ as in *yarn* as they trace each letter.

y /y/ yarn 

Identify the pictures with children. Have them circle the pictures in each row that begin with /y/ as in *yarn*.

y /y/ yarn 

Identify the pictures with children. Tell them to start at the dot next to the yarn and draw a line to the picture that begins with /y/ as in *yarn*.

y /y/ yarn 

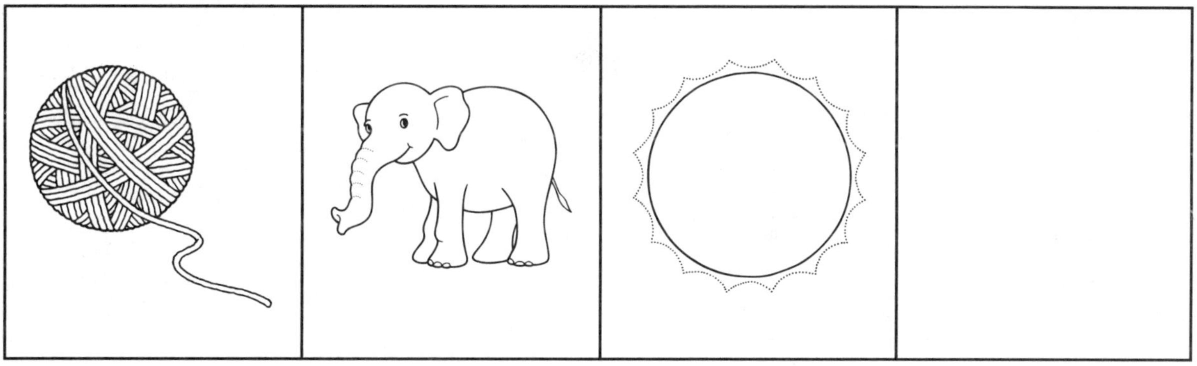

Identify the pictures in row 1 with children. Have them say the beginning sounds and blend them together to make a new word. Follow the same procedure with rows 2 and 3. Help children cut out the pictures at the bottom of the page and paste each next to the blended word it matches.

y /y/ yarn

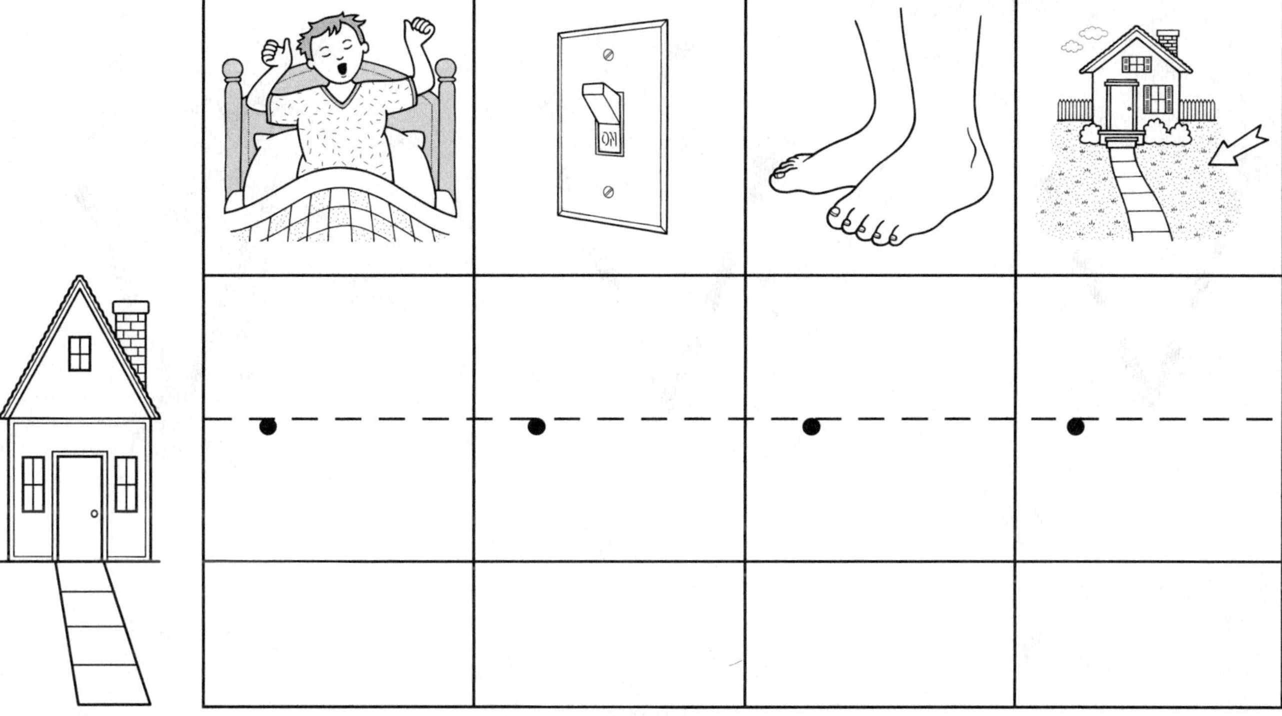

Identify the pictures with children. Direct them to circle each picture that begins with /y/ as in *yarn* and print the letter *y* under it, starting at the dot.

Lesson 23

v /v/ vase

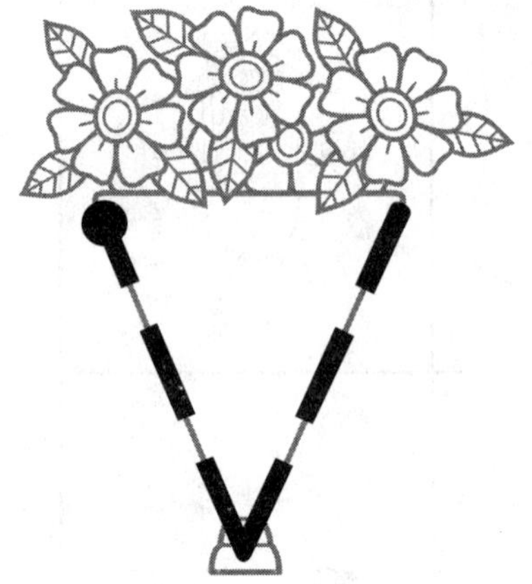
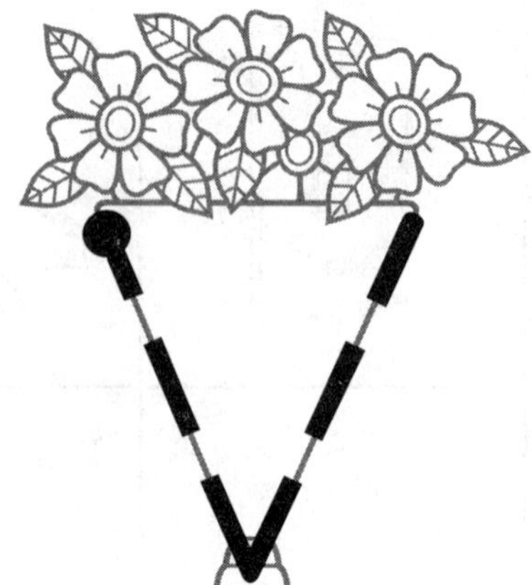

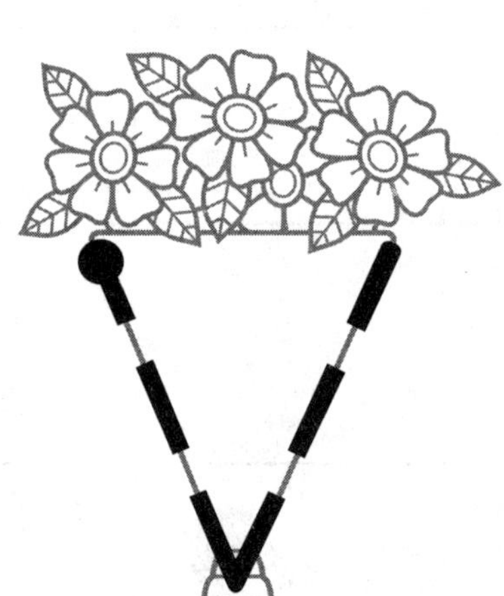

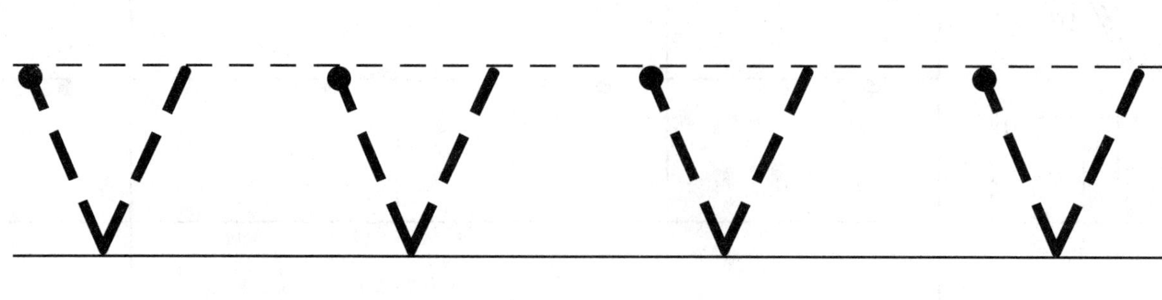

Have children trace all of the *v*'s on this page. Tell them to start at the dot and say /v/ as in *vase* as they trace each *v*.

v /v/ vase

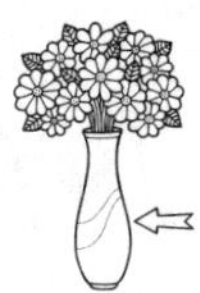

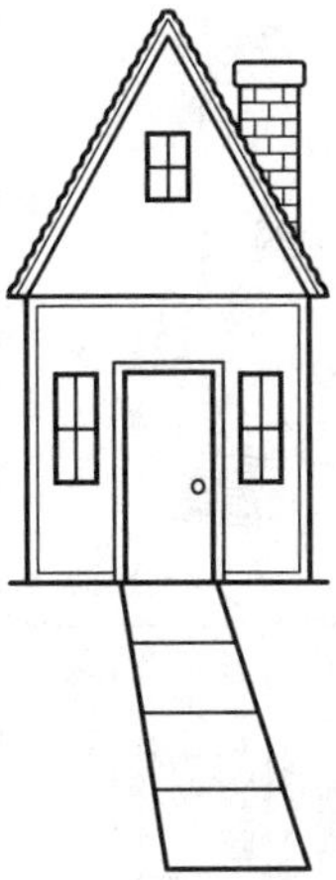

v v v v

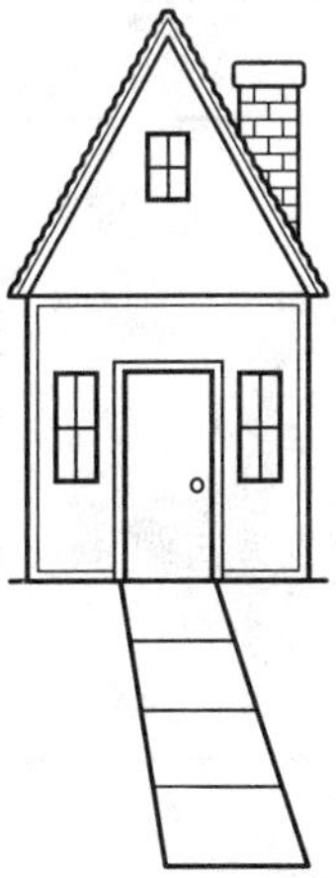

v v v v

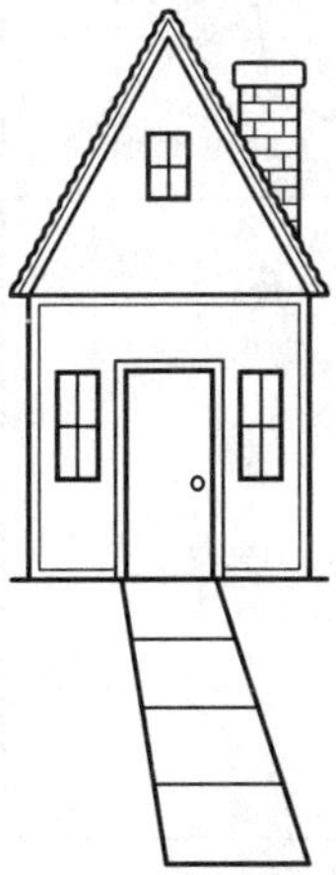

v v v v

Direct children to trace the *v*'s and say /v/ as in *vase* as they trace each letter.

v /v/ vase 

Identify the pictures with children. Have them circle the pictures in each row that begin with /v/ as in *vase*.

v /v/ vase

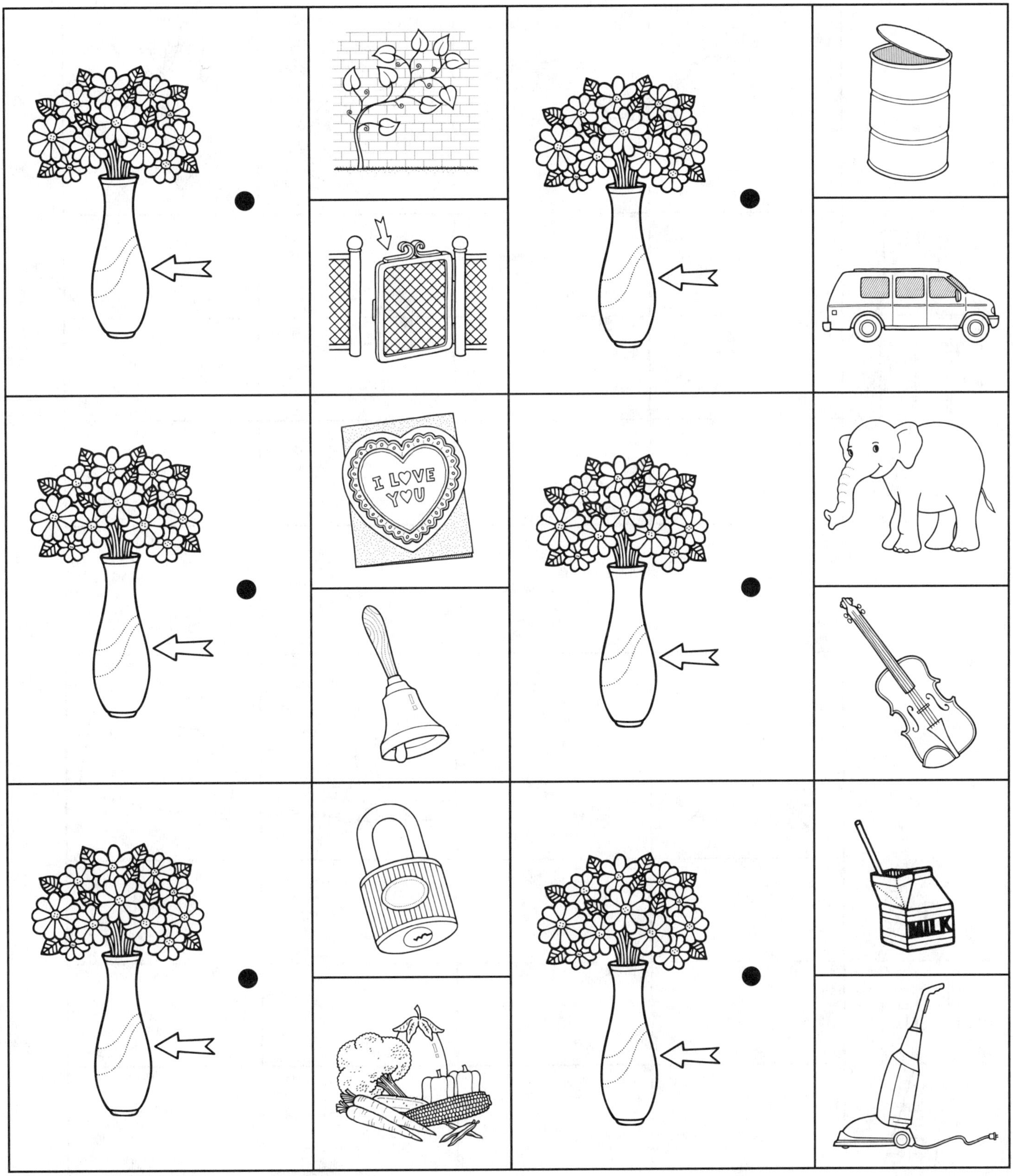

	I LOVE YOU		
			MILK

Identify the pictures with children. Tell them to start at the dot next to the vase and draw a line to the picture that begins with /v/ as in *vase*.

v /v/ vase 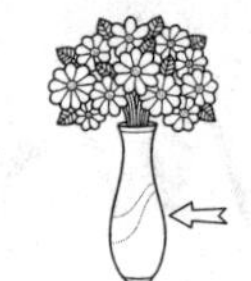

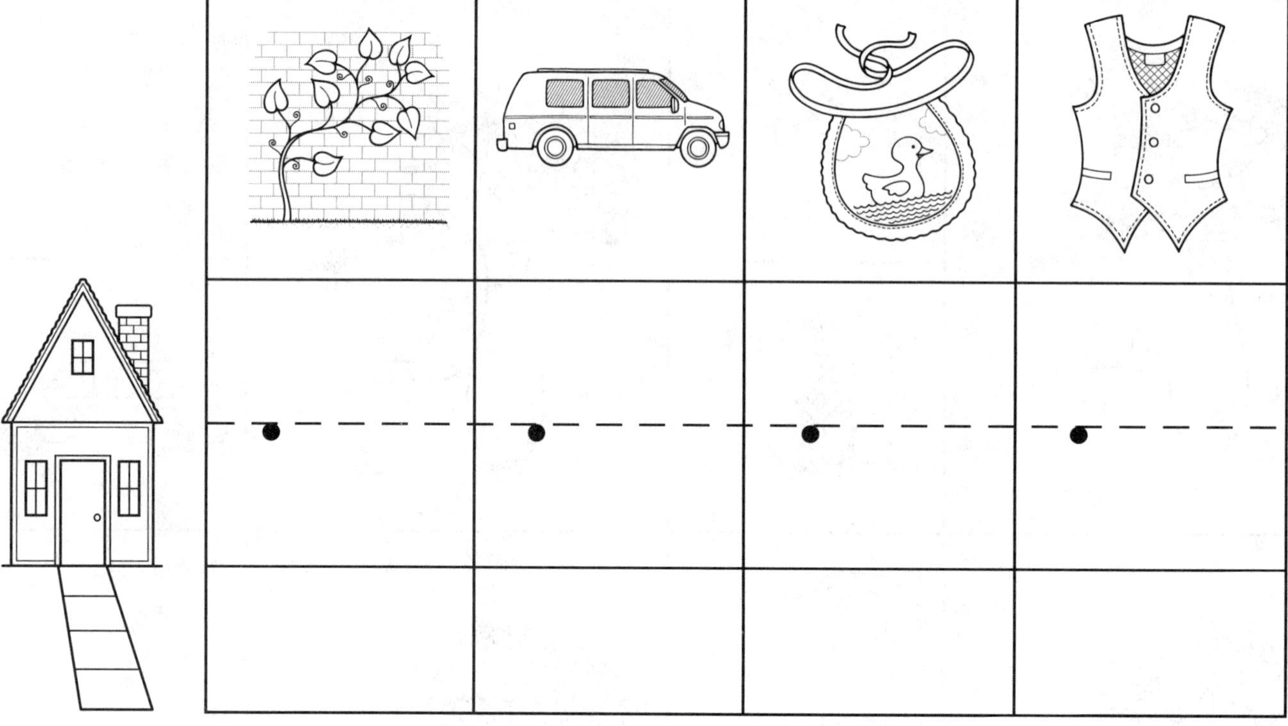

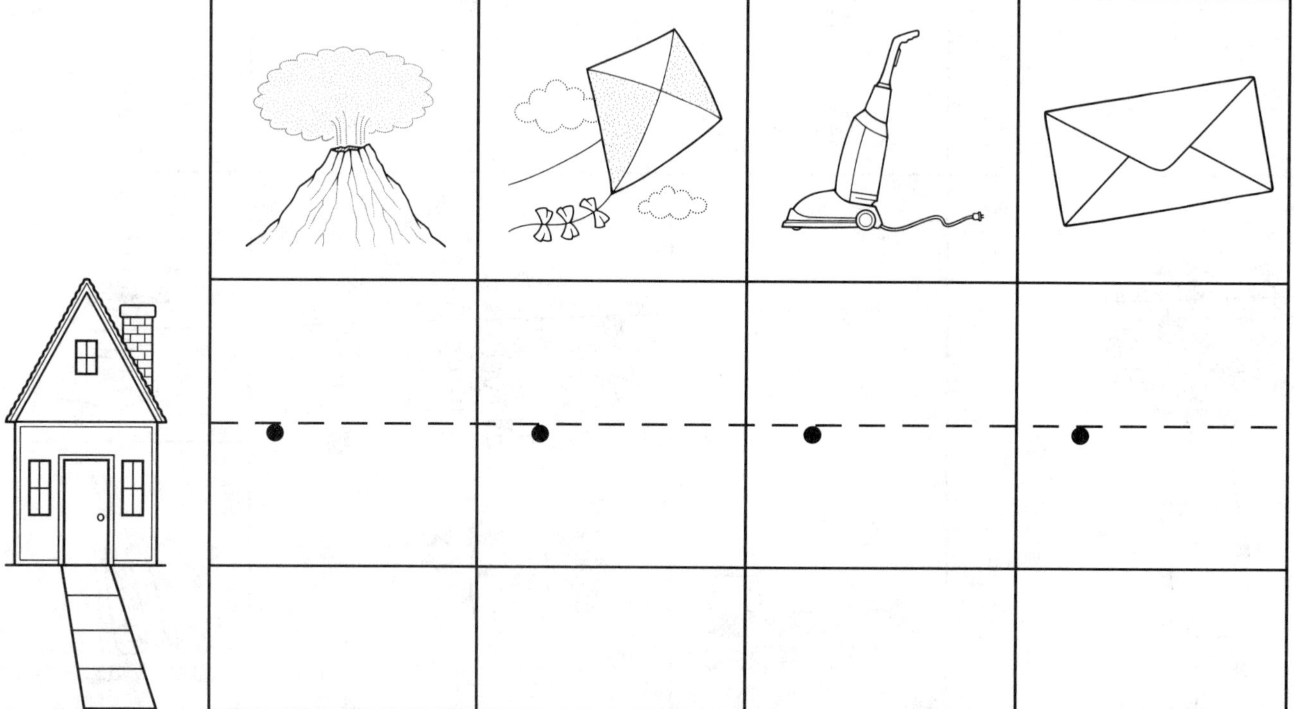

Identify the pictures with children. Direct them to circle each picture that begins with /v/ as in *vase* and print the letter *v* under it, starting at the dot.

v /v/ vase

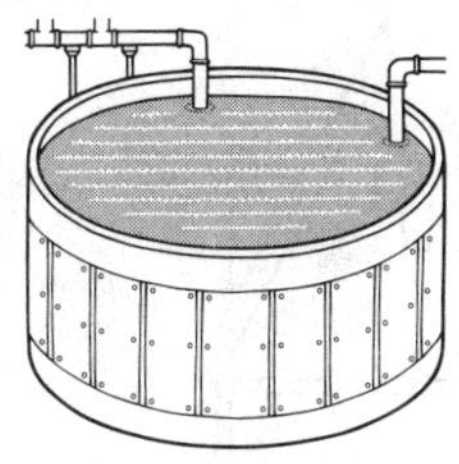

Identify the pictures in row 1 with children. Have them say the beginning sound of each. Then help children blend those sounds together to make a new word and draw a line to the picture of that word. Follow the same procedure with rows 2 and 3.

Lesson 24

z /z/ zebra

Have children trace all of the *z*'s on this page. Tell them to start at the dot and say /z/ as in *zebra* as they trace each *z*.

z /z/ zebra

Direct children to trace the *z*'s and say /z/ as in *zebra* as they trace each letter.

z /z/ zebra

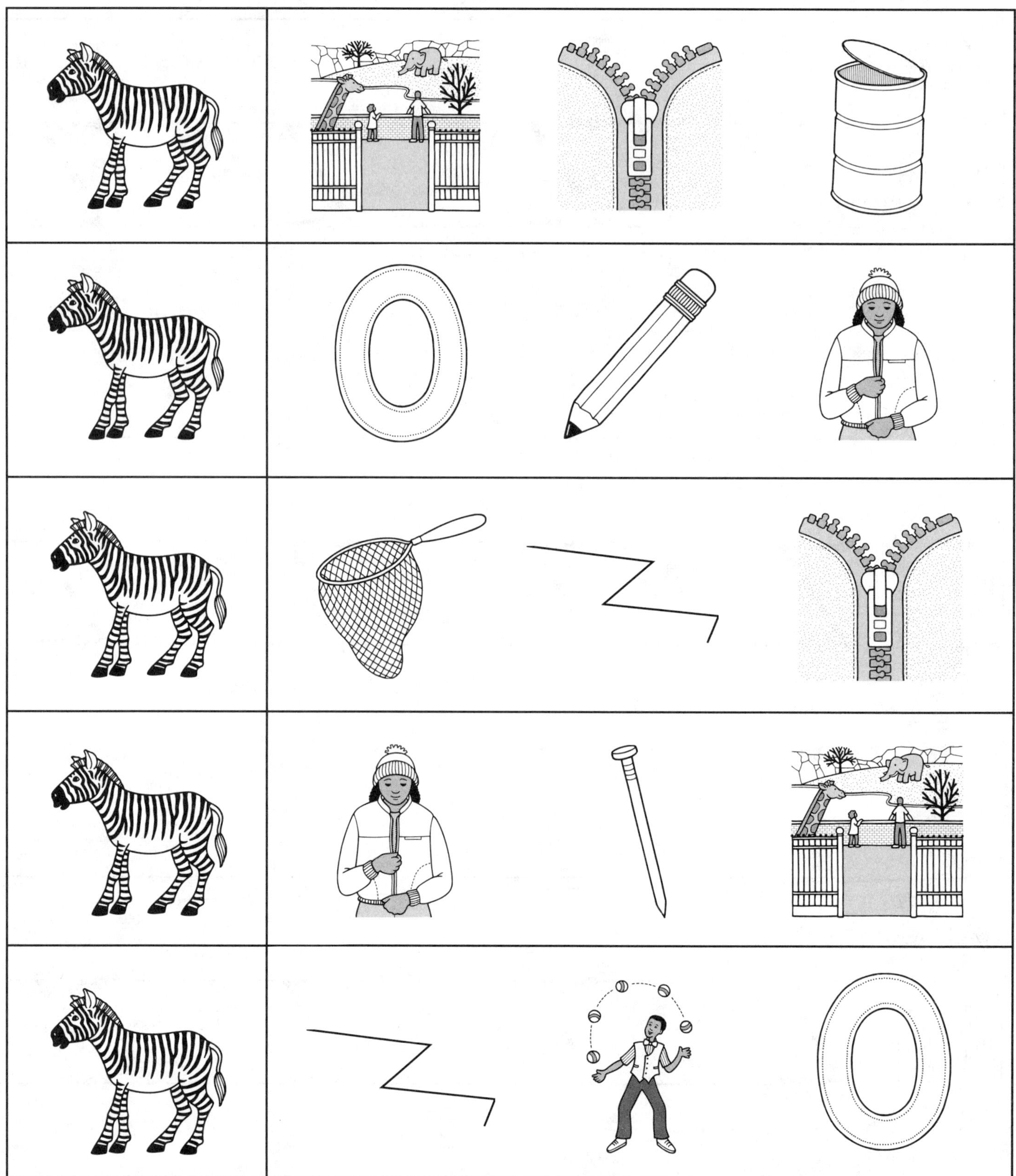

Identify the pictures with children. Have them circle the pictures in each row that begin with /z/ as in *zebra*.

z /z/ zebra

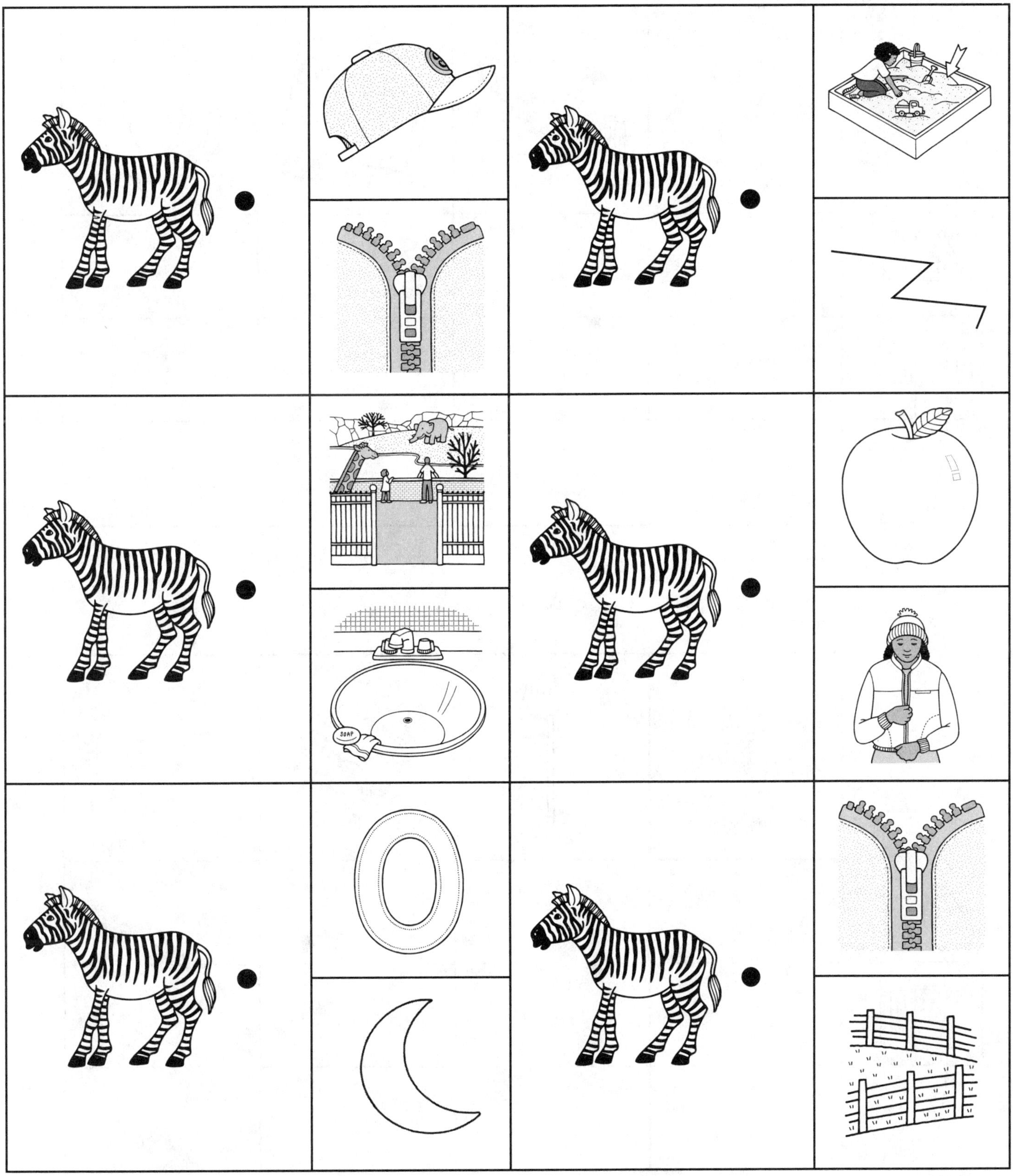

Identify the pictures with children. Tell them to start at the dot next to the zebra and draw a line to the picture that begins with /z/ as in *zebra*.

z /z/ zebra

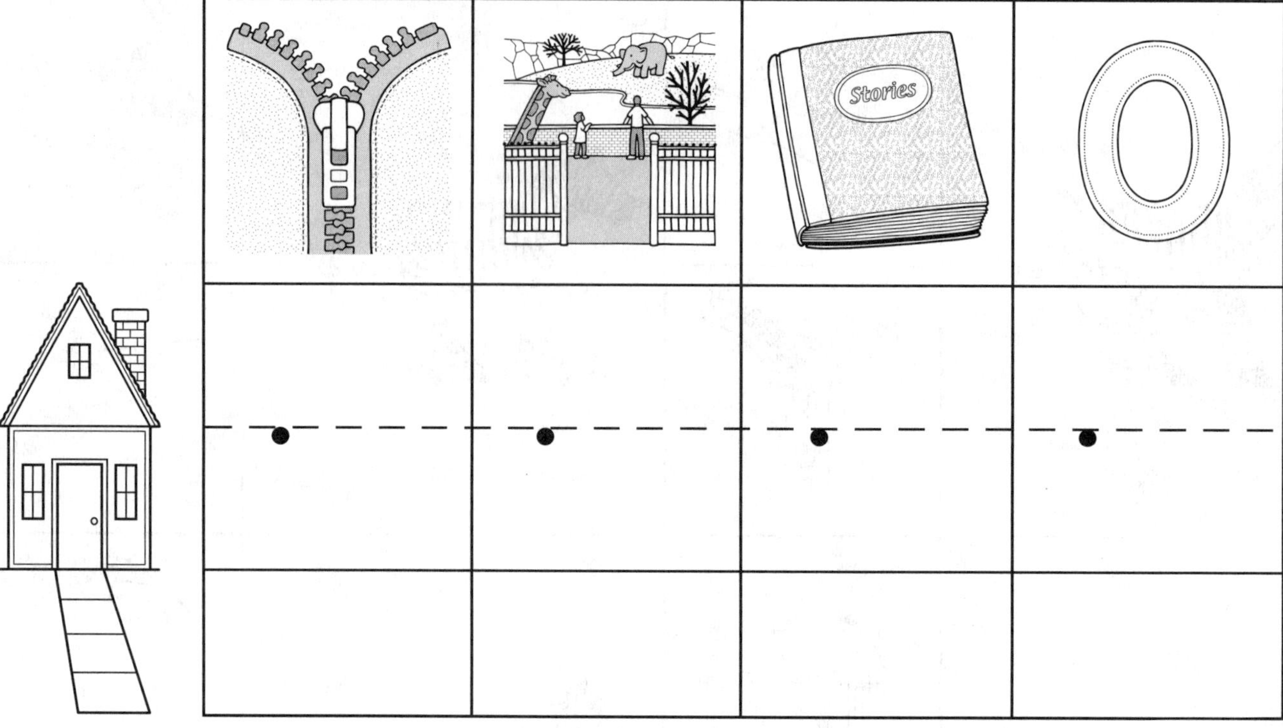

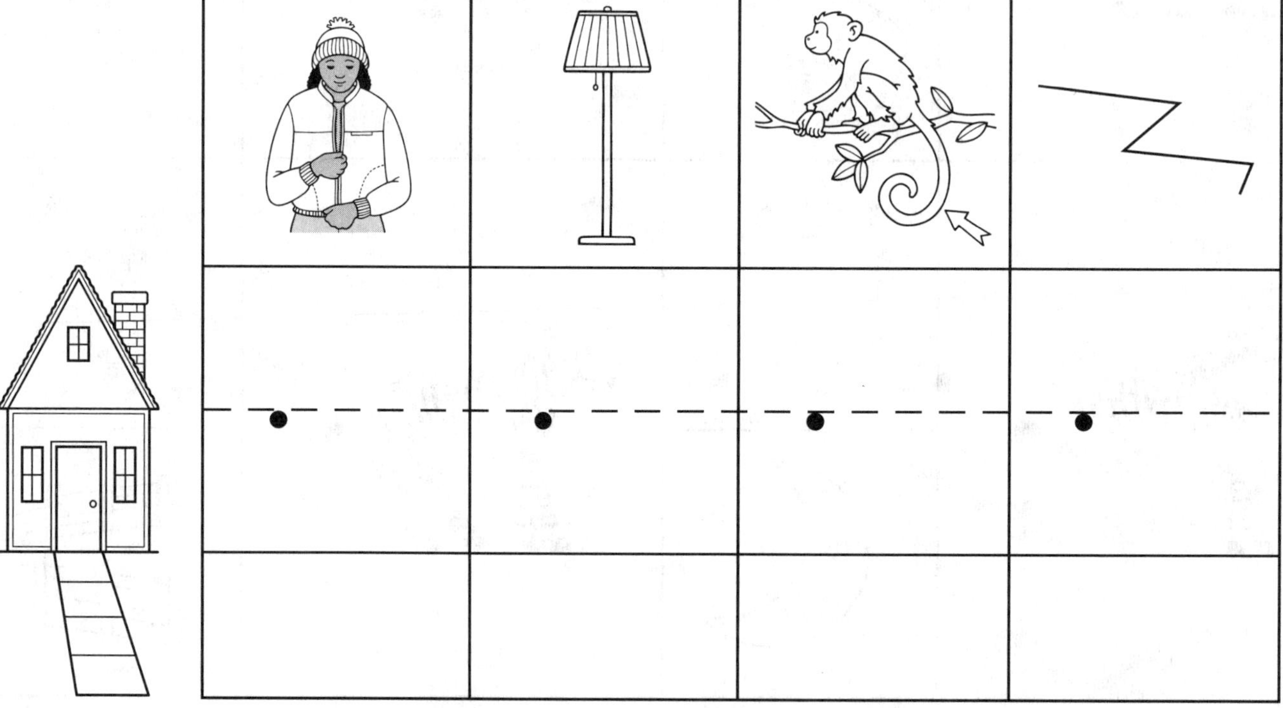

Identify the pictures with children. Direct them to circle each picture that begins with /z/ as in *zebra* and print the letter *z* under it, starting at the dot.

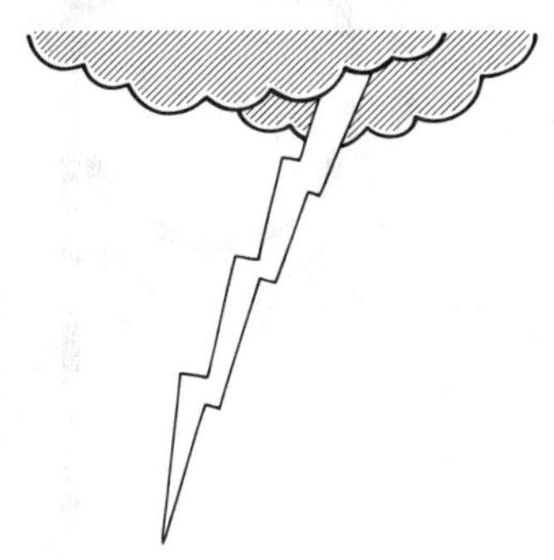

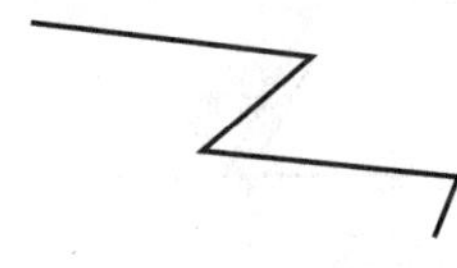

Identify the pictures in row 1 with children. Have them say the beginning sound of each. Then help children blend those sounds together to make a new word and draw a line to the picture of that word. Follow the same procedure with rows 2 and 3.

Lesson 25

qu /kw/ queen

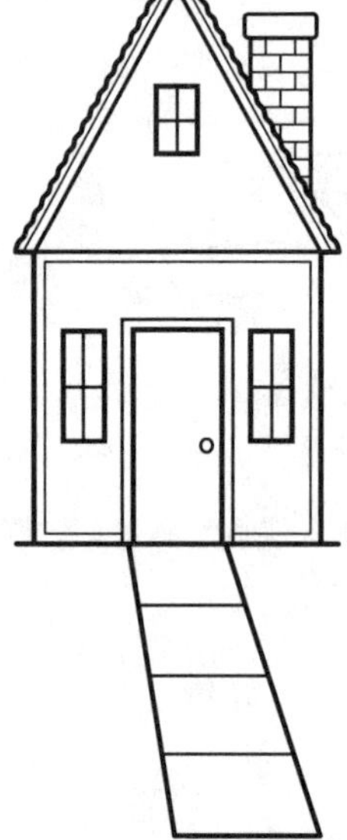

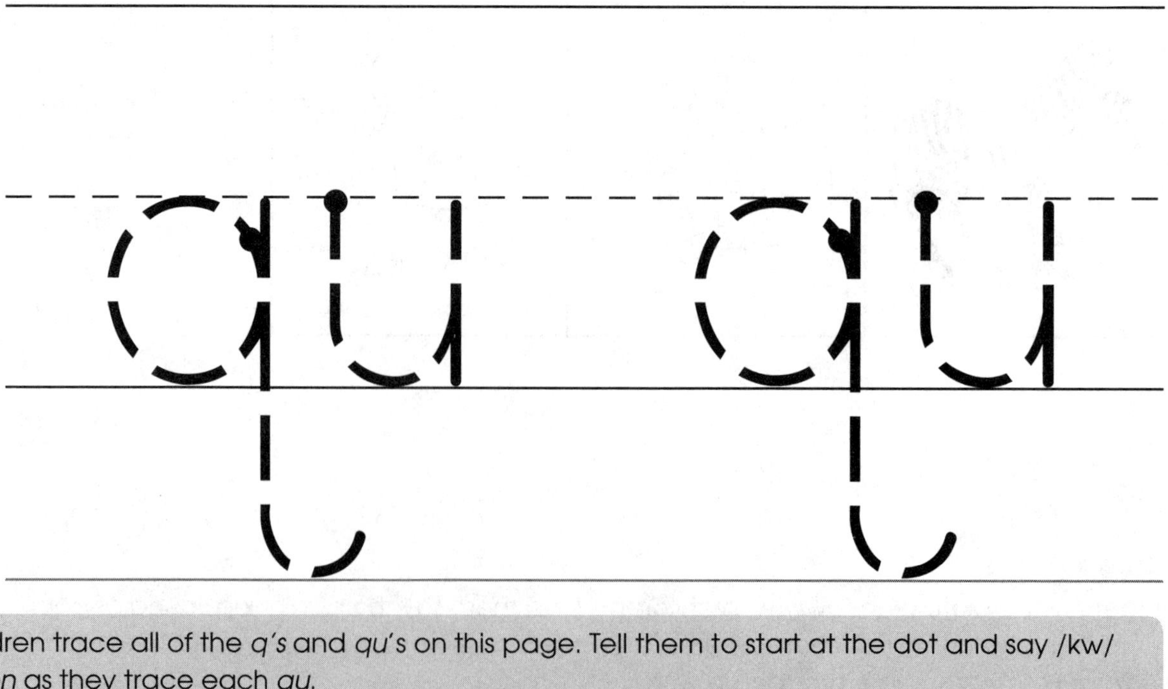

Have children trace all of the *q's* and *qu*'s on this page. Tell them to start at the dot and say /kw/ as in *queen* as they trace each *qu*.

qu /kw/ queen

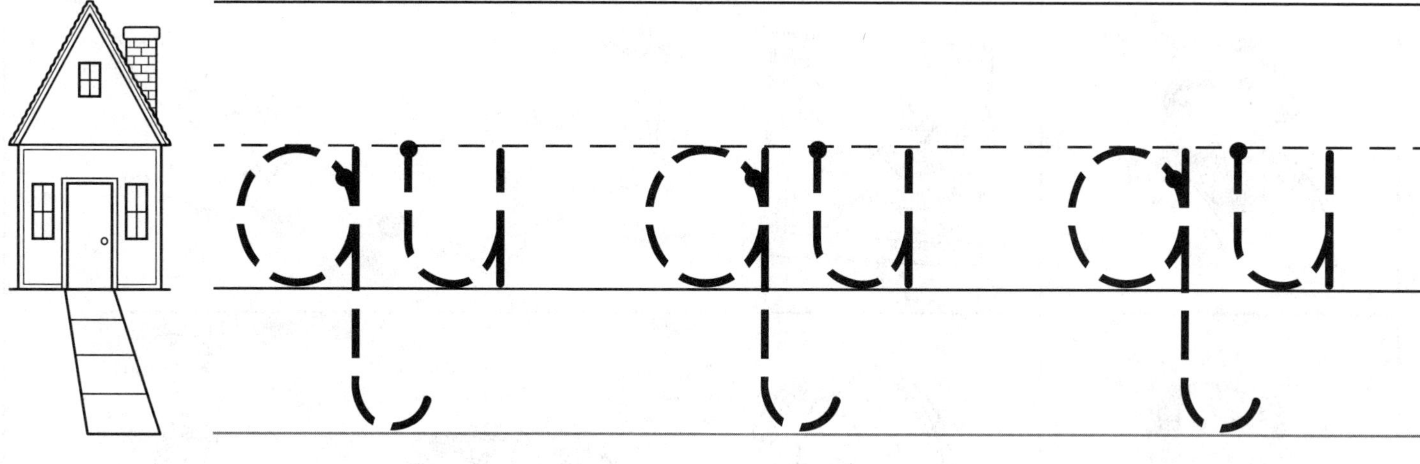

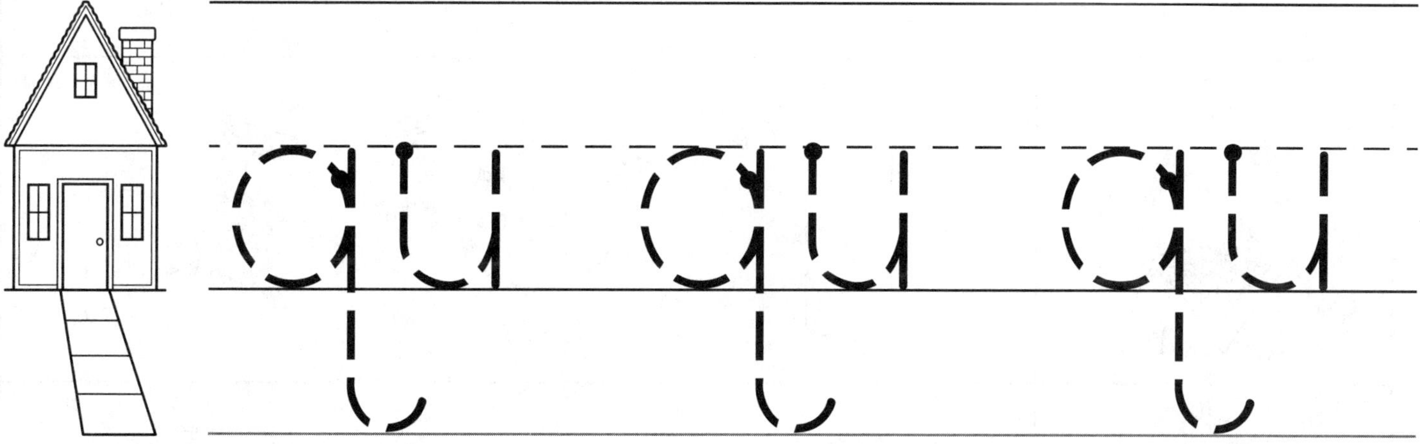

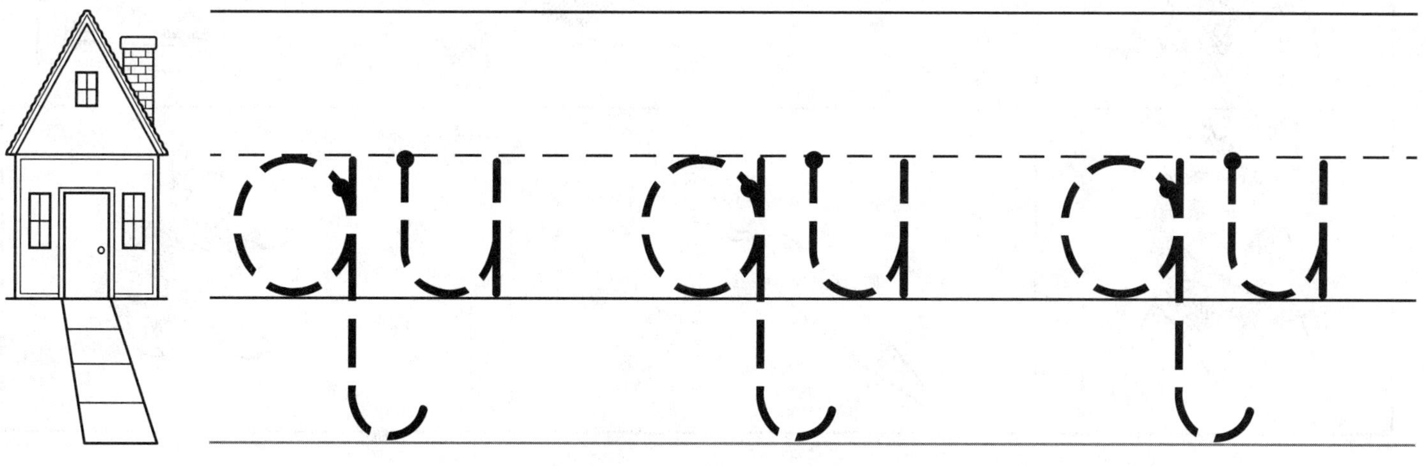

Direct children to trace the *qu*'s and say /kw/ as in *queen* as they trace each letter pair.

qu /kw/ queen 

Identify the pictures with children. Have them circle the pictures in each row that begin with /kw/ as in *queen*.

qu /kw/ queen

Identify the pictures with children. Tell them to start at the dot next to the queen and draw a line to the picture that begins with /kw/ as in *queen*.

qu /kw/ queen 

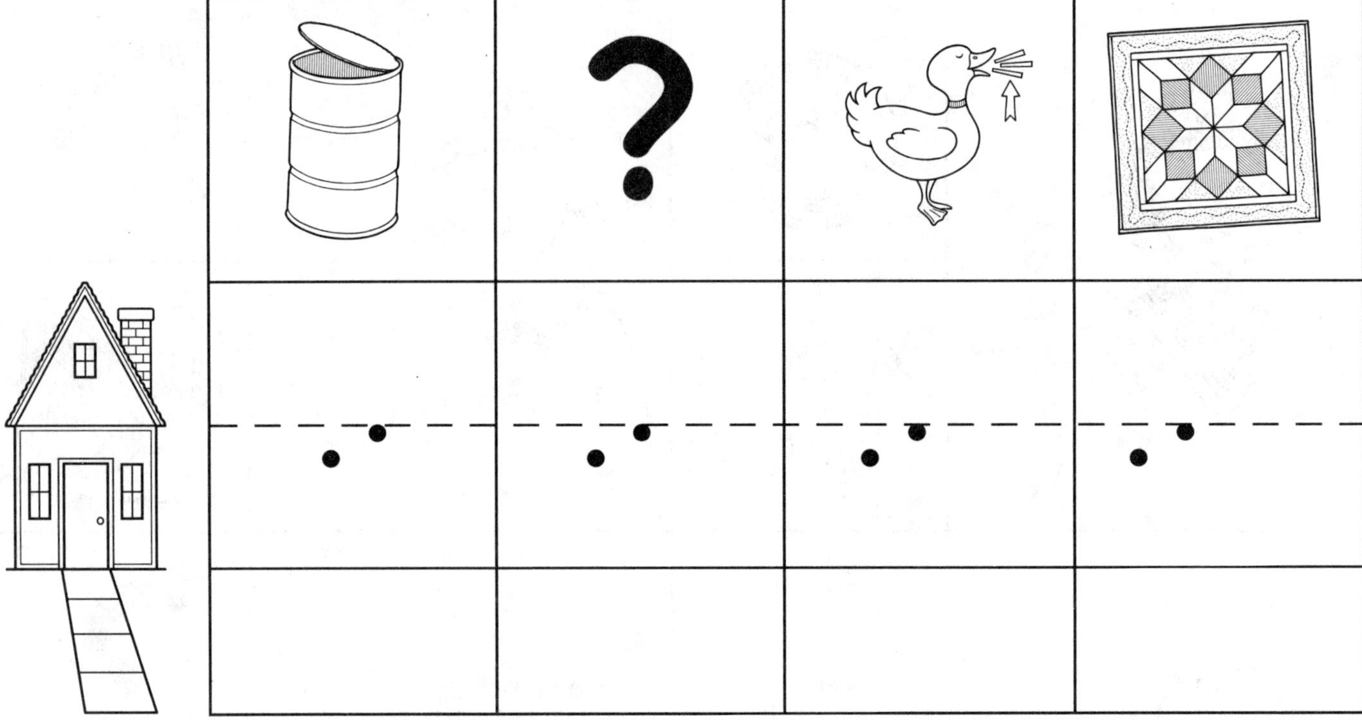

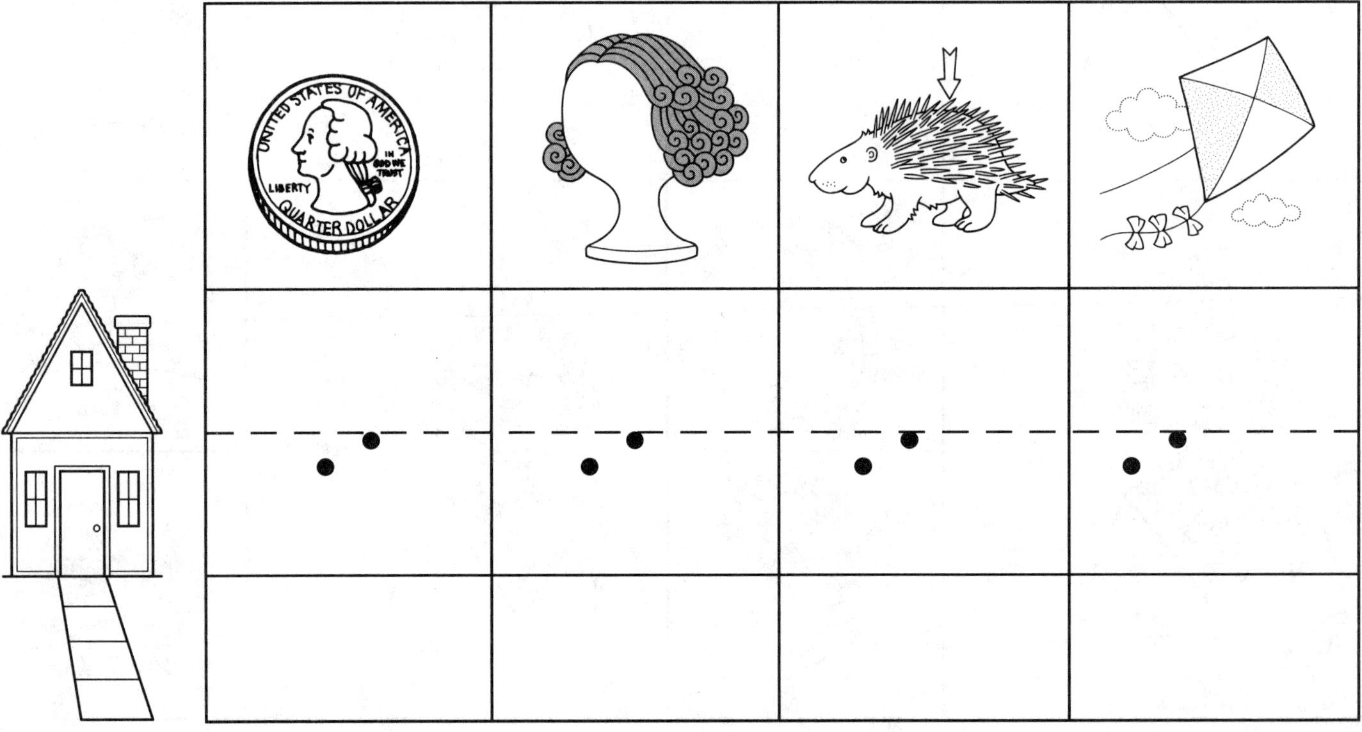

Identify the pictures with children. Direct them to circle each picture that begins with /kw/ as in *queen* and print the letters *qu* under it, starting at the dots.